50p   08/11 R

BTEC national

2nd Edition

Uniformed Public Services

Book 2

Debra Gray

Dave Stockbridge

John Vause

www.heinemann.co.uk

✓ Free online support
✓ Useful weblinks
✓ 24 hour online ordering

D0318371

01865 888118

Heinemann is an imprint of Pearson Education Limited, a company incorporated in England and Wales, having its registered office at Edinburgh Gate, Harlow, Essex, CM20 2JE. Registered company number: 87282

www.heinemann.co.uk

Heinemann is a registered trademark of Pearson Education Lim

Text, Unit 14 © John Vause, 2008
Text, Unit 15 © John Vause, 2008
Text, Unit 16 © Debra Gray, 2008
Text, Unit 17 © Debra Gray, 2008
Text, Unit 18 © Debra Gray, 2008
Text, Unit 20 © Dave Stockbridge, 2008
Text, Unit 21© Dave Stockbridge, 2008
Text, Unit 22 © Debra Gray, 2008

First published 2008

12 11 10 09 08
10 9 8 7 6 5 4 3 2 1

British Library Cataloguing in Publication Data is available from the British Library on request.

ISBN 978 0 435499 46 4

Typeset by Tek-Art, Crawley Down, West Sussex
Original illustrations © Pearson Education Limited, 2008
Illustrated by Tek-Art
Picture research by Kath Kollberg
Cover photo/illustration © Alamy/Jack Sullivan
Printed in the UK by Scotprint

Websites
The websites used in this book were correct and up-to-date at the time of publication. It is essential for tutors to preview each website before using it in class so as to ensure that the URL is still accurate, relevant and appropriate. We suggest that tutors bookmark useful websites and consider enabling students to access them through the school/college intranet.

Crown copyright
Crown copyright material reproduced with permission of the Controller of Her Majesty's Stationery Office and the Queen's Printer for Scotland

Contents

Acknowledgements

I should like to thank the following people who have helped with the production of this book:

From Heinemann – Pen Gresford and Iain Ross, whose editing skills, patience and support have been invaluable.

From Dearne Valley College – Julie Williamson, Charlotte Baker, Paul Meares, Boris Lockyer, John Vause, Mick Blythe, Barry Pinches, Kelly Ellery, Dave Stockbridge and Nick Lawton; you make me proud to be part of the public services team at DVC.

From the Services – PC Paul Jenkinson, South Yorkshire Police; Lance Corporal Kelly Stevens, 38 Signal Regiment; Lis Martin, Skills for Justice. A really big thank you to all the services who have contributed their knowledge and skills to the development of the public service programmes at DVC over the years. Phil Campbell, Jack Mitchell, Jonty Morissey and all the other members of Justice UK for the endless quests they completed on my behalf.

The biggest thank you of all goes to my family, Ben, India and Sam, who make every day brighter.

Debra Gray

I wish to thank my wife and my wider family for their continued support through the whole writing and editing process. The experience has taught me many new skills, such as being able to balance a baby on my lap while typing and being able to drink numerous cold cups of tea.

Dave Stockbridge

I should like to thank all the Public Service team at DVC for their input, guidance and wonderful sense of humour. A special thank you goes to Lynne and Nicola for their love, patience, support and understanding.

John Vause

The author and publisher would like to thank the following individuals and organisations for permission to reproduce photographs:

Alamy / David Hoffman Photo Library pp 113, 143, 150–1, 182; Alamy / Huw Jones p 129; Alamy / Tom Keane pp 124–5, 147; Alamy / Gianni Muratore p 68; Alamy / Photofusion Picture Library p 204; Alamy / PHOTOTAKE Inc. p 108; Alamy / SHOUT pp 51, 73, 107; Alamy / David Taylor p 157; Crown p 95; Getty Images pp 36–7, 52, 64, 69, 78, 105, 117, 118, 126, 135, 174, 184–5, 215, 223, 224, 226; Getty Images / AFP pp 56, 162; Getty Images / Photonica p 39; David Hoffmann p 208; iStockPhoto.com / George Cairns pp 102–3, 121; iStockPhoto.com / Sharon Dominick p 91; iStockPhoto.com / David Pedre p 177; iStockPhoto.com / Kirstin Reuber p 131; iStockPhoto.com / Michael Westhoff p 242; Pearson Education Ltd / Debbie Rowe pp 218–19, 250; Pearson Education Ltd / Jules Selmes p 44; Pearson Education Ltd / Tudor Photography p 211; Rex Features pp 2–3, 4, 8, 19, 23, 33, 76, 187; Rex Features / Ted Blackbrow p 229; Rex Features / Nils Jorgensen p 234; Rex Features / Sipa Press p 27; Rex Features / The Travel Library pp 66–7, 99; Rex Features / Roger Viollett p 127.

'Consider this' icon – Corbis; 'Case study' icon – Corbis; 'Grading tips' icon – iStockPhoto.com / Nick Schlax; 'Knowledge check' icon – Photos.com; 'Remember!' icon – Richard Smith; 'Theory into practice' icon – Harcourt Education Ltd / Debbie Rowe; 'Thinking points' icon – Harcourt Education Ltd / Jules Selmes

Thanks to the British Red Cross for permission to reproduce the emblem on p 54. The British Red Cross helps vulnerable people in crisis, whoever and wherever they are. In its role as an auxiliary to government, it offers support to statutory authorities by providing humanitarian assistance to individuals affected by emergencies. The red cross emblem is a protective symbol, whose use is restricted by international and national laws. It may not be reproduced without prior authorisation. For further information, please contact the British Red Cross, International Law Department at info@red.cross.org.uk.

Every effort has been made to contact copyright holders of material reproduced in this book. Any omissions will be rectified in subsequent printings if notice is given to the publishers.

Introduction

Welcome to this BTEC National Uniformed Public Services course book, specifically designed to support students on the following programmes:

- BTEC National Award in Uniformed Public Services
- BTEC National Certificate in Uniformed Public Services
- BTEC National Diploma in Uniformed Public Services.

This book includes specialist units not covered by Book 1 for the BTEC National Award, Certificate and the Diploma.

The aim of this book is to provide a comprehensive source of information for your course. It follows the BTEC specification closely, so that you can easily see what you have covered and quickly find the information you need. Examples and case studies from the public services are used to bring your course to life and make it enjoyable to study. We hope you will be encouraged to find your own examples of current practice too.

You will often be asked to carry out research for activities in the text, and this will develop your research skills and enable you to find many sources of interesting information, particularly on the Internet.

In some units of the book you will find information about different jobs, roles and responsibilities across the range of uniformed public services. We hope that this information will be of practical help when making your career choices.

Unit	Unit title	Award	Certificate	Diploma
14	The planning for and management of major incidents	Specialist	Specialist	Specialist
15	Responding to emergency service incidents	Specialist	Specialist	Specialist
16	Uniformed public services employment	Specialist	Specialist	Specialist
17	Understanding the criminal justice system and police powers	Specialist	Specialist	Specialist
18	Understanding behaviour in public sector employment	Specialist	Specialist	Specialist
20	Communication and technology in the uniformed public services	Specialist	Specialist	Specialist
21	Custodial care of individuals	Specialist	Specialist	Specialist
22	Understanding aspects of the legal system and law making process	Specialist	Specialist	Specialist

Guide to learning and assessment features

This book has a number of features to help you relate theory to practice and reinforce your learning. It also aims to help you gather evidence for assessment. You will find the following features in each unit.

Assessment features

Activities and assessment practice

Activities are provided throughout each unit. These are linked to real situations and case studies and they can be used for practice before tackling the preparation for assessment. Alternatively, some can contribute to your unit assessment if you choose to do these instead of the preparation for assessment at the end of each unit.

Grading icons

Throughout the book you will see the **P**, **M** and **D** icons. These show you where the tasks fit in with the grading criteria. If you do these tasks you will be building up your evidence to achieve your desired qualification. If you are aiming for a Merit, make sure you complete all the Pass **P** and Merit **M** tasks. If you are aiming for a Distinction, you will also need to complete all the Distinction **D** tasks. **P1** means the first of the Pass criteria listed in the specification, **M1** the first of the Merit criteria, **D1** the first of the Distinction criteria, and so on.

Preparation for assessment

Each unit concludes with a full unit assessment, which taken as a whole fulfils all the unit requirements from Pass to Distinction. Each task is matched to the relevant criteria in the specification.

Case study: Using psychology to improve leadership

Penny is the leader of a tightly knit and highly effective team of workers who are widely respected within the educational organisation they inhabit. Penny's team sits within a larger management structure headed by Rhys, who is Penny's line manager. Rhys has poor relations with Penny's team largely because he accords them no professional respect, constantly criticises them and ensures Penny does a great deal of the work that is actually within his remit to do.

Penny is justifiably proud of her team and the achievements they have earned and she understands their resentment, as she has also had to deal with unfounded criticism from Rhys. Penny suspects that Rhys feels threatened by the success of the team and is trying to consolidate his own leadership position by putting others down.

1. How could an understanding of psychology help Penny understand and deal with Rhys' behaviour?

2. How could an understanding of psychology be used by Rhys himself to understand his actions?

3. What aspects of psychology could Penny use to motivate her disgruntled team?

4. How could psychology improve the flow of communication between all concerned?

5. What aspects of psychology could help Penny deal with the conflicts she faces?

Assessment activity 18.2

In this assessment you are required to show how understanding the approaches to psychology can benefit the public service and the impact this will have on public service employees.

1. Research, prepare and present a PowerPoint presentation that describes the benefits of understanding the approaches to psychology within the public services. **P3**

2. Produce some supporting notes that assess how the different approaches to psychology will have an effect on employees in any public service employment. **M2**

Grading tips

P3 These are straightforward criteria. Describe in your own words the benefits that understanding the approaches to psychology can bring to an organisation in terms of improved efficiency and a motivated workforce.

M2 Your notes should clearly outline how the different approaches will affect employees.

The current debate centres not around nature or nurture alone, but how these two different perspectives could be combined to explain criminal behaviour. This of course would have tremendous use in public services such as the police, courts, prison and probation.

Remember!

- Nature is the argument that criminals are born.
- Nurture is the argument that criminals are made.
- There is evidence on both sides of the debate.
- The real relationship between nature and nurture is still unknown.

Theory into practice

Saara and Sureya are non-identical twins who are raised in the same home environment, with their younger brother Parvis and mother and father. When the twins are 16 their younger brother, who is 14, begins to get into trouble at school. This trouble eventually becomes more serious and Parvis is sent to a young offender institution at the age of 15. The twins' father also had a history of petty crime in his youth, but is a responsible and upstanding citizen now. The twins' mother has never been involved in crime.

- How would supporters of the nature argument explain how Parvis became involved in breaking the law? What about supporters of the nurture argument?
- What is the likelihood that the twins will engage in criminal activity?
- How might Saara and Sureya differ in concordance from identical twins?
- Would the twins' mother be likely to become criminal?

Knowledge check

1. Which psychological theory is Carl Rogers associated with?
2. Who developed the pyschoanalytic theory?
3. What are the benefits of understanding psychology to individuals?
4. Describe the key features of aggressive communication.
5. How does assertive communication differ from submissive?
6. What types of conflict are the public services likely to encounter?
7. What are the most common reasons for conflict?
8. Describe two informal actions someone could take that might reduce or prevent conflict.
9. What is the buddy system?
10. What is a mentor?

Consider this

If crime is linked to genetic inheritance, how might this affect:

- The way criminals are sentenced?
- The way crime is prevented?
- What impact would it have on the services?

Learning features

Case studies

Interesting examples of real situations or companies are described in case studies that link theory to practice. They will show you how the topics you are studying affect real people and the services they provide.

Theory into practice

These practical activities allow you to apply theoretical knowledge to travel and tourism tasks or research. Make sure you complete these activities as you work through each unit, to reinforce your learning.

Knowledge check

At the end of each unit is a set of quick questions to test your knowledge of the information you have been studying. Use these to check your progress, and also as a revision tool.

Remember! and Key terms

Issues and terms that you need to be aware of are summarised under these headings. They will help you check your knowledge as you learn, and will prove to be a useful quick-reference tool.

Consider this and Take it further

These are points for individual reflection or group discussion. They will widen your knowledge and help you reflect on issues that impact on public services. The 'Take it further' activities in particular will help you to obtain the knowledge and practice the skills required for the higher levels of achievement.

The planning for and management of major incidents

Introduction

This unit will enable you to increase your awareness and understanding of the different aspects of major incidents.

In the first section you will be able to investigate the different causes and types of recent major incidents and see what effects they have in terms of loss to the individual and the wider community. You will also see how major incidents have brought about a change in legislation and procedures.

The second section will develop your understanding of the work carried out by various agencies during major incidents. You will learn how they cooperate with each other, what each agency is responsible for and the specific roles they have in dealing with major incidents, as well as the relevant legislation and chains of command.

In the third section you will examine emergency planning, from which you will learn how our country prepares itself for major incidents. You will look at the main points of an emergency plan and the organisations involved in preparing for major incidents.

In the last section you will look at how organisations prepare simulation exercises in order to deal with real major incidents should they arise. This will involve you taking part in a mock scenario.

After completing this unit you should be able to achieve the following outcomes:
- Understand the effects of recent major incidents
- Know the type of work carried out by the public services during major incidents
- Understand the considerations for emergency planning and preparation for possible major incidents
- Be able to prepare for a particular major incident by using tabletop scenarios.

The terms 'major incident' and 'disaster' are often used to refer to the same thing, though there is a difference. 'Disaster' seems to have become a media term that is used to describe a serious emergency, whereas the emergency services refer to a serious emergency as a 'major incident.'

Major incident

For the purposes of this unit, an emergency is defined as: 'an event or situation which threatens serious damage to human welfare in a place in the UK, the environment of a place in the UK, or war or terrorism which threatens serious damage to the security of the UK.' This includes an emergency outside the UK that has consequences in the UK. For example, if known terrorists were boarding a plane in, say, Germany, and heading for the UK to commit an act of terrorism, then this would be classed as an emergency.

Whether there is a threat to human welfare, the environment, or security, the emergency services are obliged to respond, and it is the number of emergency personnel who respond to the emergency, and the special arrangements they need to make, that makes it a major incident. In other words, a major incident is an emergency situation that demands special arrangements by one or all of the emergency services for:

- the rescue and transport of a large number of casualties
- the organisation and mobilisation of the local authority and other organisations to respond to the threat of death, injury or homelessness on a large scale.

This means that one or more of the emergency services attend the incident in greater numbers than would normally attend a routine incident on a day-to-day basis, putting a strain on the emergency services.

British major incidents

Look at the following two case studies of recent major incidents in the United Kingdom.

Case study:
The Boscastle floods 2004

Boscastle is a coastal village in north Cornwall, with sea on one side and high ground with a river valley on the other, which relies on the tourist industry for its economy. During the afternoon of Monday 16 August 2004, record levels of torrential rain (3.5 inches in one hour) fell on the village, while a short distance up the valley twice as much rain fell. This caused the river to rise and within an hour it had risen seven feet but the real problem was that just up from the village debris had collected under a bridge and was holding back water coming from higher ground, thus causing a blockage. The bridge collapsed under pressure, releasing the debris and an estimated two million tonnes of water, which surged through the village, causing trees to be uprooted, boats to be lost, and cars and buildings to be washed into the sea.

Many buildings and businesses were damaged by the force of the water and had to be demolished because they were unsafe.

The emergency services, including seven helicopters from the Royal Navy and Royal Air Force, dealt with

the immediate response until 2.30am the following morning, rescuing people from treetops, roofs of buildings and cars.

There were no deaths or serious injuries reported, though approximately 60 people were evacuated from the village and taken to hospital. This was one of the largest maritime operations ever carried out.

1. **There was no loss of life at Boscastle but why was it a major incident?**
2. **Having regard to the location of Boscastle, what other threats were there?**
3. **What problems would there have been in the immediate aftermath, to both villagers and tourists?**

Case study: The London bombings July 2005

During the rush hour of 7 July 2005, a series of coordinated terrorist explosions killed a total of 52 people and injured 700, 22 of them seriously. The explosions also killed four suicide bombers.

At 8.50am that morning, three bombs were exploded on three trains in the London Underground within 50 seconds of each other. The first two bombs exploded on two trains travelling on the Circle Line, one eastbound and the other westbound, and the third on a train travelling on the Piccadilly Line. Two of the trains were travelling through underground tunnels at the time of the explosions and another one had just left a platform. Almost an hour later, a fourth bomb exploded on a London bus in Tavistock Square, causing extensive damage to the top and rear of the bus. Some of those who boarded the bus had been evacuated from a nearby station because of the earlier explosions.

The explosions brought London's transport system to a halt for over a day and the emergency services were stretched to deal with the situation.

1. **Given the devastation, shock and confusion brought about by these bombings, what do you think would have been one of the main priorities of the emergency services?**

2. **Why would the rescue attempts have been particularly difficult?**

3. **Apart from the obvious effects on individuals, what effect would the incidents have had on London?**

Take it further

1. Carry out some research from the Internet into the foot and mouth outbreak of 2001 and consider how different the method of dealing with it would have been to the Boscastle Floods.

2. Carry out some research from the Internet into the Hatfield Rail Disaster and the Selby Rail Crash and compare the different causes.

3. Carry out some research from the Internet into the Kegworth Air Disaster and compare the rescue effort to that of the Selby Rail Crash.

Causes and types of major incidents

There are many causes of disasters but they generally fall into one of the following categories:
- natural causes
- hostile acts
- technological
- health-related
- epidemics/pandemics.

Natural causes

Disasters with natural causes can be some of the most devastating in terms of loss of life, loss of property or damage to the environment, not to mention the economy. Volcanic eruptions, for instance, can have terrible consequences, like the one at Mount St Helens in 1980 where ten million trees were destroyed leaving a desolate and infertile landscape.

Volcanoes are caused when magma is formed deep within the earth and then rises to the surface and is erupted as lava.

Another cause of natural disasters is earthquake, which is the violent shaking of the ground as a result of the movement of tectonic plates. Whilst some earthquakes are worse than others, they can all have dreadful consequences if they occur in heavily populated areas, such as the one in Kobe City in Japan in 1995, for instance.

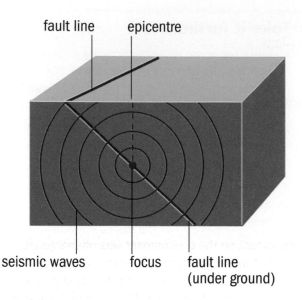

seismic waves   focus   fault line (under ground)

▲ Figure 14.1 How an earthquake happens

Consider this

What is it that makes earthquakes dangerous? Is it the shaking of the ground or something else?

Hostile acts

These are aggressive or violent acts that can cause havoc to communities or even nations. Such acts can involve terrorism, where buildings or civilians are attacked with bombs or missiles. For example, the Twin Towers attack on 11 September 2001 was an act of terrorism where four planes were hijacked in the United States of America and two of them were flown into the Twin Towers in New York, killing almost 3,000 people.

Civil war

This is a war between people of the same country and causes members of society to live in constant fear because of the threat of harm, or theft, or damage, or loss of property. People will naturally become anxious because they cannot expect the same protection that they can in peacetime and there could be a strong temptation to take the law into their own hands. Civil war can stretch the emergency services and military to their absolute limit.

Technological

Technological disasters are those that result from, say, defective rail tracks, faulty components of an aeroplane, or it could be the emission of radiation, because all of these involve mechanisation or applied science.

Consider this

1. Which category of disaster was the Hatfield Train Crash and why?
2. Which category of disaster was the Kegworth Air Disaster and why?

Health-related causes

Some major incidents can result from the spread of infectious diseases, which can be either **epidemic** or **pandemic**.

Key terms

Epidemic An epidemic is the spread of a disease throughout a community and is normally contained within that area.

Pandemic A pandemic is the spread of disease over a much larger area, possibly an entire country or even the world, for instance, avian flu or SARS.

Case study: The Chernobyl nuclear power plant

Chernobyl is located in north central Ukraine, quite near to the border with Belarus, in the former Soviet Union.

In the early hours of Saturday 26 April 1986, one of the plant's nuclear reactors exploded causing clouds of radioactive fallout to contaminate huge areas of the northern hemisphere, including parts of the Western Soviet Union, Eastern Europe, Western Europe, Northern Europe and parts of North America. The contamination was so severe in Ukraine, Belarus and Russia that over 300,000 people had to be evacuated and re-housed.

This incident is regarded as the worst accident in the history of nuclear disasters and this particular incident resulted in a dramatic increase in thyroid cancer in young people. A report by the Chernobyl Forum in 2005 stated that as many as 9,000 people, who were highly exposed to the radiation, may die from cancer. However, according to Greenpeace, there is likely to be 270,000 cases of cancer as a result of the accident, 93,000 of which will probably be fatal.

Apart from the increases in cancer, people developed psychological problems because of the effects of radiation, social upheaval and lack of communication regarding the economic situation since the division of the Soviet Union.

Chernobyl

The impact on the environment was phenomenal, with evidence of radiation pollution covering the entire northern hemisphere. This pollution meant the contamination of soil, water systems (including drinking supplies), vegetation and animals. Restrictions were placed on the sale and movement of livestock and these restrictions even reached as far as Western Scotland, North Wales and Cumbria, where levels of contamination were above the recommended dose.

1. **What would you say were the worst effects of the Chernobyl disaster?**

2. **Could this ever happen in the UK? Carry out some research using the Internet to see if we have nuclear power plants and any history of leaked radioactive materials.**

Avian flu, otherwise known as 'bird flu,' is one of many different types of flu that is common in birds but it is the H5N1 flu virus strain that is the biggest concern. This is highly contagious, especially with poultry, and it can be fatal to humans. So far, avian flu H5N1 has claimed 164 lives from 270 reported cases in Azerbaijan, Cambodia, China, Djibouti, Egypt, Indonesia, Iraq, Thailand, Turkey and Vietnam. Some experts predict that if the virus mutates, so that it can be passed from human to human, then an outbreak of avian flu could kill between 5 million and 150 million people.

Severe Acute Respiratory Syndrome (SARS) is a respiratory disease in humans caused by the coronavirus, a family of viruses that causes the common cold but which has mutated to become dangerous to humans, killing almost 800 people so far. The first SARS epidemic is believed to have started in a province of China in 2002 but there have been reported cases in over 25 countries, including the USA, the UK and India.

Effects of major incidents

Effects on individuals

The effects of major incidents on individuals can be devastating. Floods, for instance, could ruin a person's business, meaning a loss of income for the owner of the business, as well as a loss of income for anyone employed by that business. Similarly, an outbreak of avian flu could mean the destruction of thousands of birds; again, meaning loss of income for the owner, as well as the threat to human health or life.

In some areas of the world, people lose their homes as well as their businesses. For example, the tsunami in South East Asia in 2004 not only destroyed homes and businesses it also destroyed entire villages. The same destruction could happen in the event of an earthquake or the eruption of a volcano.

Effects on rescue workers

At many major incidents, people die or are seriously injured; some are trapped in wreckage, whilst others might be badly burned or bleeding. People of all ages can be casualties in disaster situations; this includes young children and even babies. The emergency services and other rescue agencies witness all kinds of injuries to victims of major incidents. They will see casualties suffering from mild shock and others suffering terrible injuries; unfortunately, they also see people dying as a result of their injuries.

When responding to an incident, the emergency services' priority is to deal with it as efficiently as possible; they do not have time to consider their own feelings or emotions. However, when the incident has been dealt with and the individual members of the emergency services have had time to reflect on the horrendous scenes they have witnessed, then it is possible that they become psychologically stressed. This is known as post-traumatic stress disorder (PTSD), which can make an individual mentally and physically ill, and unfit for duty.

Effects on communities

■ Loss of law and order

During a major incident, it is inevitable that a strain is placed on the uniformed public services because the incident is using most of their human resources and normal routine is disrupted. This means that, the police, for instance, whilst directing their efforts on dealing with the major incident, cannot control their area as normal. Consequently, there could be a temporary loss of law and order and an increase in crime, such as theft and looting, especially where buildings or vehicles have had to be abandoned.

Different types of major incidents, however, can have different effects on communities. Civil wars, for instance, can bring about loss of law and order to a community or even a country; but natural causes of major incidents can also bring about civil unrest, especially where victims become agitated because they believe that the government is not doing enough to help them, as in the floods in Kentucky in the USA in 2005, for example. This could lead people to believe that they can take the law into their own hands.

▲ Rescue workers witness very distressing situations

■ Disease

Any major incident is bad enough for a community, but there can be prolonged periods where normality cannot be restored because of secondary effects. Floods, for example, can lead to disease where flood water, with all its contaminants, such as sewage, mixes with tap water, which is then drunk. Typhoid and cholera are two serious, infectious diseases caused by drinking contaminated water.

Wider impact of incidents

Reviews of disasters

After a major incident, the emergency services and other agencies involved hold a review, which is a form of assessment, to determine if the incident was responded to in the most efficient way. A review is part of a process for improving performance, where questions are asked and suggestions for improvement put forward. There are several components to the reviewing process.

■ Public enquiry

A public enquiry is an open enquiry in front of a public audience into a major incident. The purpose of such an enquiry is to allow people to seek information about the major incident. Members of the audience are free to ask questions and raise issues about what they may have read or heard and to voice their concerns regarding any short- or long-term effects the incident is likely to have. An enquiry may be adjourned because further information might be needed regarding issues that may have been raised at the enquiry.

Public enquiries have a chairperson and a panel, usually consisting of heads of personnel who attended the major incident, representatives of government departments, specialist agencies, such as Aviation Authority representatives, medical personnel and other interested parties.

■ Debriefs of incidents by agencies

A debrief is a method of analysing the response by an agency to an incident, by means of question and answer. Debriefs are common practice throughout all uniformed public service organisations and they are intended to assess the efficiency of how a particular service responded to an incident, with the intention of highlighting mistakes and thereby improving future performance.

Debriefs may be headed by the senior officer attending the incident, though not necessarily so, and they take the form of question and answer followed by an evaluation and recommendations for future major incidents.

At a debrief following a major incident, the emergency services (police, fire and ambulance) would give their response times and an account of their actions in dealing with the incident.

Other agencies, such as local authority emergency teams, also have debriefs where they answer questions regarding their involvement in major incidents.

Prevention

It is impossible to prevent some serious events from happening, since some phenomena are beyond human control, like earthquakes and volcanoes, which are part of the nature of the earth and cannot be controlled. However, not all emergencies are bound to turn into disasters where human life or the environment is threatened.

Planning

With careful consideration, an emergency situation can be prevented from turning into a disaster. In areas where earth tremors and earthquakes occur frequently, for instance, it would be prudent to construct buildings and bridges that can withstand them. Indeed, in certain areas of the world, like Japan, it is a legal requirement that buildings are constructed to withstand earthquakes.

In the United Kingdom, especially after the floods of June and July 2007, better planning consideration needs to be given to the construction of new homes and communities so that they are not being built on flood plains, for instance. However, where flooding is prevalent in established housing and communities, then plans could be put in place to ensure the safety of residents and communities.

Consider this

What preventative measures could be put in place to reduce the risk of a repeat of the floods in the UK in the summer of 2007?

Improved technology

Technology plays a large part in most people's lives these days and technology can help in the prevention of disasters in several ways.

Highly technical equipment can forecast severe storms, gales and snow, just as it can, with some accuracy, track earthquake and volcanic movement. Furthermore, government and military intelligence have the technology to intercept emails and telephone calls from terrorist suspects, all of which serve to make a safer world. However, if the information gleaned from technology is to prove useful then it has be collated, disseminated and acted upon.

Better funding

Since the bombings of the Twin Towers in September 2001, more government funding has been given to emergency planning, including training of the fire and rescue services in chemical and biological contamination techniques, as well as the restructuring of the government's emergency planning department. However, the recent flooding in the UK has highlighted the fact that funding is needed not only to defend against acts of terrorism; it is also needed to rebuild businesses and communities following any disaster.

Government funding is given to those areas where disasters have occurred and immediate aid is required. The floods in the UK in 2007 resulted in the government distributing £3.6 million between 21 local authorities, with the largest payments going to Worcestershire, Gloucestershire and Warwickshire. Further funding can be obtained through the Bellwin Scheme, which is an emergency assistance fund set up to help those local authorities who have experienced sudden and extensive upheaval as a result of an unforeseen event, such as flooding. Funding is also available from the European Union Solidarity Fund (EUSF) and in August 2007 the British government applied for £46 million to help with the recovery from the extensive flooding in the UK. Whilst funding from the EUSF would help enormously, it could take up to one year for the funding to be approved and granted.

Other sources of funding include grants from the Lottery Fund and donations through national appeals. For example, by November 2004, Boscastle had £200,000 through an appeal that was set up by the local council and local trustees.

Environmental initiatives

Many disasters have an effect on the environment, whether these are oil spillages at sea, air pollution from nuclear fallout, contamination of rivers or foot and mouth outbreaks. The government department responsible for the environment is the Department for the Environment, Food and Rural Affairs (otherwise known by the acronym, DEFRA, or, the Environment Agency). DEFRA has the authority to take whatever action is necessary in order to prevent a disaster, or to stop its escalation. For example, during the foot and mouth outbreak of 2001, it ordered the closure of footpaths in many parts of the countryside, compulsory disinfecting of vehicles and footwear when entering controlled areas, the prohibition of the movement of certain farm animals and the eventual slaughter and burning of thousands of cattle.

DEFRA also has the authority to prevent access to certain areas of open moorland in periods of prolonged hot, dry weather if there is a high risk of fire, which could threaten the moorland environment. Whilst such measures may appear to be more like coping strategies, they are, nonetheless, initiatives that are designed to prevent potential disasters from becoming reality.

Theory into practice

DEFRA is the key agency in an initiative that involves major alterations in Boscastle. The river is currently being widened and deepened to reduce the risk of it bursting its banks, the steepness of river banks has been reduced and bridges reinforced.

action to take during an emergency. However, whilst local authorities and the emergency services prepare emergency and contingency plans, some would say that not enough has been done to educate the public, and that this was evident from terrible scenes in the recent media coverage of the floods in the United Kingdom. The problem with educating the public is that authorities have to balance the likelihood of causing panic, by constantly telling the public what steps they should take to prevent a disaster, with information about what they should do in the event of a disaster.

Education by authorities

Part of the fire service's role is community education in the prevention and detection of fire, and in 2004 the government issued a leaflet to all householders on the

general advice about what to do in an emergency

If you find yourself in the middle of an emergency, your common sense and instincts will usually tell you what to do. However, it is important to:
- Make sure **999** has been called if people are injured or if there is a threat to life
- Not put yourself or others in danger
- Follow the advice of the emergency services
- Try to remain calm and think before acting, and try to reassure others
- Check for injuries - remember to help yourself before attempting to help others

If you are not involved in the incident, but are close by or believe you may be in danger, in most cases the advice is:
- Go inside a safe building
- Stay inside until you are advised to do otherwise
- Tune in to local radio or TV for more information

Of course, there are always going to be particular occasions when you should not "go in" to a building, for example if there is a fire. Otherwise: **GO IN, STAY IN, TUNE IN.**

The **GO IN, STAY IN, TUNE IN** advice is recognised and used around the world. It was developed by the independent National Steering Committee on Warning and Informing the Public as being the best general advice to give people caught up in most emergencies

Go in, Stay in, Tune in

There is an agreement with radio and TV companies that if there is a major emergency they will interrupt programming to give public safety advice and information about the incident, so that when you **TUNE IN** locally or nationally anywhere in the UK you'll get the advice you need.

Tune in

▲ *Preparing for Emergencies*, a leaflet issued to all householders in 2004

Source: Cabinet Office. Crown Copyright material reproduced with permission of the Controller of HMSO and the Queen's Printer for Scotland.

Costs

In terms of hardship, suffering and personal loss, it is impossible to calculate the cost of major incidents on a personal level. In monetary terms, however, the cost is calculated according to the amount of damage, the cost for rebuilding and any compensation that might be owed. The cost of the damage caused by flooding in the UK in 2007 is estimated at £3 billion in insured properties and £3 billion in uninsured properties.

Insurance companies are facing their heaviest losses in history and whilst they have promised to pay claimants, the process is slow because properties cannot be assessed until they have completely dried out. Furthermore, many insurance companies are considering refusal to cover flood damage claims if the government fails to invest in flood prevention.

New investments

The government has promised to invest in building better flood defences but some experts estimate that the investment falls short by more than £8 billion. However, it is not only defences to floods that need investment; it is needed for the prevention of other major incidents, such as terrorism, which means investment in security and the uniformed public services.

Lack of investment can have a drastic effect on a country's economy, as well as preventing the rapid recovery of a major incident.

Firstly, it is in the interests of private companies to invest in such things as defence and security systems so that their businesses are affected as little as possible in the event of a major incident.

Secondly, utilities, such as water and electricity companies, need to invest in their infrastructure so that they can provide adequate services during times of need. For instance, water companies need to invest in draining systems that are capable of carrying away excessive amounts of rainfall, thus minimising the risk of flooding, while electricity companies need to ensure that power stations are located in areas that are not prone to flooding.

Furthermore, with the growing concerns over the effects of global warming, careful consideration needs to be given to the location of the development of housing. The English Partnership is The National Regeneration Agency that aims to bring together the public and private sector in providing safe, sustainable housing and amenities.

Resultant legislation

Legislation is designed to give the security services, police and other organisations the authority to take whatever measures they deem appropriate to prevent a major incident or to prevent an emergency from escalating into a disaster. Not all new legislation is the result of potential or actual major incidents, however; it is often the case that they are upgraded or amended to deal with any inadequacies that may have been highlighted in view of recent events, like the London bombings, for example.

Since the year 2000, there have been several Acts of Parliament designed to give police and the security services the authority to prevent terrorism. The latest statute is the Terrorism Act of 2006, which became law in March 2006 and made amendments to previous statutes, namely the Prevention of Terrorism Act 2005 and the Terrorism Act 2000.

The Terrorism Act 2006 makes it a criminal offence to:

- directly or indirectly incite or encourage others to commit acts of terrorism
- sell, loan, or distribute terrorist publications, including publications that encourage terrorism or assist terrorists
- give or receive training in terrorist techniques
- attend at a place of terrorist training
- possess or make any radioactive device
- sabotage nuclear facilities
- make threats or demands to be given radioactive materials.

■ Procedures

The new laws give the police extra powers, including:

- warrants to search any property owned or controlled by a terrorist suspect
- extending stop and search powers to cover bays and estuaries
- to detain suspects after arrest for up to 28 days
- improved search powers at ports
- the power to prosecute groups that glorify terrorism.

Home Office ministers want to make it a criminal offence where people, who have been stopped by the police, fail to answer questions about their movements and their identity.

Processes

Since the events of September 11 2001, airport security at home and abroad has increased with searching and scanning of passengers, X-raying hand luggage and personal items prior to checking in for a flight; similar processes apply at ferry ports. On long haul flights, all luggage is X-rayed and searched at random. The tighter security measures inevitably brought long delays at all airports.

In August 2006, following an alleged plot to detonate bombs on up to nine aircraft, airport security was again increased whereby liquids, other than essential medication, were prohibited from being taken onto aircrafts. Hand luggage was also banned and essential travel documents had to be carried in clear, plastic bags.

■ Improvements

In order to deal with security risks, airports have had to make improvements and these have included screening of employees and better training of staff, as well as improvements in security equipment, such as communications and closed-circuit television.

In the United States of America, airports are taking advantage of technology by using biometric testing in the form of iris recognition, thus trying to eliminate human error in identifying suspects who may attempt facial disguise. Heathrow airport is conducting fingerprint and iris recognition tests with a view to strengthening security and reducing the queuing time.

Assessment activity 14.1

For this activity you are required to prepare and deliver a presentation that will show that you understand what is meant by a major incident and show the cause and effects of three recent major incidents. You should ensure that you cover the content in the following four sections:

1: Major incident
   Definition; British major incidents

2: Causes and types
   Natural causes; hostile acts; technological; health-related and epidemics/pandemics

3: Effects
   On individuals; on rescue workers; on communities

4: Wider impact of incidents
   Reviews of disasters; prevention (better planning, improved technology, better funding, environmental initiatives, education by authorities); costs (damage, rebuilding, compensation, insurance); new investment; resultant legislation; procedures; processes; improvements.

You should use this content so that your presentation will:

1. Describe the term 'major incident,' including three different causes or types giving relevant examples for each. **P1**

2. Describe three different recent major incidents/disasters, one of which must have occurred in the UK, showing the cause of each and the effects they have on the people, communities, environment involved and other wider impacts they have had. **P2**

Grading tips

P1 To achieve this grade you should use the content in sections 1 and 2, and give relevant examples.

P2 To achieve this grade you must choose three recent disasters (one of which must have occurred in the UK) and use the content in sections 3 and 4.

Inter-agency cooperation

There are many agencies involved in major incidents and disaster recovery. Here is a list of just some of them:

- emergency services (police, fire and ambulance)
- Red Cross
- military
- local authorities
- utilities (gas, water and electricity companies)
- WRVS.

Take it further

1. Carry out some research using the Internet to see how the Red Cross and WRVS may be involved in major incidents.

2. Name three other agencies that could be involved in major incidents.

Interaction between emergency and other services

Agencies involved in major incidents know how to interact with each other through liaison, cooperation and careful planning. Within each police area, representatives from the agencies likely to be involved in major incidents attend Emergency Planning Resilience Forums where they produce a comprehensive, multi-agency emergency procedures guide. The guide clearly states the aims and objectives of the forum and defines the responsibilities of the agencies involved, the use of voluntary agencies, as well as recommendations for training. The emergency procedures guide is, essentially, an emergency plan, or a collection of plans, that the emergency and other services follow in the event of a major incident. Therefore, before the onset of a major incident, the agencies involved know their roles and responsibilities, and will have carried out joint training so that they have each other's cooperation in the event of a major incident.

Responsibilities at scene

Regardless of the agencies' specific roles and responsibilities, they all share common objectives when dealing with major incidents. These include:

- saving life and lessening suffering at the scene
- protecting property
- preventing the escalation of a disaster
- protecting the environment
- sharing information between all agencies involved in the incident
- protecting and preserving the scene
- contributing to debriefing and subsequent investigation and inquiries into the incident
- restoring normality
- maintaining normal services where possible
- providing whatever resources are necessary for the recovery of the incident.

Agency specific objectives

Apart from the common objectives, each agency has specific responsibilities and objectives to ensure an efficient response to a major incident.

Local authority

Major incidents always bring disruption to the community, and since the community is the focus of social, family, educational and spiritual well-being, it is important for normality to be restored as quickly as possible. Whilst it is the responsibility of the emergency services and other organisations to respond to the major incident, it is the responsibility of the local authority to ensure, as far as possible, that the needs of the community are met by maintaining normal services. For example, during the event of a major incident, certain members of the community may still be reliant on community and social care, such as catering services.

In some cases, particularly severe flooding, members of the community may have to be evacuated and the local authority is responsible for providing rest and reception centres, or temporary accommodation; these might be located in schools and leisure centres.

Major incidents not only cause distress and anxiety for everyone directly involved, they are also a source of great concern for friends, relatives and loved ones who are living out of the area or may be on holiday and have heard about the incident through the media. It is vital that there is a contact number so friends and relatives can find out the information they require, and this is usually provided by the local authority.

Local authorities have emergency planning teams (Local Authority Emergency Planning Officers) and they play an important role in the coordination and recovery of a major incident by:

- establishing a Local Authority Control Point to ensure a standard response procedure for the smooth operation of the incident
- providing a Site Officer to deploy and coordinate on-site resources
- providing extra resources for the emergency and other services.

Police

The specific aims of the police service at a major incident are to:

- collate and distribute casualty information
- preserve the scene for evidence
- investigate the cause
- identify the dead
- ensure the entry and exit at the incident
- control the cordons
- control crowds and sightseers.

Fire and rescue service

The specific aims of the fire service are to:

- fight fires and investigate the cause in a fire situation
- conduct search and rescue using specialist equipment
- ensure the site is safe before other emergency personnel attempt rescue
- establish decontamination units where necessary.

The ambulance service

The specific aims of the ambulance service are to:

- perform triage
- establish a casualty loading area
- transport casualties to designated hospitals
- order adequate medical resources.

Duties under law

The Civil Contingencies Act 2004 and the Civil Contingencies Act 2004 (Contingency Planning) Regulations 2005 set the statutory guidance for civil protection in the UK at local level. It places a legal obligation on local authorities and other organisations to cooperate in responding to, and preparing for, major incidents. The Act is in two parts, with the first part detailing the duties of those who respond and prepare, while part two makes provision for the making of special emergency regulations in order to assist with the most serious incidents.

The responders fall into two categories.

1. Category 1 responders – these are the organisations that are at the centre of planning and responding, and they are the emergency services (police, fire and ambulance), local authorities and the Health Protection Agency.
2. Category 2 responders – these are the organisations that are not directly involved in planning, but play a vital part in dealing with incidents. Category 2 responders include:
   - utilities (gas, electric, water and sewage, and telephone service providers)
   - transport (train operating companies, Transport for London, airport operators, harbour authorities and Highways Agency)
   - government agencies (Health and Safety Executive)
   - strategic Health Authorities.

Emergency powers

Emergency powers invoked under the Civil Contingencies Act will be only temporary and used as a last resort and will be available only:

- for serious incidents that threaten human welfare, the environment or national security
- if it is necessary to make urgent provision in order to resolve the emergency and existing powers are inadequate
- if the emergency powers to be invoked are proportionate to the incident.

The legislation makes it compulsory for Category 1 responders to provide an integrated response to emergency planning. They must hold a meeting at least once every six months in the form of a local resilience forum. Category 2 responders must attend at the invitation of Category 1 responders or, if it is not possible, ensure a representative attends.

Cooperation is needed between Category 1 and 2 responders and other organisations to ensure that the legal duties placed on them can be effectively managed and executed. Cooperation is only one of the duties placed on organisations by the legislation. The table below shows the legal duties placed on responders.

Duty	Responders
Cooperation	1 and 2
Information sharing	1 and 2
Assessing the risk of hazards and emergencies and their impact on the community	1
Maintaining emergency plans for preventing, reducing and controlling emergencies, as well as dealing with the secondary effects	1
Business continuity management	1
Communicating the risk to the public and how it will be responded to	1
Advice and assistance to commercial or voluntary organisations, including management issues should the need arise during an emergency	Local authority only

Table 14.1 Legal duties of responders to major incidents

Chains of command

When dealing with major incidents, the emergency services use three levels of command:

- operational (bronze)
- tactical (silver)
- strategic (gold).

Operational command is concerned with dealing with events at the immediate scene of an incident, and could involve such things as fire fighting, rescuing trapped victims from wreckage, treating the injured, and so on. An inner cordon is established around the incident to prevent unauthorised access to the disaster site while operational personnel carry out their work. Operational staff includes the emergency services, local authority representatives and other organisations as demanded by the nature of the incident.

Tactical command consists of a member from each of the emergency services who takes charge of the scene and creates tactics for his or her service, at operational command, to successfully deal with the incident. Tactical command, unlike operational command, is not directly involved in the hands-on approach but is normally established further away from the scene, possibly in mobile units designated as special operations rooms.

Strategic command is formed if the incident is very serious and cannot be resolved by tactical command, though in cases of pandemic disease or predicted incidents, such as floods, the strategic team may be the first command to be established.

This command comprises senior officers from the emergency services and other organisations as required. Their role is to form a strategy to deal with the incident and to support tactical and operational commands. Gold Command, as it is more often called, is located away from the incident, possibly at a police station or council building.

Organisation

It is common practice that major incidents are coordinated by the police service, though strategic commanders from the other services would advise on matters where they had specialist knowledge. For instance, the Gold Fire

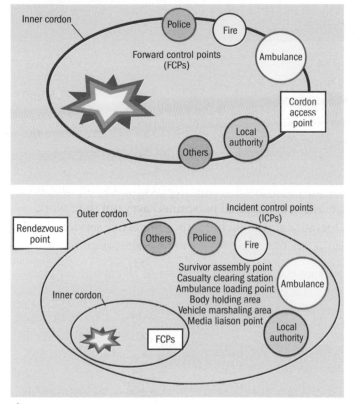

▲ Figure 14.2 Inner and outer cordons at an emergency scene

Source: Cabinet Office, *Dealing with Disaster*, rev 3rd ed., pp. 23, 24. Crown Copyright material reproduced with permission of the Controller of HMSO and the Queen's Printer for Scotland.

Commander would have better knowledge of how to deal with a fire incident than a Gold Police Commander.

Each of the emergency services is coordinated and organised by their respective service commanders within the levels of command already outlined.

As for the organisation and involvement of local authorities, a Local Authority Liaison Officer would visit the scene to assess the level of support required by the local authority. If necessary, the Local Authority Liaison Officer would visit Silver Command to provide cooperation between the emergency services and the local authority.

In the event of a minor incident, which is unlikely to escalate, the Emergency Planning Duty Manager may coordinate the local authority's response, but at large incidents the local authority will establish its own Emergency Control Centre and coordinate the local authority's response to the incident. This would include Chief Officers from the local authority who act at Gold Level, as well as Chief Officers from Council Departments, who act at Silver Level.

Assessment activity 14.2

This activity requires you to write an article for a magazine, entitled 'Major Incidents', which will inform the public of three specific incidents and how different agencies responded to them. You should cover how the agencies worked together, making reference to how their duties are governed by law. You should ensure that you include the content in the following five sections:

Section 1: Inter-agency cooperation
Agencies involved in major incident/disaster recovery.

Section 2: Responsibilities at scene
Common objectives (save lives, prevent escalation, protect environment, restore normality, contribute to debriefing process).

Section 3: Agency-specific objectives

Section 4: Duties under law
Civil Contingencies Act 2004 including any subsequent amendments; emergency powers, duties of cooperation placed on agencies by law.

Section 5: Chains of command
Operational (bronze), tactical (silver) and strategic (gold); organisation of the local authorities and emergency services.

You should use this content in your article so that it will:

- Identify agencies that were involved in the response to three specific incidents/disasters, one of which must have occurred in the UK, describing the work of agencies at UK incidents with reference to any appropriate duties under law. **P4**

Grading tips

P4 You should make reference to the content in all five sections.

M2 This is an extension of P4 but instead of describing the work of agencies at UK incidents you should:

- Explain how agencies involved in a specific UK incident/disaster worked together with reference to any appropriate duties under law. **M2**

Emergency plans are designed to increase resilience by ensuring that all the agencies involved in responding to the incident:

- know their roles
- are competent to carry out their assigned tasks
- have access to available resources and facilities
- have confidence that other responders are prepared.

When emergency planning is undertaken by Category 1 responders, a great deal of thought is given to identifying possible risks and how they could be efficiently dealt with. A risk includes hazards (e.g. floods) and threats (e.g. terrorist atacks) that could adversely affect organisations, the community, an individual, the nation or the environment.

Assessment

The purpose of emergency planning is to provide an integrated response to major incidents with a view to bringing about a successful end to the incident. However, before an emergency plan can be prepared, possible risks need to be identified and assessed, including:

- large-scale road traffic collisions
- possible plane/train accidents
- terrorist activities
- flooding
- diseases.

Thinking points

1. From the list of incidents, give a brief explanation for each scenario saying what the main problems would be with each incident.

2. Which organisations would you expect to deal with them and why?

3. If you were Gold Commander, which incident would cause you most concern?

Risk assessments

Risk assessments include:

- **risk evaluation** – the identification of significant risks by analysing their likelihood and impact, and formulating an overall risk score
- **risk treatment** – involves deciding which risks are unacceptably high, and devising strategies to reduce them.

Risk assessments form the basis of all emergency plans, the main considerations of which are: prevention, preparation, response and recovery.

Hazard prevention options

Once a potential hazard or threat has been identified, its impact and scope is evaluated and if it is a significant or unacceptable risk, then measures have to be taken to try to prevent it from causing harm. This is done by examining the possible options and selecting those that are the most suitable by sharing information amongst agencies at the planning stage.

At the scene of an actual major incident, however, hazard prevention could be undertaken by prompt and decisive action. For example, in the East Midlands Air Disaster, where a passenger aircraft landed on the motorway a short distance from the runway, a worse disaster was prevented when the fire service covered the fuselage of the aircraft with foam to prevent the risk of fire.

Hazard minimisation options

Hazards cannot always be predicted or prevented, for example the UK floods in 2007, and sometimes the next best thing is to consider options for minimising harm to the public.

Flooding is a serious hazard for individuals and in order to minimise the threat there are several options that could be put in place. Sandbags could be issued to residents, for instance, and boats could be made available to evacuate the more vulnerable members of the community, as well as making arrangements for fresh drinking water in the event of domestic supplies becoming contaminated. This would minimise the risk of disease that is caused by drinking contaminated water.

Hazard prevention and minimisation are part of the risk assessment.

Preparedness

Preparedness can prevent an emergency from turning into a serious disaster but this can only be done if there has been a proper risk assessment.

Besides planning for known hazards, such as an explosion at a chemical plant, Category 1 responders plan for unforeseen events. These are known as 'contingency plans,' or back-up plans and they provide options for dealing with circumstances that were not catered for by the original emergency plan.

Contingency plans (or back-up plans) need to be put into place so that if prevention and minimisation fail, then the incident can still be prevented from turning into a disaster by employing different options. For example, in the event of a chemical leak or biological attack, the fire service has a mobile decontamination facility, which can be used if evacuation is not an option.

Preparation can also involve other measures, such as public awareness and community education and self-help groups – something the fire service is actively engaged in. If people are aware of possible hazards and how to react to them, then they are more prepared.

Response by the emergency services

Response to an incident means the manner in which organisations respond; the way in which they set about dealing with the incident.

■ Police

The police service normally coordinate the activities of other organisations at a major incident that is based on land. Their primary aim is the saving and protection of life in conjunction with other emergency services, as well

▲ Hazard prevention by the fire service at Kegworth prevented a worse disaster

as preserving the scene to safeguard evidence because it could be that criminal proceedings follow.

Where it is possible, the police will establish and protect inner and outer cordons to enable other responders to carry out their duties safely. The police, in conjunction with other agencies, for instance, the Highways Agency, will establish traffic cordons and diversions to keep traffic away from the scene.

It is also the duty of the police to take witness statements, control onlookers, safeguard victims' personal property, gather evidence and oversee any criminal investigation. They also have responsibility for the identification of fatalities on behalf of HM Coroner.

■ Fire and rescue services

The primary function of the fire and rescue services at a major incident is the rescue of people trapped by fire, wreckage or debris. They have the necessary skills and equipment to search confined and dangerous areas for survivors as well as having the expertise to deal with casualties. Fire service personnel are also trained in removing large quantities of flood water, evacuation procedures and advising the other emergency services on health and safety issues at the scene. They are also equipped to undertake mass decontamination of people who have been exposed to chemical, biological, radioactive or nuclear (CBRN) substances.

■ The ambulance service

The ambulance service's primary role at a major incident is to coordinate the NHS response through an Ambulance Incident Officer. Ambulance service personnel will perform triage and designate hospitals to which injured people are taken, as well as ensuring there are sufficient human and medical resources at the scene.

Some major incidents require the provision of specialist medical staff and scientific advice, and these are provided by the Health Protection Agency. Where an emergency is on a national or international scale, the Department of Health will take on the role of coordinating the NHS response.

■ Response by local authorities

Local authority planners coordinate the emergency response throughout their area, giving support to the emergency services and other organisations, as well as ensuring that sufficient resources are available to deal with the incident. Local authorities assume a community leadership role and their services, such as social services and housing, are crucial to the response by providing temporary accommodation and rest centres for victims.

■ Response by the voluntary sector

Within the voluntary sector, several organisations respond to major incidents and provide an array of skills and qualities. St John Ambulance, for instance, offers extra medical resources. Other voluntary services include the WRVS, who offer counselling, food and rest

stations, while Mountain and Cave Rescue offer expert search and rescue support in difficult and inaccessible areas.

Recovery

The recovery phase is the dealing with the aftermath and returning the community to normality. This can take several forms, depending on the type and scale of the incident and could involve several agencies. The local authority takes a leading role in restoring the community to normal but large-scale incidents, such as foot and mouth disease or extensive areas of flooding, will require the intervention of government agencies, such as DEFRA, as well as some voluntary organisations.

Where there has been soil contamination, the local authority, under the guidance of DEFRA, might excavate and replace contaminated soil, and in cases of damage to wildlife because of, say, an oil slick, the RSPCA and RSPB might become involved.

■ Government agencies involved in recovery

- **DEFRA** – for incidents affecting the environment (flood or pollution incidents)
- **Health and Safety Executive** – for ensuring the health and safety of the responding emergency services and its specialist expertise in CBRN (chemical, biological, radiation or nuclear attack) and major hazard industrial sites
- **Highways Agency** – for incidents affecting the road network in England
- **Maritime and Coastguard Agency** – in incidents requiring civil maritime search and rescue
- **Government Decontamination Service** – for providing advice and guidance to those responsible for dealing with decontamination following a major hazardous materials incident.

Types of emergency plans

It is quite common for organisations to have more than one emergency plan, depending upon the risks and threats of their particular area. Different types of plans are described below.

Multi-agency emergency procedures guides

These are comprehensive guides which are produced by Category 1 and Category 2 responders at emergency planning forums at Metropolitan District Council level. The guides include the roles, responsibilities and procedures to be followed by responding agencies to a variety of major incidents. However, such guides are not plans and they have no operational status; they are prepared so that responders can fulfil their obligations under the Civil Contingencies Act 2004.

Generic plans

These are general plans that include procedures for organisations to respond and deal with a wide range of possible emergencies. Such plans include the strategy which would be used in all instances, such as ensuring sufficient resources are made available for those responding to, say, a road traffic collision.

Specific plans

These are specific and detailed plans that relate to particular types of incidents, or to a specific site or location for which generic plans would be insufficient. For example, an incident involving toxic chemicals would require a more detailed plan than a road traffic accident in terms of dealing with the chemicals and minimising risk.

Specific plans may be used in conjunction with generic plans for incidents where, say, an evacuation procedure would be covered in a generic plan, but the response and recovery of an incident would be covered in a specific plan.

Multi-agency plans

These are required for an integrated response.

Single-agency plans

These are plans prepared by a single organisation, for instance, mountain and cave rescue.

Organisations involved in planning

- Local authorities
- NHS
- Inter-faith groups
- DEFRA
- Fire
- Police
- Ambulance
- Military
- Red Cross and Red Crescent
- Radio Amateur's Emergency Network (RAYNET)
- Coroner
- Salvation Army
- Casualties Union
- Mountain and cave rescue teams
- Utilities.

Organisations' roles, responsibilities and objectives during planning

It is the objective and responsibility of all organisations involved to contribute to reducing the effects of a major incident and preventing its escalation. It is important to consider the roles of different organisations so that their skills and expertise can be called upon immediately to bring about a successful response.

■ Local authorities

Local authorities have large numbers of employees with skills and expertise, including structural engineers, who can advise on the safety of buildings after an incident, and social workers who can assess the counselling needs and emotional support required by victims. Local authorities also have access to a variety of equipment which might be required for different types of emergencies, as well as buildings, such as depots, recreation centres and schools, all of which could be called into use during and after an emergency.

Part of the preparation and prevention planning involves making lists of what resources are available and how they could be used, should an emergency arise.

■ NHS

Primary Care Trusts (PCTs) are responsible for local health care throughout England and they have a key role to play in emergency planning. It is the responsibility of PCTs to ensure that there are adequate community resources at any time in response to a major incident. Therefore, PCTs need to outline how they can contribute in responding positively to a major incident and what their role will be. For example, it could be the case that in the event of, say, a train crash involving many casualties, a strain is placed upon receiving hospitals. The pressure could be released by the PCTs discharging less seriously ill patients to make room for those in urgent need of medical attention.

Depending upon the type of incident, PCTs may need to administer drugs to people who have come into contact with the accidental or deliberate release of hazardous materials into the environment, or vaccinate people in the event of a disease outbreak.

■ Military

The military has a wide selection of vehicles (helicopters and reconnaissance aircraft), which may be available in an emergency. In incidents such as flooding and foot and mouth outbreaks, the services of the military prove particularly valuable. However, military assistance to the civil community can never be guaranteed because of operational commitments, though where it is possible, military assistance will be provided. Hence, the military are not directly involved in planning for major incidents in the civilian community.

■ Casualties Union

When plans have been prepared they have to be tested otherwise there is no way of telling if they are adequate.

Take it further

Carry out some research using the Internet into the Casualties Union and answer the following:

1. What is the Casualties Union?

2. How can the Casualties Union help with emergency planning?

■ Voluntary organisation involvement

Voluntary organisations, such as the Red Cross and Red Crescent, RAYNET, Salvation Army, and mountain and cave rescue teams are involved in emergency planning with Category 1 and 2 responders so that they can share information and make other organisations aware of the resources they have to offer.

The main objectives, as far as voluntary organisations are concerned with emergency planning, are:

- at which phase of an emergency they may be called upon to assist
- what is expected of them
- who will call them out.

Response from voluntary organisations can be either operational or supportive. Operational response would involve direct assistance in dealing with the emergency by, say, taking part in a search and rescue operation or providing comfort and guidance to casualties. Supportive response might include an organisation, such as the Women's Royal Voluntary Service (WRVS), providing care and refreshments for the operational teams at a disaster site.

Multi-agency involvement in real-life exercises

A real-life exercise involving multi-agencies is a live rehearsal of a scenario and is a means of testing and validating an emergency plan. It will test such things as logistics, communications, adequacy of resources, cooperation and physical capabilities. Such exercises are helpful, especially for inexperienced personnel, because they develop confidence and provide a realistic insight into what real incidents are like.

Planning for a multi-agency response is very difficult and requires care and cooperation, which is encouraged through local resilience forums under the Civil Contingencies Act. Category 1 responders are responsible for their own plans but it is essential that the different responders' plans complement each other. Category 2 responders are governed by their own legislation in regard to emergency planning, but under the Civil Contingencies Act they are also obliged to provide Category 1 responders with information regarding their duties.

Regulations require that plans include provision for carrying out exercises and it is only by doing this that organisations can test their plans.

Exercises may focus on a number of aspects, including:
- all aspects of a generic plan
- all aspects of a specific plan
- those plans that address most probable risks
- those plans where the least training has been done.

A real-life exercise is designed to make responders aware of other responders' roles and responsibilities, and to build morale.

Other organisations involved in prevention

Health and Safety Executive

The Health and Safety Executive (HSE) is a government agency, and the enforcing authority, that supports the Health and Safety Commission (HSC) in ensuring that risks to workers and members of the public are properly controlled by:
- conducting and sponsoring research
- promoting training
- providing an information and advisory service
- submitting proposals for new or revised regulations and approved codes of practice.

It is the duty of the HSC to look after many aspects of health and safety, including:
- nuclear installations
- mines and factories
- farms
- hospitals and schools
- offshore gas and oil installations
- the gas grid
- the movement of dangerous goods and substances.

Large and small businesses

Any business, large or small, can experience a serious incident that can prevent it from continuing its business. For example, the floods of 2007 have had a drastic impact on both small and large businesses throughout the United Kingdom. In Sheffield, South Yorkshire, the cost to businesses from the floods of 2007 is in the region of hundreds of millions of pounds, and this does not include the loss to the economy.

Business managers have a responsibility to prevent the impact of major incidents from causing major disruption, not only to their business but also to their employees and members of the public. Furthermore, businesses have a duty to protect their employees and members of the public from the threat of terrorism.

Case study: Manchester bomb explosion

At 11.20am on Saturday 15 June 1996, a bomb exploded in a busy shopping area in the centre of Manchester. Two hundred and seven people were injured, some of them seriously, by flying glass as shop windows shattered.

Police evacuated hundreds of people from the city centre as army bomb disposal experts used a remote-controlled device to examine a suspect van parked outside one of the stores as the bomb exploded.

Many of those injured were outside the police cordon and suffered deep glass wounds, which required surgery. Seventy bystanders were ferried to three hospitals in ambulances, while others walked or were taken by friends.

1. What was the problem with the police cordon?
2. Could the management have done anything?
3. What would you have done if you had been in charge?

Media agencies play an important role in the preparation and prevention of major emergencies because the Civil Contingencies Act requires Category 1 responders to communicate with the public regarding emergencies. Communicating with the public has two aims:

- to warn the public of any potential or current emergencies
- to provide information and advice to the public, including how they will be responded to.

Media management involves releasing factual information to warn, inform and advise the public but without causing alarm. Where casualties are involved, only numbers are given to the media; no initial statements are made about the condition of casualties, numbers of dead or their identities.

Possible future disasters

Earthquakes

Earthquakes are not something that springs to mind when considering emergency planning in the UK but look at the case study below.

2001: Chile – 9.5 on Richter scale – 2,000 killed	2001: Leicester – 4.1 on Richter scale – shook Melton Mowbray
1976: China – 8.3 on Richter scale – 240,000 people killed	2000: Warwick – 4.2 on Richter scale
1960: Chile – 9.5 on Richter scale – 2,000 people killed	1990: Bishop's Castle, Shropshire – 5.1 on Richter scale
1906: California – 8.3 on Richter scale – 3,000 people killed	1984: Lleyn, North Wales – 5.4 on Richter scale – biggest on land
	1931: near Great Yarmouth – 6.1 on Richter scale (biggest ever recorded)

Table 14.2 Comparison of UK earthquakes to world's worst earthquakes

Case study: Earthquake strikes UK

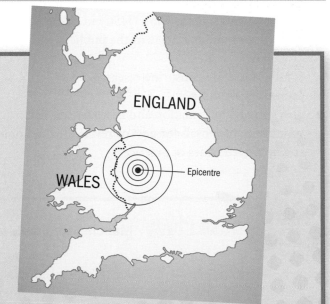

At 12.53am on Monday 23 September 2002, buildings shook for up to 30 seconds in parts of the West Midlands, Wales, North Yorkshire, London and Wiltshire, as a result of an earthquake measuring 4.8 on the Richter scale. The epicentre was in Dudley in the West Midlands, and whilst this was believed to be the UK's largest earthquake for ten years, structural damage was only minor and there were no injuries.

A senior seismologist at the British Geological Survey (BGS), said: 'It's an extremely large earthquake in UK terms but not large in world terms; we'd only classify it as a light earthquake.' Another spokesman for the BGS said that an earthquake of this magnitude is equivalent to the power of a small nuclear weapon. The whole length of Wales was shaken and people over 120 miles (190 km) apart felt two sudden shocks.

Earth tremors are not uncommon in the UK but it certainly caused concern for people in the West Midlands with 5,000 calls made to the West Midlands Police switchboard within an hour of the tremors and 12 people walking into their local police station in their nightclothes.

According to the Environment Agency, buildings are considered to be at risk from earthquakes over 5 on the Richter scale. There are between 200 and 300 quakes each year in Britain but only about 10% are strong enough to be felt. One such hit the UK on 27 February 2008, measuring 5.2 on the Richter scale. Its epicentre was in Lincolnshire.

Coastal erosion

The main cause of coastal erosion is the action of waves, tides and currents on the foreshore, though it can also be affected by rainfall, drought, and freezing and thawing cycles in coastal cliffs.

Besides being a natural defence against the sea, our coastlines serve as natural habitats for a variety of birds and other wildlife. Coastal erosion is relatively slow to develop, and whilst it may not always seem proper to describe it as a major emergency, it is, nonetheless, a serious incident that has a drastic impact on the environment.

Flooding

In 2007 there was extensive flooding in Gloucestershire and Oxfordshire, as well as other parts of the UK.

Take it further

Carry out some research using the Internet into the summer floods in Gloucestershire and Oxfordshire and answer the following:

1. Has flooding occurred in Gloucestershire before? If so when?

2. Is it possible for it to happen again?

3. What has been done to prevent future flooding in these areas?

Assessment activity 14.3

For this activity you are to prepare a leaflet for public distribution that will explain emergency planning. You should include the content in the following four sections:

1: Main considerations
Assessment – identification of possible incidents; hazard prevention options; prevention – hazard minimisation options; preparedness – plan for known hazards as well as for unforeseen events; responses (by emergency services, by local authorities, by voluntary organisations); recovery – activities required to return to normality; types of plans

2: Organisations involved in planning
Organisations' role, responsibilities and objectives during planning; multi-agency involvement in real-life exercises

3: Other organisations involved in prevention
Health and Safety Executive; large and small businesses; media agencies

4: Possible future disasters
You should use this content in the leaflet so that it describes the main considerations that need to be taken into account when developing the major incidents guide/plan **P3**. However, if you elaborate on this and explain how emergency planning could have reduced the impact of one specific UK major incident, then you should achieve **M1** (you could refer to a major incident that you have already covered in **P2**. If you analyse the importance of inter-agency emergency planning for major incidents you will achieve **D1**. **D1** is a continuation of **M1** and **M2**.

A tabletop exercise is a simulation of a realistic scenario that is designed to:

- test the effectiveness of an emergency plan
- test the effectiveness of response
- provide an opportunity for those involved to interact with other agencies
- understand the roles and responsibilities of other agencies.

These exercises are not necessarily based around a tabletop, though they are usually conducted indoors. A timeline is involved and as the simulation unfolds the participating responders are expected to implement the emergency plan. An element of media participation may be added to simulate enthusiatic reporters, eager for a news report.

Tabletops are effective in that once different organisations have exercised together they are more likely to provide an effective response to a genuine disaster than if they had come together for the first time when a disaster occurs.

Take it further

From the information provided, try to formulate a definition of 'tabletop scenario.'

Agencies that may be involved

In accordance with the recommendations of the Civil Contingencies Act, all Category 1 responders may be involved and Category 2 responders may be requested to participate. Voluntary services would be expected to participate, depending on the type of scenario (for list of agencies see 'Organisations involved in planning' in 14.3).

Types of tabletop scenarios

- Chemical/fuel spillages
- Train/plane crash
- Building collapse
- Terrorist attacks.

Each scenario will be driven by an emergency plan, which could be generic, site specific, multi-agency, single-agency or an Emergency Procedures Guide. For example, whilst a train/plane crash scenario might test a multi-agency plan as well as the emergency procedures guide, a building collapse might test a specific and single-agency plan. The fire service prepares such plans as they are the emergency service that would deal with such an incident. It is only when exercises are simulated that plans can be validated.

Issues for consideration in the scenario

■ Cause of incident

The cause and type of an incident will have a bearing on how organisations respond.

■ Chemical/fuel spillages

The release or potential release of hazardous chemicals into the atmosphere can be dangerous to the public and the environment. A chemical or fuel spillage could be caused by a road traffic collision involving a vehicle transporting hazardous chemicals or fuel. Alternatively, it could be a chemical spillage from a COMAH site (location of a site where hazardous chemicals are manufactured or stored under the Control of Major Accident Hazards Regulations 1999), or even the result of a terrorist attack.

■ Train/plane crash

Such incidents could be caused by a technical fault, human error, or act of terrorism. Train/plane crashes are always very serious and require an immediate, combined response.

■ Building collapse

Building collapse can have several causes, including:

- faulty construction
- coastal erosion
- earthquake
- terrorist attack
- flooding
- fire.

■ Terrorist attacks

Terrorist attacks can take several forms, including bombings of busy public places, biological weapon attacks and sabotage of public transport. Terrorist attacks are usually committed with the intention of causing the maximum harm and disruption to members of the public, the government or the economy.

Likely agency response

The emergency services would always respond to all of the above scenarios but some of them would call for different specialist organisations, as shown in the table below.

The first priority of the emergency services is the safety of personnel and of the public, as well as trying to ensure, as far as possible, that the incident does not escalate. Following an initial assessment, a major incident may be declared unless the incident is such that no disruption or further assistance is required by other organisations. However, if the incident is declared a

▲ The army bomb disposal unit can identify a suspicious device

major incident then procedures are followed according to the emergency or contingency plans. For example, most bomb threats are dealt with by the police and they fall into three stages as follows:

Stage 1: possibility of a bomb

If the police suspect the threat is not a hoax they may decide to evacuate the public and staff and call upon the local authority to arrange temporary accommodation, though evacuation may not be deemed necessary at this stage. The local authority would assist the police in diverting the traffic and providing barriers to control crowds and liaise with local transport companies for the removal of the public from the scene.

Chemical/fuel spillages	Train/plane crash	Building collapse	Terrorist attacks
Health and Safety Executive	Health and Safety Executive	Health and Safety Executive	Health and Safety Executive
DEFRA	DEFRA	Local authority	DEFRA
Local authority	Local authority	Utilities	Local authority
Health Protection Agency	Health Protection Agency		Health Protection Agency
Water authority	Salvation Army		Salvation Army
Highways Agency	WRVS		WRVS
	Network Rail		Network Rail
	Utilities		Utilities
	Civil Aviation Authority		Civil Aviation Authority
	British Transport Police		British Transport Police
			Military

Table 14.3 Organisations that may respond to different types of incident

At this stage, the police may carry out a search of premises to identify any suspicious packages.

Stage 2: suspected device identified

Where a suspicious device has been identified, the police would contact the Explosive Ordnance Disposal Team (Army Bomb Disposal Unit), who would decide if the device was a real threat.

Stage 3: bomb explodes

The police would work closely with the fire service in securing the area with an inner cordon and assisting in fire fighting and rescue operations. A security cordon would be established to protect the scene for evidence, as well as protecting the emergency services and members of the public from the possibility of a secondary device.

The ambulance service would be on hand, outside the protected area, to perform triage and transport any casualties to hospital.

Resources that may be required

Where an incident involves chemicals or hazardous materials, the fire service will mobilise a HAZMAT (hazardous materials) unit so that victims who have come into direct contact with hazardous materials can be decontaminated.

Where incidents, such as train/plane crashes, are prolonged or a rescue is required during the hours of darkness, then lighting and generators will be required at the site.

In the case of building collapse, props and supports will be required, as well as oxygen supplies for victims trapped in confined spaces with little oxygen.

Extra human resources are often called for at very serious incidents, including voluntary services such as the WRVS and Salvation Army, to provide support and counselling, as well as refreshments to victims and emergency personnel.

Inner and outer cordons

Inner cordons protect the safety of personnel where operational command is situated. The outer cordon contains the following posts while others are located outside of the cordons, as shown in the diagram.

■ **Casualty clearing station –** this is an area that is established by the ambulance service in consultation with the medical incident officer, within the outer cordon, where triage is performed and a decision made as to the medical condition of casualties, before they are evacuated.

■ **Rendezvous point –** this is an area that is located close to or within the outer cordon where vehicles attending the incident are directed. Rendezvous points are staffed by police who receive the vehicles and direct them to the site of the incident or the vehicle marshalling area.

■ **Marshalling area –** this is an area inside the outer cordon that is set aside for emergency vehicles and any specialist vehicles required to deal with the incident. Therefore, the marshalling area should be large enough to accommodate several vehicles and in close proximity to the rendezvous point.

■ **Press information centre –** this is an area outside the outer cordon where press, television reporters and radio reporters gather for a press release.

Command and control

Where the incident is very serious and on a large scale, the three levels of command and control need to be established so a strategy can be formulated to deal with it effectively. Do you remember what the three levels of command are?

Communications network

Good communications are essential at the scene of an incident and all the emergency services have direct access to their control room through radio communication, as well as radio handsets which enable them to coordinate other agencies at the site. Along with local authorities, emergency services and the health service have mobile telephones which are protected under the Access Overload for Cell Phones scheme (ACCOLC), which enables mobile phones to continue operating when restrictions have been imposed on the

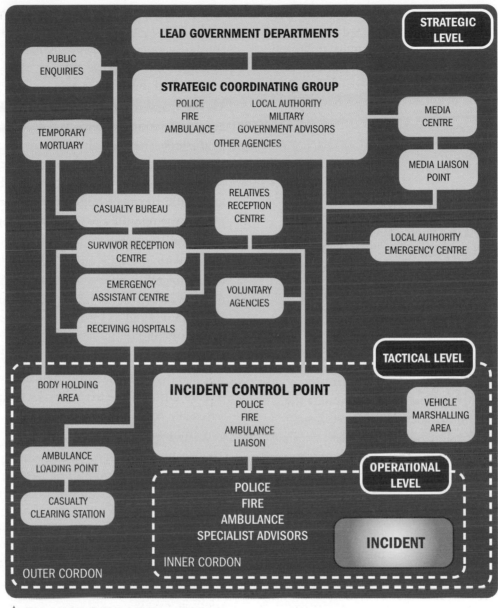

▲ Figure 14.3 Division of responsibilities at the emergency scene

Source: Home Office, *Dealing with Disaster*, 3rd ed., p. 10.
Crown Copyright material reproduced with permission of the Controller of HMSO and the Queen's Printer for Scotland.

use of mobile phones. Major incidents often bring severe congestion to telephone networks, but the government Telephone Preference Scheme allows essential users to make and receive calls by placing restrictions on non-essential users.

The Internet also provides organisations with an effective means of communication, information and electronic mailing system.

Environmental considerations

It is difficult to say which type of incident can do most environmental damage because whilst chemical spillage can pollute watercourses, the atmosphere, plant and animal life, so, too, can acts of terrorism. Train/plane crashes can also affect the environment adversely, especially where plane crashes spill large amounts of aviation fuel over land and water.

Other forms of environment, such as wetland areas, Sites of Special Scientific Interest (SSSI) with rare fauna and flora, can all be threatened with chemical pollution. Furthermore, marine life and beaches can suffer pollution from such incidents as oil tankers running aground and breaking up.

■ Chemical/fuel spillage

It is the common objective of all responding agencies to save lives and prevent the incident from escalating. However, they all have different skills which enable them to carry out specific responsibilities at the scene.

■ Chemical spillage

Specifically, the police would inform the various statutory bodies, such as the local authority, Environment Agency, water authority and Health and Safety Executive. They would also coordinate the response outside the immediate area of the spillage. Other specific responsibilities would include:

- controlling and diverting traffic
- making public announcements
- undertaking casualty identification
- preserving the scene for investigative purposes.

The fire service's specific response would be to protect and control entry and exit from the immediate scene, thereby ensuring that safety procedures are followed and that the scene is preserved as much a possible. They would liaise with onsite chemists to identify the hazardous substance, and assist other emergency services to recover casualties from the scene. The service has direct access to a computer system, called Chemdata, which contains data on thousands of chemicals and trade name products, including essential information for emergency response, such as physical properties, hazards, containment, decontamination, basic first aid, protective measures and action in the event of fire.

The ambulance service's specific responsibilities include triage, the immediate treatment of casualties and transportation to receiving hospitals. The service is responsible for coordinating the health service response to the incident.

The Environment Agency has the responsibility of advising and giving information on the disposal of the substance, once it has been identified. The agency will also work with the local authority and water authorities to safeguard the water supply.

The local authority has the responsibility of providing accommodation for persons temporarily displaced by the leak. They will also assist in the monitoring of chemical dispersal, advising the public, and helping to reduce the pollution to watercourses. Furthermore, the local authority has a responsibility to assist the police in implementing traffic diversions and signposting.

Public health doctors have a responsibility to work closely with hospitals, environmental health and other bodies to gather information on patients receiving medical care, either at hospitals or their own General Practitioners and to identify chemicals present in the environment.

Where there is a threat to SSSI, country parks and woodlands, the local authority will work in consultation with English Nature to undertake to preserve, and where necessary, replace flora and fauna affected by chemical contamination.

The Health Protection Agency would provide a Consultant in Communicable Disease Control (CCDC) to assess the problem and the long-term consequences.

Post-incident responsibilities

When the emergency services have dealt with the major incident, there are still lots of things to be done by certain organisations. The Health and Safety Executive, for instance, carries out extensive enquiries into the causes of major incidents to ensure that the risk of future incidents of a similar nature is reduced. In the event of air crashes, the Aviation Authority has a responsibility to investigate the cause and where there has been a chemical spillage, the local authority, together with the Environment Agency, has a duty to ensure that soil and water courses are restored to normality. The local authority also has the responsibility of monitoring air quality.

Debrief of situation by all agencies

A debrief is held after all major incidents in order to assess effectiveness of agency response. Debriefs may be held separately, that is, gold command, silver command and bronze command may have their own debriefs but they could also involve a joint debrief of all commanders. (For further information on debriefs see page 9.)

Reviews of response procedures

Remember, a review is an assessment of how efficiently a major incident was responded to. Part of the review involves taking statements of witnesses and members of the organisations involved in the incident. Some reviews are carried out by independent police services, that is, a police service that was not involved in the incident.

When the statements have been analysed, a report is compiled and this is dispatched to the senior ranks of the emergency services so that good practice can be disseminated or lessons learnt can be taken on board.

Consider this

You should understand that a review of a disaster is not meant to be a critical analysis; it is meant to serve as a learning aid with the intention of making organisations more efficient in future.

Scene investigation

Scene investigation is necessary to determine the cause of an incident and to see if criminal proceedings are necessary, so the more a scene is protected during the incident, the better the likelihood of finding the cause. In some cases, air crashes, for instance, the pieces of wreckage are collected and reassembled like a huge jig-saw puzzle. Scenes may be investigated by the following:
- Police (CID or SOCO)
- Fire service

- Forensic scientists
- Civil Aviation Authorities
- Health and Safety Executive.

Long-term social service and NHS aftercare of victims and relatives

Physical and mental injuries may mean that individuals need long-term support from the social services and NHS because they are no longer able to look after themselves. This long-term care can also extend to relatives of victims who, whilst not suffering from any physical disability, may have become so traumatised by witnessing the injuries to their loved ones that they too have become unable to look after themselves.

Criminal and inquest proceedings support

When the scene of a major incident has been investigated and there is sufficient evidence to suggest criminal intent or negligence, then proceedings are brought against the person or organisation responsible. This could mean, as with the case of the Lockerbie air disaster, that the people responsible are extradited to stand trial.

An inquest is held into all sudden, suspicious, and unnatural deaths by HM Coroner and if, during the course of the evidence, the coroner decides that there has been criminal negligence, then they can direct that a person be investigated and charged.

Clear up of scene and/or environment

We have already mentioned that several agencies are involved in the clear up of the scene. The main organisations, depending on the type of incident, are the Environment Agency and the local authority.

Evaluation

When everything has been done to recover the community to normality, an evaluation of the incident is prepared by the coordinating officer and the local authority. The evaluation will highlight the things that went well and the things that did not go so well, together with recommendations for the future.

Assessment activity 14.4

For this activity you are to participate in a tabletop scenario of a major incident. You should ensure that you cover the content in the following four sections:

Section 1: Tabletop scenarios

Definition; agencies that may be involved.

Section 2: Types of tabletop scenarios

Section 3: Issues for consideration in the scenario

Cause of incident; likely agency response; resources that may be required; inner and outer cordons; casualty clearing stations; rendezvous points and marshalling areas; press information centre; command and control; communication network; environmental considerations; common and agency-specific responsibilities at the scene.

Section 4: Post-incident responsibilities

Debrief of situation by all agencies; reviews of response procedures; scene investigation; long-term social service and NHS aftercare of victims and relatives; criminal and inquest proceedings support; clear up of scene and/or environment; evaluation.

You should use the content to prepare and demonstrate a simulation of one of the following scenarios:

1. Chemical/fuel spillage
2. Train/plane crash
3. Building collapse
4. Terrorist attack

You should make the exercise as realistic as possible and ensure that you carry out a tabletop scenario of a major incident, describing its cause and identifying the responsibilities of the responding agencies, both within the cordons and beyond. **P5**

Grading tips

You could cover the content by way of narration as you participate in the tabletop scenario.

M3 This is an extension of P5 where you should analyse the tabletop scenario, explaining the roles and responsibilities of the agencies during and after the major incident.

D2 You should produce a brief report that will evaluate the tabletop scenario, making recommendations for consideration for future planning.

Knowledge check

1. What is meant by a 'major incident'?
2. List four different causes of major incidents.
3. What is the difference between epidemic and pandemic?
4. What is PTSD and how is it caused?
5. What does DEFRA stand for?
6. List six new offences created by the Terrorism Act of 2006.
7. Give three responsibilities of the police, fire and ambulance services at a major incident.
8. What is meant by 'Category 1' and 'Category 2' responders?
9. Which legislation creates such responders?
10. What are the three chains of command and where would they be located in the event of a major incident?
11. What is the purpose of a risk assessment?
12. What is the difference between the Red Cross and the Red Crescent?
13. What does RAYNET stand for?
14. What is the role of HM Coroner?
15. What is a tabletop exercise?
16. Where would you expect to see a casualty clearing point and a marshalling yard in the event of a major incident?

End of unit assessment

Preparation for assessment

Write an article for an emergency planning forum that will cover the following:

1. Describe the term 'major incident,' including three different causes or types giving relevant examples for each. **P1**

2. Describe three different recent incidents/disasters, showing the cause of each and the effects they had on the people, communities, environment involved and other wider impacts they had. **P2**

3. Describe the main considerations that need to be taken into account when developing the major incidents guide/plan, and explain how emergency planning could reduce the impact of one specific major incident. **P3 M1**

4. Identify agencies that were involved in the response to three specific incidents/disasters, describing their work throughout with reference to any appropriate duties under law, and explain how agencies involved in a specific incident/disaster worked together with reference to any appropriate duties under law. **P4 M2**

5. Analyse the importance of inter-agency emergency planning for major incidents. **D1**

In groups of four, hold a discussion to determine how you could:

6. Carry out a tabletop scenario of a major incident, describing its cause and identifying the responsibilities of the responding agencies, both within cordons and beyond. **P5**

7. Analyse the tabletop scenario, explaining the roles and responsibilities of the agencies during and after the major incident. **M3**

8. Evaluate the tabletop scenario, making recommendations for consideration for future planning. **D2**

Grading criteria	Activity	Pg no.	To achieve a merit grade the evidence must show that the learner is able to:	To achieve a distinction grade the evidence must show that the learner is able to:
To achieve a pass grade the evidence must show that the learner is able to:				
P1 Describe the term 'major incident,' including three different causes or types giving relevant examples for each	14.1	13		
P2 Describe three different recent incidents/ disasters, showing the cause of each and the effects they had on the people, communities, environment involved and other wider impacts they had	14.1	13	**M1** Explain how emergency planning could reduce the impact of one specific major incident	**D1** Analyse the importance of inter-agency emergency planning for major incidents
P3 Describe the main considerations that need to be taken into account when developing the major incidents guide/ plan	14.3	25		
P4 Identify agencies that were involved in the response to three specific incidents/ disasters, describing their work throughout with reference to any appropriate duties under law	14.2	17	**M2** Explain how agencies involved in a specific incident/disaster worked together with reference to any appropriate duties under law	
P5 Carry out a tabletop scenario of a major incident, describing its cause and identifying the responsibilities of the responding agencies, both within cordons and beyond.	14.4	32	**M3** Analyse the tabletop scenario, explaining the roles and responsibilities of the agencies during and after the major incident.	**D2** Evaluate the tabletop scenario, making recommendations for consideration for future planning.

Responding to emergency service incidents

Introduction

This unit will give you an insight into and understanding of the roles and responsibilities undertaken by the emergency services when responding to various emergency situations.

In the first outcome you will learn how reports of incidents are classified, processed and responded to. You will also look at different types of incidents and see how some of them require the additional response of public services with specialist skills and knowledge. Included in this section are emergency vehicle equipment, driver training and standards, and public perceptions of emergency response vehicles.

The second section deals with the roles and responsibilities of key services when attending the scene of an emergency response incident. These include the initial actions of those first in attendance, as well as the specific roles and responsibilities of the emergency services at the scene. Also included in this section are the roles of other statutory and voluntary organisations attending the scene of emergency response incidents.

In the third outcome you will examine why it is necessary to preserve the scene of incidents and the need for accident investigation. You will also look at the various ways of collecting evidence and the assistance given by voluntary organisations.

The fourth outcome will allow you to understand the health and safety considerations when dealing with a variety of emergency incidents and the safety measures taken for self-preservation as well as public information. This section also includes relevant legislation and regulations that govern the manner in which emergency response situations are dealt with.

After completing this unit you should be able to achieve the following outcomes:
- Know the use of incident grading and the importance of responding to emergency incidents safely in response vehicles
- Understand the roles and responsibilities of key services when attending the scene of an emergency response incident
- Understand the necessity for scene preservation and the service provisions of specialist units at emergency incidents
- Understand the health and safety considerations when attending the scene of an emergency response incident.

Emergency incident definition

According to the Civil Contingencies Act 2004, an emergency is defined as:

- an event or situation which threatens serious damage to human welfare, or
- an event or situation which threatens serious damage to the environment, or
- war or terrorism, which threatens serious damage to security.

Incident grading

The emergency services (police, fire and ambulance) are duty bound to respond to all emergency situations, but because they have different roles and responsibilities, they have different graded response policies. You should understand that emergencies are graded by the call handler, according to the information provided by the caller, and not by the means of reporting the incident, for instance, by a '999' call.

Police

The police services of England and Wales grade their response in accordance with the *National Call Handling Standards*, published by the Home Office in conjunction with the Association of Chief Police Officers. Incidents reported to the police are graded as emergency or non-emergency and there are four grades, as follows:

■ Grade 1: Emergency

A grade 1 incident is where a report is received of an incident currently taking place and in which there is, or is likely to be, a risk of:

- danger to life
- the use or immediate threat of use of violence
- serious injury to a person and/or serious damage to property.

Where the incident relates to criminal conduct, it will also be classified as grade 1 if:

- it involves crime which is likely to be serious and in progress
- an offender has just been disturbed at the scene
- an offender has been detained and poses, or is likely to pose, a risk to other people.

Where the incident relates to a traffic collision, it will also be classified as grade 1 if:

- it involves or is likely to involve serious personal injury
- the road is blocked or there is a dangerous or excessive build up of traffic.

Notwithstanding the conditions just mentioned, an incident may be classified as grade 1 if the call handler has strong and objective reasons for believing that the incident should be classified as an emergency.

■ Grade 2: Priority

This grade is where the call handler acknowledges that the incident requires a degree of importance or urgency but an emergency response is not required. It includes incidents such as:

- a genuine concern for somebody's welfare
- an offender has been detained and does not pose, or is unlikely to pose, a risk to others
- a road traffic collision that involves injuries or serious obstruction
- the likelihood that a witness or evidence might be lost
- a person involved is suffering extreme distress or is believed to be vulnerable.

■ Grade 3: Scheduled response

This grade is used where it is believed that the needs of the caller can be best achieved through scheduling because:

- the response time is not critical in apprehending offenders
- better quality of initial police action can be given if it is dealt with by a pre-arranged response by a police officer or other appropriate resource, or attendance at a police station.

▲ Emergencies are graded by the call handler according to certain response policies

■ Grade 4: Resolution without deployment

This grade is used where the incident can be adequately resolved through telephone advice, Help Desk intervention, frequently asked questions or the involvement of other appropriate agencies or services.

Ambulance

The ambulance service grades incident responses into three categories, as follows:

- Category A – this is a priority category and refers to an incident that is considered to be immediately life threatening
- Category B – this is where an incident is serious but not immediately life threatening
- Category C – this is the category where an incident is neither serious nor life threatening.

You should note that it is not only calls from members of the public that are categorised in this way; it also applies to urgent calls from GPs and other health professionals.

Fire

Incidents are graded by the fire service according to their risk category, of which there are five, as follows:

- Risk Category A – this normally refers to large cities and towns, and includes shopping areas, business, entertainment or industrial centres
- Risk Category B – this category normally refers to large cities and towns with multi-storey buildings, and includes large areas of residential accommodation, as well as industrial trading estates containing high-risk occupancies
- Risk Category C – this category normally refers to the suburbs of larger towns and the built-up areas of smaller towns, including terraced and semi-detached dwellings, as well as low-risk industrial and residential areas
- Risk Category D – this category refers to all areas that do not come within Categories A to C
- Remote Rural – this is a separate category and has no pre-determined response.

Inter-agency approaches/ agreements

The emergency services are known as Category 1 responders under the Civil Contingencies Act 2004 and they are legally bound to cooperate in inter-agency approaches to emergency situations. Approaches and agreements are determined at Local Resilience Forums, which are located within the boundary of police areas. Emergency service personnel must attend a forum at least once every six months where they cooperate with other personnel in both preparing for and responding to emergencies. This is done by assessing local risks, emergency planning, sharing information, joint training and exercises with agencies such as utilities companies, local authorities and voluntary agencies, who would be involved in emergency incidents.

Local Resilience Forums are the key to emergency preparedness and they bring together all the agencies who have a duty to cooperate by giving consideration to producing multi-agency plans and agreements, and the coordination of multi-agency exercises and training events.

Role of call centres and incident managers

Most emergency call centre staff work in the control room of one of the emergency services and deal with both emergency and non-emergency telephone calls from members of the public. They identify the needs of the caller through careful listening and effective questioning so they may assess the urgency of the call before deciding upon the most suitable course of action.

Depending upon the nature of the call, the call handler has the responsibility to:

- direct the emergency services to deal with the incident
- direct non-emergency calls to the appropriate telephone number or agency
- monitor progress by maintaining contact with the incident team and ensure staff safety
- ensure the effective use of resources

- ensure that response time standards are met where possible
- ensure regular communication with the emergency services using telephone, radio and computer systems
- ensure, as far as possible, that other resources are available to respond to other incidents.

Call handlers work under the supervision of team leaders and incident managers, though all emergency call handlers are involved in incident management. It is the role of incident managers to liaise with other organisations such as local authorities, utilities companies, local transport companies, voluntary agencies, the Environment Agency, and any other agency whose services may be required in order to provide an efficient response to the incident.

Policies and procedures for dealing with incidents

When attending emergency incidents, all the emergency services follow their own service policy and procedures but where a joint response is required at, say, a major incident, then all responders should be aware of joint policy and procedures of the joint emergency plan, as decided at the Local Resilience Forum. For example, each service would be aware of the common objectives as well as their own specific objectives.

Common objectives include such things as:

- saving life and alleviating suffering at the scene
- protecting property
- mitigating the incident and preventing its escalation
- safeguarding the environment
- restoring normality
- maintaining normal services where possible
- providing resources.

Each of the services is aware of the protocol of establishing command and control of the incident, namely, Gold, Silver and Bronze, and personnel for each level of command is predetermined before the onset of a major incident.

It is generally accepted that the police will coordinate the incident but with the fire service taking a lead role in fire situations or incidents involving hazardous materials.

Key terms

Emergency response There are two meanings of the term 'emergency response.'

Firstly, emergency response is the fifth of six related activities that make up Integrated Emergency Management (IEM) when dealing with major incidents; the other elements being: anticipation, assessment, prevention, preparation and recovery.

Secondly, an emergency response is the manner in which an emergency service responds to a Class A or Category 1 incident. It is the immediate, safe response in accordance with authorised driver grades and may require the use of blue lights and audible siren.

Response times

Emergency response times vary from service to service and from area to area. Government guidelines for response times of the different emergency categories are outlined below.

Police

Grade 1: Emergency
Urban Response Times – 10 minutes.
Rural Response Times – 17 minutes.

Grade 2: Priority
Resources will be deployed as soon and as safely as practicable and in any case within 15 minutes.

Grade 3: Scheduled Response
These incidents must be fully resolved to the satisfaction of the caller, as soon as possible and in any case within 48 hours of initial contact.

Grade 4: Resolution without deployment
Advise caller of agreed call back time which must be as soon as possible but in any case within 24 hours.

Ambulance

Category A (life-threatening) calls within 8 minutes or less.

Category B calls within 14 minutes in urban areas or 19 minutes in rural areas.

Fire

Risk Category A: Two appliances should arrive within 5 minutes and a further one within 8 minutes.

Risk Category B: One appliance should arrive within 5 minutes and a further one within 8 minutes.

Risk Category C: One appliance should arrive within 8 to 10 minutes.

Risk Category D: One appliance should arrive within 20 minutes.

Initial response services

Out of the three emergency services, it is normally the police who respond first to most incidents. This is because they are constantly on patrol, whereas the fire and ambulance service are on call at stations or strategic locations where they are ready to respond to emergency calls. There are few incidents to which the police do not respond initially because even if they attend in a supporting role, say, for an injury that requires the skills of the ambulance service, they may still be required in some capacity. For example, they might have to break into a house because the owner has collapsed, or they might have to attend a traffic collision where the fire service take the lead role in a rescue operation but there is still the problem of controlling traffic, taking witness statements and investigating the cause.

Additional public services offering specialist knowledge

Despite the skills and abilities of the emergency services, some incidents cannot be resolved without the specialist knowledge and expertise of additional public services. For example, the services of the military would be required in the event of a suspicious package that was believed to be an explosive device.

Accountability

All emergency service personnel are accountable for their actions whilst performing their duty. They are governed by the rules and regulations and codes of conduct of their respective services, for the good of the service and the safety of the public, as well as themselves. The fact that emergency personnel have to respond quickly to emergencies does not give them any special dispensation whilst driving at high speeds, even when using flashing lights and sirens.

Emergency vehicles and equipment

When responding to emergency incidents, the emergency services must do so quickly and safely, and they must also have the necessary equipment so that they can deal efficiently with the incident. Emergency equipment is carried as standard in all emergency vehicles and, obviously, some vehicles are larger than others and carry more equipment because of the nature of that service. Whilst the emergency services in the UK have different policies, their types of vehicles and equipment are very similar.

Ambulance service vehicles and equipment

Most ambulance services have a range of vehicles and transportation, including:

- ambulances with two crew members
- rapid response cars with one crew member
- paramedic motorcycles.

Some services even have bicycles for paramedics to respond to emergency incidents in busy towns and cities, as well as air ambulances for responding to really serious incidents or incidents that are not easily accessible by any other means. The South Western Ambulance Service even has an ambulance boat for incidents in the Isles of Scilly.

Emergency equipment carried by the ambulance service includes:

- electrocardiograph machines
- immediate aid response kit (resuscitation bag/valve with adult and child masks, hand-held suction, airways, burns gel packs, assorted dressings)
- portable oxygen sets with a range of face masks
- battery operated suction unit
- pulse oximeter
- manual sphygmomanometer and stethoscope
- defibrillator with accessories
- drugs packs, intravenous fluids and cannulae
- rigid neck collars
- long spinal board, orthopaedic stretcher
- vacuum splints and fracture splints
- moving and handling equipment, pillows, blankets and carrying chairs
- universal precaution equipment including disposable gloves, face masks, aprons, waste bins and sharps boxes
- maternity pack and blankets
- tissues and incontinence pads.

Police service vehicles and equipment

Police services throughout the UK use a vast range of vehicles but for responding to emergency situations, the following vehicles are commonly used:

- Volvo V70 T5
- Vauxhall Omega
- BMW 5 Series
- BMW X5
- Vauxhall Vectra
- A selection of 4x4 vehicles.

Most police services also use motorcyles and have access to a force helicopter.

Emergency equipment carried by such vehicles includes:

- traffic cones and cone lamps
- accident signs (slow, diversion, 'use hard shoulder' and 'rejoin main carriageway')
- tow ropes
- fire extinguisher
- crowbar, hacksaw and axe
- industrial gloves
- first aid kit, resuscitation kit and infectious diseases kit
- space blankets
- water container
- 'stinger' tyre deflation unit.

Fire service vehicles and equipment

Whilst the fire service do not have the range of operational vehicles that police services have, they, nonetheless, have specialist vehicles and a wide variety of specialist equipment. Besides the standard fire engines (or fire tenders), some brigades have Incident Support Units (ISUs) that have been especially designed to deal with certain types of incidents. For example, Water/Ice Rescue Units that are fully equipped with boats for rescues from deep water, and Heavy Rescue Units that contain necessary cutting and lifting apparatus for incidents involving building collapse or large-scale road traffic accidents. Furthermore, the fire service has Pollution Containment Units for dealing with chemical or hazardous material incidents.

Emergency equipment carried by the fire service includes:

- flat-head and pick-head axe
- fire-retardant, pathogen and chemical resistant and water-resistant boots with steel toe and a full-length steel sole
- flashlight
- self-contained breathing apparatus (SCBA)
- helmet, face mask and/or visor
- fire-resistant work gloves
- PASS device (Personal Alert Safety System)
- hand-held radio
- hydraulic rescue tools
- duck-bill lock breaker
- spanner wrench

- circular saw ('K-12')
- cutters edge
- laser heat gun
- thermal imaging camera (infrared)
- pager/receiver (for fire alerts).

Driver training and driving standards for emergency response vehicles

In the year 2000, the Driving Standards Agency (DSA) became responsible for assessing the standards and training needs of all drivers who are entitled to drive emergency response vehicles that are fitted with blue lights and sirens. The vehicles included:

- Ambulance Service
- Bomb Disposal Teams
- Coastguard Service
- Fire and Rescue Service
- Human Tissue Transplant Vehicles
- Life Boat Launching Vehicles
- Mines Rescue Service
- Mountain Rescue Teams
- National Blood Service
- Police

In consultation with other agencies, the DSA drew up a document that contained a list of expectations of the core competencies that drivers should meet before being allowed to drive emergency vehicles in response to emergency calls. That document has been accepted by the three main emergency services (police, fire and ambulance) and is the basic standard that has to be met by all emergency services.

The competencies consist of three elements, and include performance criteria, as well as underpinning knowledge, as follows:

- **element one** – the ability to assess the need for an emergency response
- **element two** – the ability to drive the vehicle safely to emergencies
- **element three** – the ability to demonstrate the correct attitude when responding to emergencies.

Police

Besides the standards set by the DSA, the police services in England and Wales have their own driving centres where police drivers are trained and graded in accordance with National Training Standards, which are approved by the Association of Chief Police Officers (ACPO). The type of driver training is dependent upon the job role of the police officer. For example, police drivers can be graded as:

- standard response drivers
- advanced drivers
- pursuit drivers.

Advanced drivers and pursuit drivers receive intense training, using high-powered vehicles and advanced techniques in responding quickly and safely to emergency calls.

Fire

The fire service has its own driver training centres, and drivers are trained to the standards set by their Fire Authority. In order to drive an Emergency Fire Appliance, drivers must hold a Large Goods Vehicle (LGV) licence and have received the appropriate training and assessment. They are then permitted to drive whilst responding to emergency situations, provided the vehicle is fitted with audible/visual warning devices.

Ambulance

Ambulance authorities require drivers to hold C1 (medium-sized vehicle) and D1 (minibus) licences and to receive the appropriate training as specified by the DSA. However, some ambulance services, London, for instance, require drivers to hold a LGV licence.

Driver training and assessment is not normally conducted by the ambulance service but by independent driver training centres.

Public perception and reaction to emergency response vehicles

What do you think when you see an emergency vehicle speeding through traffic with sirens sounding and blue lights flashing? When people see emergency vehicles responding to incidents they have very mixed views and reactions. Some perceive the police, for instance, as abusing their powers and believe that they speed through traffic with their lights flashing simply because they do not want to queue in traffic like everyone else. There have been instances when drivers have followed emergency vehicles through congested areas to avoid queues. Others believe that pursuing drivers of stolen vehicles causes more danger than not pursuing them. There are even others who believe that there is one law for the emergency services and one law for the public when it comes to speeding or driving dangerously. The following case study highlights this.

▲ People can have mixed responses to emergency vehicles in a hurry

Case study: Speeding police officer cleared of dangerous driving

In 2003 a police constable appeared in court charged with dangerous driving when his police vehicle was recorded travelling at 159 mph on a motorway in the early hours of the morning. He also drove at 120 mph in a 60-mph zone and at 60 mph in a 30-mph zone.

The officer, who was trained in advanced driving as well as the use of firearms, denied the charge and told the court that he was testing the new car and wanted to familiarise himself with it so that if he had to respond to an emergency he would know its capabilities.

The District Judge accepted his reason for breaking the speed limit and said that the officer was the 'crème de la crème' of police drivers.

The Royal Society for the Prevention of Accidents was shocked that such a speed was not regarded as dangerous by the court, and the head of road safety did not believe that 159 mph can ever be justified on public roads.

At the time the officer was driving, the roads were free from other traffic and driving conditions were good.

1. Do you think the officer was driving dangerously?
2. How do think the public reacted to the verdict?
3. Do you think the verdict would have been different if the officer was in his own car?

Take it further

Visit the following website to find out how the public perceive emergency services when responding to incidents: http://news.bbc.co.uk/1/low/talking_point/4619055.stm

Emergency service driver accountability

Drivers of emergency response vehicles are subject to the same traffic laws as everyone else. However, while using blue lights and audible warnings in response to an emergency call they are exempt from a number of motoring regulations and they may:

- treat a red traffic light as a give way sign
- pass to the right of a keep left bollard
- drive on a motorway hard shoulder (even against the direction of traffic)
- disobey the speed limit.

If it can be shown that a driver of an emergency service vehicle drove without due care and attention, or that they drove in a dangerous manner, then they can be prosecuted, just the same as a member of the public, because they are accountable to the laws of the land. Furthermore, if convicted of a serious traffic offence, they may be disqualified from driving, not only emergency vehicles but also privately owned vehicles.

When drivers of emergency vehicles are involved in accidents they always attract media coverage.

Case study: Accused paramedic had two hours training

Paramedic kills motorist

A paramedic appeared in the Crown court in September 2003 charged with causing the death of a motorist whilst attending an emergency call. The court was told that the paramedic had only received two hours training on how to drive an ambulance in response to an emergency.

It was alleged that the paramedic approached a busy junction too fast and went through some traffic lights at red when he collided with the other vehicle.

The paramedic pleaded not guilty to the charge and the court heard from police investigators that the ambulance should have been going much slower than the estimated 30 mph when the collision occurred, though some witness said he was driving 'like a nutcase.'

He was cleared of causing death by dangerous driving but found guilty of driving without due care.

Assessment activity 15.1

For this activity you are required to prepare and deliver a presentation that will show that you understand how emergency incidents are graded by a selected public service control room. You should ensure that you cover the following content:

Emergency incident: definition.

Incident grading: how incidents are graded by emergency services; inter-agency approaches/agreements; role of call centres and incident managers; policies and procedures for dealing with incidents; definitions of emergency response; response times; initial response services; additional public services offering specialist knowledge, e.g. bomb disposal, underwater search; accountability.

Emergency response: emergency vehicles and equipment; driver training and driving standards for emergency response vehicles; public perception and reaction to emergency response vehicles, e.g. other road users' behaviour; emergency service driver accountability, e.g. bad driving causes accidents and deaths, media coverage when mistakes are made.

Grading tips

To achieve this grade you should use the content so that your presentation will:

- Describe how emergency service incidents are graded by a selected public service control room. **P1**

All of the emergency services know each other's roles and responsibilities as well as those of other organisations, including voluntary agencies. Because of this knowledge, the first member of the emergency services to attend the scene can make an assessment of the situation and request the services of other organisations as demanded by the incident.

Initial actions of first in attendance

One of the reasons why it is important that emergency responders arrive at the scene safely is because the information they relate to their control room is vital for the effective recovery of the incident, especially if the incident calls for an integrated response by the emergency services. As mentioned earlier, it is normally, but not always, a police officer who first attends the scene and they follow a routine procedure.

Information update (actions of first police responder at the scene)

If the incident is of a minor nature and there is no need for further assistance, then this will be relayed to the control room. However, if the incident is serious where immediate assistance is required, then this is transmitted to the control room using the following mnemonic:

- **C**asualties – number or estimated number
- **H**azards – present or potential
- **A**ccess – routes in and out for the emergency and other services
- **L**ocation – exact location of incident
- **E**mergency services – present and needed
- **T**ype of incident – e.g. building collapse, traffic collision, fire, chemical hazard
- **S**afety – that of colleagues and self.

In serious incidents, the first officer at the scene does not become involved in rescue work because they need to assess the situation and maintain contact with control in order to coordinate the response. The first officer takes command of the incident until the formal control structure is established, using their vehicle as the forward control point and making a note of messages passed and received, as well as decisions taken.

Actions of first fire responder at the scene

The first officer to arrive at a fire incident assumes the role of Fire Incident Commander and they, just like the first police officer to attend, must not become personally involved in rescue or fire fighting efforts. Their immediate function is to:

- complete a dynamic risk assessment
- instigate Incident Command
- determine the size and nature of the emergency and communicate the information to control
- form a plan of action to deal with the developing situation
- continue the risk assessment process and issue instructions to implement the plan
- designate a suitable rendezvous point
- establish communications and liaison with the other emergency services
- implement a restricted zone and cordons.

Actions of first ambulance service responder at the scene

In really serious incidents, the ambulance service will be coordinated by an Ambulance Incident Officer (AIO) but until their arrival at the scene, the first ambulance or paramedic response unit will:

- report arrival on scene to Ambulance Control
- liaise with other emergency service Incident Officers
- provide control with details of the incident
- request ambulance/medical resources as required
- confirm incident appears to be 'A major incident'
- commence a log of all communications and actions
- ensure that the nearest appropriate receiving hospitals are aware of the incident.

Roles and responsibilities of key emergency services attending incident

The following table shows the roles and responsibilities of the three main emergency services at an emergency response incident.

Police	Fire	Ambulance
Provide and update control room with clear information	Fight fires in a fire situation	Provide emergency aid and triage
Direct and divert traffic	Minimise risk of fire by removing combustible materials or using foam	Resuscitate where necessary
Ensure access and exit routes are clear	Advise other services on health and safety at the scene	Establish casualty loading point
Cordon off the immediate area	Search for and rescue of casualties using specialist equipment	Establish casualty clearing area
Control crowds, sightseers and onlookers	Identify hazardous substances	Transport casualties to designated hospitals
Obtain witness statements	Dilute or neutralise harmful chemicals	Order medical resources where necessary
Coordinate other services	Establish decontamination units	
Preserve the scene for evidence	Assist in salvage operations	
Identify dead on behalf of HM Coroner	Provide first aid at the scene	
Inform and warn the public through media	Use pumping apparatus for removal of water	
Investigate the cause	Investigate the cause in case of fire	

Table 15.1 Roles and responsibilities of key emergency services at an emergency response incident

Other statutory or voluntary agencies

■ Highways Agency

Where an incident causes or is likely to cause serious disruption to the major roads network, then the Highways Agency should be contacted. This is an executive agency of the Department for Transport (DfT), which is responsible for managing traffic, dealing with congestion and informing road users of problems on the major roads of England. The Highways Agency is responsible for maintaining all motorway systems and 'A' class roads throughout England, while local authorities are responsible for other roads.

Congestion is monitored and managed through the agency's Regional and National Traffic Control Centres, with detailed information readily available to the public. The agency has the technical capability to close roads and divert traffic quickly.

■ Local radio

Local radio stations provide information and regular updates of incidents that are in the public interest. They can be used to warn of dangers, any action the public needs to take, school closures and any disruptions to services as a result of the incident. In serious incidents, local radio stations also give out useful telephone numbers, as well as advising on evacuation arrangements.

Theory into practice

Look at the following scenario and answer the questions at the end.

The Runaway Lorry

At 3.30am a fully laden petrol tanker developed a mechanical fault whilst descending a steep hill on the outskirts of a heavily populated town. The driver struggled in vain to control the vehicle and after demolishing a set of traffic lights and a lamp-post, it eventually collided into the side of an elderly care home, causing serious structural damage to the building and extensive damage to the tanker.

Petrol from the tanker is spilling onto the floor near the building and some of the residents have been disturbed by the collision but it is not known how many residents live in the home, though it is believed that several are physically disabled and are unable to walk. A member of staff from the home runs outside and screams uncontrollably but has the presence of mind to make an emergency telephone call.

The driver of the tanker is breathing but is unconscious and has a laceration to his head.

1. You are the first emergency responder at the scene. What would be your initial response?
2. Using the mnemonic of CHALETS, what precise information would you transmit to your control room?
3. What other information would you require before a combined response could be effectively mounted?
4. Apart from other emergency services, what other agencies would you request?
5. What would be the role of the police, fire and ambulance services at this incident? Explain.

■ Bomb disposal

Many calls are made to the police claiming that a bomb has been planted somewhere, and whilst most calls are hoax calls, threats have to be taken seriously and correct procedures followed.

Where there is good reason to believe that a package is suspicious, or that an object is an unexploded bomb,

then bomb disposal experts need to be requested. Bomb disposal (or explosive ordnance disposal) is normally carried out by Bomb Disposal Engineers of the British Army's Royal Engineers, who will clear any suspicious areas before allowing members of the public to return to the area.

Influenced by the London bombings, the man made the fake device by pouring coloured cooking oil into a container and wiring it to a mobile phone. He then taped a note to the device, which read: 'Any more and we start. This is the last warning.' After placing the device opposite an Asian restaurant, he sat in his car and watched people pass by it.

Later that evening the device was spotted and when the police responded they closed nearby roads and cordoned off an area of 100 metres, where several restaurants and takeaways were situated. An army bomb disposal team attended and carried out a controlled explosion.

The man was arrested when his other mobile phone was traced after he telephoned an emergency operator with further threats.

Assessment activity 15.2

This activity requires you to produce a leaflet for public distribution that shows the initial actions of emergency responders at the scene of an incident, as well as the roles and responsibilities of the key services at the scene. You should ensure that you include the following content:

Initial actions of first in attendance: information update (casualties, hazards, access, location, emergency services required, type of incident (CHALET))

Roles and responsibilities of key emergency services attending incidents: police (for example, clearing access and exit routes, directing traffic, providing clear information, public order, crowd control, cordons); fire service (for example, extinguishing fires, rescuing casualties, removing harmful by-products of combustion, diluting or neutralising harmful chemicals);

ambulance service (for example, providing emergency aid, resuscitation, transportation of casualties).

Other statutory or voluntary agencies: for example, Highways departments to assist with road closures, local radio to advise of traffic problems or evacuations, bomb disposal to investigate suspicious packages.

You should use this content in your leaflet so that it will:

- Identify the initial actions, roles and responsibilities of the key services when attending at the scene of an emergency incident **P2**
- Describe the importance of responding safely to emergency incidents as an emergency response driver **P3**

Grading tips

You should make reference to the content in all sections.

M1 This is an extension of P2 but instead of just identifying the initial actions and roles and responsibilities of the key agencies you should:

- Explain the roles and responsibilities of the key services attending an emergency incident.

D1 This is an extension of P2 and M1 but instead of explaining, you should:

- Evaluate inter-agency cooperation of the emergency response services.

Scene preservation for scene investigation

All incident scenes are potential crime scenes and, as such, they need preserving so that any vital evidence can be collected. Scene preservation may often prove difficult at large incidents because the first priority of the emergency services is the protection of life and the care of casualties. Inevitably, the rescue and treatment of casualties, as well as establishing control posts and taking whatever measures are necessary to prevent an escalation of the incident, will mean considerable disturbance of the ground at the immediate site of the incident. This is why the incident must be coordinated and the scene protected as far as is practical.

Need for traffic accident investigation

All serious and fatal road traffic collisions are thoroughly investigated by the police so that the exact cause can be known. This is particularly important in fatal collisions since the evidence will be required for a Coroner's Court (Inquest), which is an enquiry into sudden, unnatural and suspicious deaths.

Where a traffic collision occurs and the driver of a vehicle involved alleges mechanical failure, or if it is suspected that the vehicle is faulty, then the vehicle will be examined by an officer of the Accident Investigation Branch. The examination of the vehicle is necessary to either corroborate or negate the allegation, or to determine the roadworthiness of the vehicle.

Investigations into accidents include:
- the condition of component parts of vehicles (e.g. faulty brakes or worn tyres)
- any contributory factors (e.g. weather or road conditions)
- the length of any brake or skid marks
- type of road and speed limits
- witness statements

- evidence of reckless or dangerous driving
- evidence of driving whilst under the influence of drink and drugs.

When the investigation is complete, a conclusion can be drawn as to the cause, and if anybody is found to be guilty of causing it, then they can be brought to account through prosecution. However, accident investigations not only serve to apportion blame, they are also needed to see if road safety can be improved and accidents prevented.

Need for fire investigation

Just as there is a need for the cause of serious accidents to be investigated, there is also a need to investigate the cause of fires to see if they were started intentionally or accidentally. Fires, unlike road traffic collisions, tend to destroy any evidence or clues as to the cause, but specialist fire investigation officers can say what the likely causes of fires are, as well as where the fire started.

▲ Specialist fire investigation officers find out if a fire has started accidentally or intentionally

For all fires they attend, fire officers are required to complete a fire data report, which asks for the most likely cause of the fire; though this level is not conclusive and neither is it intended to serve as evidence for a prosecution. However, officers who are very experienced in fire investigation may be able to say with some certainty what the cause of a fire is, though the Home Office recommends the use of forensic scientists and scenes of crime officers to examine the causes of some fires.

Role of Health and Safety Executive

The Health and Safety Executive (HSE) is a government agency, and the enforcing authority that supports the Health and Safety Commission (HSC) in ensuring that risks to workers and members of the public are properly controlled. Specialist staff, including inspectors, scientists, engineers and medical professionals, aim to protect everyone from risk of health or safety by:

- conducting and sponsoring research
- promoting training
- providing an information and advisory service
- submitting proposals for new or revised regulations and approved codes of practice.

The HSE also has a duty to maintain the Employment Medical Advisory Service, which provides advice on occupational health matters.

It is the duty of the HSC to look after many aspects of health and safety, including:

- nuclear installations
- mines and factories
- farms
- hospitals and schools
- offshore gas and oil installations
- the gas grid
- the movement of dangerous goods and substances.

British Transport Police

The British Transport Police (BTP) is a national police service that is funded by train operating companies and the London Underground, and is responsible for providing a service to rail operators, staff and passengers throughout England, Wales and Scotland. The BTP also have jurisdiction over the following:

- Docklands Light Railway
- Glasgow Subway
- Midland Metro tram system
- Croydon Tramlink.

Prior to 2005, railway accidents were investigated by Her Majesty's Rail Inspectorate and the BTP, but following recommendations of the Cullen Report into the Ladbroke Grove rail crash in 1999, a new investigation agency was established.

▲ The Rail Accident Investigation Branch is an independent body which investigates railway accidents

The Railways and Transport Safety Act 2003 created the Rail Accident Investigation Branch (RAIB), which is an independent body with the responsibility for establishing the objective facts of rail accidents and dangerous occurences which result in:

- the death of at least one person
- serious injury to five or more people
- extensive damage to rolling stock, the infrastructure or the environment.

Security for scene preservation

Incident scenes can vary greatly, not only because of the type of incident, but also because of the location and time of the incident. However, whether the incident is a train crash or a major traffic collision, the scene must be preserved for investigation because, as mentioned at the beginning of this section, all incident scenes are potential crime scenes and, as such, they need preserving so that any vital evidence can be collected.

Some scenes may be easier to secure than others and the use of police tape might be sufficient to secure the scene. Other scenes, however, may not be so easy to secure and the use of cordons, road closures, public rights of way and the use of extra police officers may be required to secure a scene.

Consider this

Look at the four examples below and then answer the question at the end.

1. A major traffic collision on the M25 at 4.30pm on a Friday evening.

2. A train derailment on the London to Scotland line at 5.30am in a remote area of Derbyshire.

3. A fire at a busy shopping complex in Birmingham city centre on a Saturday afternoon.

4. A moorland fire high on the Pennines between Yorkshire and Lancashire, with raging winds blowing the flames towards the M62.

How would you secure the scenes of each of these incidents?

■ Use of cordons

A cordon is a barrier that is used to surround the scene of an incident in order to restrict access, thereby preserving the scene. A cordon could be formed using plastic tape, rope, barriers, vehicles or human resources and it should be large enough to contain the scene of the incident and allow for emergency personnel to enter.

Cordons must be sufficiently guarded along the perimeter, as well as at entry and exit points to ensure that only authorised personnel are admitted. A rendezvous point for those services attending the incident is normally located near the entrance of the cordon with an officer designated to keep a log of personnel entering and leaving the cordon.

Scene preservation for evidence collection

Crime scene investigation

The objectives of investigating crime scenes are to:

- preserve and recover evidence and information
- minimise contamination
- discover the truth about the incident
- bring the offenders to justice
- vindicate the innocent.

The nature of some incidents makes it very difficult to preserve and produce evidence, especially evidence such as brake marks on the road, damaged rail carriages and railtracks, as well as damage to vehicles that have been involved in road traffic collsions. In such cases, it is necessary and acceptable to use photographic evidence in court, though the evidence must be provided by an authorised Scene of Crime forensic photographer, who makes a statement as to what the evidence is.

In other incidents, photographs alone would not be sufficient to prove liability, for instance, a case of dangerous driving would be better corroborated by the production of video evidence. Police traffic cars have video equipment fitted as standard so that evidence of such offences can be recorded.

Forensic scientists are often involved in the criminal investigation of serious incidents. They have the knowledge and expertise to examine scenes of crime by applying certain principles in the gathering, securing and analysing of evidence. Sources of forensic evidence include:

- fingerprints
- tool marks
- shoe prints
- glove marks
- body fluids (e.g. blood, saliva)
- glass samples
- hair
- fibres
- handwriting.

A further source of evidence that is used in crime scene investigation is the use of witness testimony. This involves taking statements from witnesses to the incident who may be able to provide:

- **direct evidence**
- **corroborative evidence**
- **circumstantial evidence**.

Key terms

Direct evidence is what a witness actually saw in direct relation to the crime or incident, and this is valuable evidence.

Corroborative evidence is that which tends to support the testimony of what another witness says.

Circumstantial evidence is evidence that when considered with other evidence tends to prove the facts of the case.

Each emergency service is made aware at the planning stage of the need for preserving evidence for a subsequent investigation, which could be for HM Coroner, Public Inquiry, or Civil or Criminal proceedings. As part of the evidence gathering process, all the emergency services participate in the debrief process, as well as compiling a report on their involvement at major incidents.

Other agencies that may carry out their own investigations, depending upon the nature of the incident, could be:

- the Air Accident Investigation Branch
- the Marine Accident Investigation Branch

- the Rail Accident Investigation Branch
- the Health and Safety Executive
- the Environment Agency.

Voluntary agencies

St John Ambulance – this is a charitable organisation which can provide first aiders, ambulances and specialist vehicles to support the emergency services at emergency incidents.

British Red Cross – this is a humanitarian voluntary agency which helps people in crisis worldwide. It is part of the International Red Cross and Red Crescent Movement, and in the UK it responds to all kinds of emergencies, from major incidents to transport accidents, evacuations, floods and fires.

✚ BritishRedCross

In times of major emergency, the British Red Cross may be called upon to staff reception centres, support the ambulance service, assist in the process of tracing all those involved and many other tasks. The British Red Cross can provide emergency response volunteers, as well as ambulances and equipment when they are required. In the aftermath of a fire incident, the organisation can offer lots of support including:

- emotional support
- support with the care of children and pets
- use of shower and toilet facilities
- provision of toiletries
- clothing
- light refreshments
- use of a telephone
- first aid.

WRVS (formerly Women's Royal Voluntary Service) – this is a voluntary service that gives support to the emergency services and the public in emergency incidents, such as floods, fires, rail disasters and evacuations.

In incidents that require evacuation, such as floods, bomb scares or fires, the WRVS can provide rest centres and shelter, with refreshments for everyone involved in the incident, including casualties and emergency service personnel. They have the capability to organise and provide food on a large scale for extended periods of time.

Assessment activity 15.3

For this activity you are to write a report for the attention of all emergency responders and other organisations involved in emergency situations, which will inform them of the importance of scene preservation. You should include the following content in the report:

Scene preservation for scene investigation: need for accident investigation, for example a serious or fatal road traffic collision; need for fire investigation, for example malicious and suspicious fires; role of Health and Safety Executive, for example accidents in the workplace; British Transport Police, for example accidents on the railways, trains and the underground network, security for scene preservation; use of cordons.

Scene preservation for evidence collection: crime scene investigation, such as the use of photographs, video, forensics, witness testimony, provisions made to each emergency service.

Voluntary agencies: other agencies who can offer assistance in the event of an emergency incident, for example the St John Ambulance (first aid), British Red Cross (first aid), Victim Support Scheme (welfare and emotional support), Women's Royal Voluntary Service (assist with welfare, provision of food and shelter).

Grading tips

You should use this content in the report so that it will:

* describe the necessity for scene preservation and the service provisions of specialist units at emergency incidents as part of an incident investigation **P4**
* identify the statutory and voluntary agencies who may work together at the scene of an emergency incident. **P5**

This is an extension of P4 but instead of describing you should:

* explain how scene preservation and the service provision of specialist units contribute to an accident/incident investigation. **M2**

It is of the utmost importance that emergency responders protect themselves from hazards and dangers; otherwise they will become part of the problem instead of part of the rescue effort.

Self-preservation

Specialist clothing

Apart from their standard uniform, the emergency services have specialist clothing to protect them from the many dangers posed by the different types of emergency incidents; this is known as Protective Personal Equipment (PPE). Some PPE is common to all the services, whilst some is exclusive to certain emergency services.

■ Ambulance service PPE

- disposable aprons or disposable overalls where there is a risk of splashing with blood or body fluids
- protective overalls where there is a risk of severe contamination
- face mask where there is a risk of transmission of a contagious disease or a risk of inhalation of dust or other particles
- protective eyewear where there is a risk that blood, body fluids or dirt may get into the eyes
- ear defenders/protection where there are noise hazards.

■ Fire service PPE

- firefighting suits, gloves and boots for fighting fires
- protective headwear for firefighting and building collapse
- self-contained breathing apparatus for entering smoke-filled buildings
- visors/goggles for various incidents
- decontamination suits.

▲ Specialist clothing is necessary to protect members of the emergency services from the hazards and dangers of their work

■ Police service PPE

- fire suits for some specialist units
- protective headwear
- goggles/visors
- specialist riot gear and shields for public order incidents.

All the emergency services wear high-visibility jackets when dealing with road traffic collisions or incidents where high-visibility jackets are required, for instance, incidents on the railway. Certain members of the emergency services have also received training for the potential threat of chemical, biological, radiation and nuclear attack, for which gas-tight suits are issued.

Scene safety measures

Safety at the scene is paramount at any incident, not only for members of the public but also for members of the emergency services. Even in an emergency, the emergency services have a duty of care to themselves, their colleagues and the public. Remember, if a member of the emergency services becomes a casualty, they are likely to make the situation worse because they are taking resources away from the incident. If the scene is not made safe, then there is a chance that someone could become an unnecessary victim of the incident.

Consider this

Look at the following scenarios and say how you could prevent harm to the emergency services and public by using:

- warning signs
- barriers
- cones
- road closures and diversions.

1. A large-scale traffic collision on a motorway where all three lanes are blocked and petrol from several crashed vehicles has spilled onto the carriageway.

2. A suspicious package has been found in a busy shopping centre following a call to the police warning them that a bomb had been planted in one of the shops. It is a Saturday afternoon and the store is very busy.

3. A light aircraft has made an emergency landing in some fields on the outskirts of a town. Unfortunately, as it landed it collided with an overhead power cable causing the live cable to come down into the field close to a local beauty spot that was quite busy with tourists.

Consideration for public welfare

There are many things to consider when there is an emergency situation, especially in large-scale incidents which could affect the welfare of the public. Some incidents can threaten the safety of the public in the immediate vicinity, like burning buildings, for instance, while other incidents, such as traffic collisions on motorways and arterial routes, can cause disruption to the road network for several hours. It is not unheard of to have miles of traffic queuing on motorways because of serious traffic collisions.

The media, in the form of local television and radio, can play an effective part in an emergency in three main ways:

- it can warn the public of an emergency that could threaten their health, and advise them to keep away
- it can warn the public of possible delays to public transport, thus allowing them to make alternative travel arrangements

- it can warn the public about congestion on certain roads so that they can plan alternative routes.

The Highways Agency has a regularly updated website, showing all motorways and main roads in England where there is congestion and how long the delay is likely to last.

Ensuring the scene is safe and will not affect the local environment and its citizens

Some incidents present a greater threat to the public and the environment than others, but whatever the threat, the scene must be made safe so that it will not affect the environment and its citizens. It is stressful enough in times of an emergency and the public need to be assured that there is no immediate threat to themselves, their families and friends, and the environment.

There are many dangers at the scene of emergency incidents, including:

- chemical spillage
- electrical cables
- railways and railway crossings
- fires
- bombs and explosive devices.

Chemical spillage

Chemicals can be extremely hazardous to the public and to the environment. If there is an incident involving hazardous chemicals, then the emergency services need to know what course of action to take to prevent danger to the public and to the environment.

All vehicles that transport hazardous substances, and all buildings that store them, must display a **Hazchem plate**.

Key terms

A **Hazchem plate** is a warning system that informs the emergency services, through an Emergency Action Code (EAC), how to deal with hazardous substances that are carried in vehicles or stored in buildings.

Emergency Action Code. The number tells the fire service which fire suppressant to use, while the letter tells them which equipment to wear, whether there will be a violent reaction and how to dispose of the substance

Warning symbol indicates the danger the substance presents

2X

0000

0808 570 293

United Nations Identification Number, which identifies the dangerous substance. These are assigned by the United Nations Committee of Experts on the Transport of Dangerous Goods

Telephone number if specialist advice is required

Company name or badge

▲ A Hazchem plate

There may be an optional second letter 'E' in the EAC, and this indicates that the incident presents a threat to the public beyond the immediate vicinity. In this case, the public may need to be evacuated or warned to stay indoors with doors and windows closed.

Number	Suppressant	Letter	Violent reaction (V)	Equipment (Liquid-tight suit (LTS), Breathing Apparatus (BA))	Disposal (dilute or contain)
1	Coarse water spray	P	V	LTS	Dilute
2	Fine water spray	R		LTS	Dilute
3	Foam	S	V	BA	Dilute
4	Dry agent	T		BA	Dilute
		W	V	LTS	Contain
		X		LTS	Contain
		Y	V	BA	Contain
		Z		BA	Contain

Table 15.2 Key to numbers and letters of EAC

■ Electrical cables

Electrical cables run above and below the ground and carry thousands of volts of electricty. Overhead cables could be brought down by, for insance, storms, air accidents, or train derailments that collide with wooden cable-bearing poles. Underground cables may be accidentally exposed by excavating vehicles. Any live cables that are on or near the ground can conduct electricity through dampness or metal objects. It would be advisable to dial 999, and ask the police to help keep passers-by well clear.

■ Railways and railway crossings

There are thousands of miles of railways in the UK, with more than 8,000 level crossings. According to HM Railway Inspectorate, 20 people died during the year 2003/2004.

Case study: Train crashes Into car

On Saturday evening, 6 November 2004, a car drove onto an unmanned level crossing and was struck by a high-speed train. Six people died, including the car and train drivers, and five were seriously injured when all eight carriages of the Paddington to Plymouth train derailed at Ufton Nervet, Berkshire.

The incident was attended by 14 fire engines and more than 20 ambulances from surrounding counties. Passengers were lifted from the wreckage and 61 injured were taken to hospitals in Reading and Basingstoke.

A thorough investigation was ordered by the Minister of Transport and teams of investigators searched the scene for evidence. Specialist search teams examined the site to collect evidence, and police made 'extensive inquiries' about the driver of the car.

Take it further

To see how often rail accidents occur in the UK, visit the Timeline of rail accidents at http://news.bbc.co.uk/1/hi/uk/3989465.stm

■ Fires

Fire is one of the largest causes of accidental death in the UK with around 500 deaths a year from house fires and 250 deaths a year from vehicle fires. Each year, the fire service attends over 600,000 fires in the home and there are around 93,000 vehicle fires.

Fire incidents are particularly dangerous because people can become trapped and lose consciousness through smoke inhalation, one of the biggest causes of death in fire-related incidents. Therefore, evacuation is often necessary for the safety of the public.

■ Bombs and explosive devices

In this age, where terrorism is always in the news, bomb threats are common and whilst there are lots of bomb hoaxes, they have to be taken seriously. Bomb warnings may or may not come with a coded message – a way of proving the authenticity of the call – but all calls have to be taken seriously.

Bomb calls may come from terrorist organisations or from individuals with a grudge against society. They may be received at police stations, newspaper companies or by businesses, and may come in the form of telephone calls, emails, text messages or faxes.

Targets of bombers vary from the government and government ministers to businesses. In the case of terrorist bombs, as mentioned previously, they are intended to cause the utmost devastation to people, the country or the economy. Therefore, when a call is received that a bomb has been planted in a busy area, or a suspect package has been found, the threat has to be taken seriously.

Case study: Suspicious package at Bristol Airport

At the beginning of July 2005, Bristol Airport was evacuated just after 6.00pm when a suspicious package was found in baggage handling. Passengers were moved away from the main terminal building to the old terminal, which is now out of use. An army bomb-disposal team were sent for to deal with the package.

Planes were still landing, but passengers were not allowed to leave the planes and roads leading to the airport became gridlocked as flights were grounded and check-in suspended.

It was believed that the suspicious package got to the airport through a connecting flight.

Police directed arrivals at the airport to the old terminal, as well as warning motorists of the congestion surrounding the airport.

Legislation and regulations

The emergency services, like all employees, are governed by legislation and regulations relating to their health and safety at work. Legislation is designed to protect workers and their colleagues from injury and hazards whilst performing their duty.

Impact of legislation and regulations

Unlike most other occupations, the work of the emergency services involves a certain amount of risk and danger. For their own protection, and that of the public, the emergency services have to manage the risks and make decisions based on an evaluation of the risk. Besides managing risks, however, the emergency services have to comply with health and safety law, which can have an impact on the way they carry out their duties. Look at the three following examples of how legislation has an impact on the fire service.

1. In 2006, firefighters in the Devon fire brigade were told to use the stairs instead of sliding down their poles because health and safety officials decided the poles were a hazard, even though using stairs would add vital seconds in responding to an emergency.

2. Firefighters in Humberside are not allowed to use stepladders to install smoke alarms in people's homes, even though this is a popular and important fire prevention method. Installing alarms in such a manner is a contravention of the Health and Safety Executive Work at Height Regulations 2005.

3. The emergency services are being told not to attempt to save drowning people because of health and safety restrictions. In September 2007, two police support officers in Wigan stood by while a 10-year-old boy drowned in a pond, because of a risk to their own safety. A fully qualified officer later plunged into the water to attempt a rescue but this was acting against force policy. The police and fire service personnel are told not to enter water in case they put themselves in danger. A firefighter in Scotland who attempted a similar rescue was later informed he could face disciplinary action.

Take it further

Carry out some research using the Internet and see if you can find another three examples of the impact of health and safety law on the emergency services.

Health and Safety at Work Act 1974 (HASAWA)

HASAWA set basic principles to be followed by both employees and employers to help ensure a safe working environment by:

- protecting the health, safety and welfare of people at work
- protecting others against risks to health or safety in connection with the activities of persons at work

- controlling the keeping, use and possession of dangerous substances.

When it became law in 1974, HASAWA did not apply to police officers but The Police (Health & Safety) Act 1997 brought all police officers within the scope of the Act.

HASAWA is an enabling act, which means that further health and safety legislation can be made law without having to pass through Parliament. New regulations made under HASAWA include:

- the Reporting of Injuries, Diseases and Dangerous Occurrences Regulations 1995 (RIDDOR)
- the Control of Substances Hazardous to Health Regulations 2002 (COSHH)
- the Management of Health and Safety at Work Regulations 1999
- the Personal Protective Equipment (PPE) at Work Regulations 1992.

Theory into practice

Police pursuits of stolen vehicles or disqualified drivers are covered under HASAWA. The control room supervisor can instruct the pursuit driver to abandon the pursuit if it is believed that the risk of danger in the pursuit is greater than the risk of bringing the pursuit to a safe conclusion. The risk is assessed by having regard to the safety of the public, the police pursuit driver and the occupant or occupants of the vehicle being pursued.

■ RIDDOR

RIDDOR enables the HSE and local authorities to identify risks in the workplace by placing a legal obligation on employers, the self-employed and people in control of premises to report:

- work-related deaths
- major injuries or injuries lasting more than three days (including fractured limbs, loss of sight, electric shock, burns)
- work-related diseases (including lung disease, skin disease and infections)
- dangerous occurences (including explosions, failure of breathing apparatus).

Near misses must also be reported under the regulations. A 'near miss' is when something happens but, luckily, it did not result in a injury or death, though it could have done. This is classed as a dangerous occurrence and must be reported under RIDDOR.

■ COSHH

COSHH is designed to protect employees from hazardous substances that are stored or used in the workplace. These include: oils, bleaches, paint, solvents and any by-products emitted from burning, as well as biological agents. The regulations require exposure to hazardous substances to be prevented or adequately controlled so that the health of workers and others exposed to them is not threatened.

Hazard Analysis Critical Control Points (HACCP)

Besides ensuring the health and safety of workers, there is also legislation that protects the consumer from contaminated or unfit food. Since January 2006, food production and preparation in the UK is subject to European Regulation on Hygiene of Foodstuffs. This requires all food business operators to implement and maintain a permanent procedure based on the principles of hazard analysis critical control points (HACCP).

HACCP is a method that relies on the identification and close monitoring of Critical Control Points (CCPs) in the production and preparation of food to ensure that food is safe and fit for human consumption. It relies on the following principles:

- identifying hazards and eliminating or reducing them to acceptable levels
- identifying the critical control points at which control is essential
- establishing critical limits of acceptability from unacceptability
- establishing and implementing effective monitoring procedures
- establishing corrective actions when CCP is not under control.

Assessment activity 15.4

For this activity you are to prepare a wall display that will describe the health and safety measures to ensure the safety of personnel attending emergency incidents. You should ensure that you cover the following content:

Self-preservation: specialist clothing, such as high-visibility clothing, footwear, eye protection, head protection, gloves

Scene safety measures: warning signs, barriers, cones, road closures and diversions

Consideration for public welfare: for example, using the media to warn the public, warning the public about possible delays to public transport, warning the public about congestion; ensuring the scene is safe and will not affect the local environment and its citizens

Dangers at the scene: chemical spillage, for example hazardous chemicals (Hazchem warning system); electrical cables; railway and railway crossings; fires, for example persons trapped, smoke inhalation, evacuation; bombs and explosive devices, for example bomb warnings, targets, terrorist activity, searching, evacuation

Legislation and regulations: impact of legislation and regulations; Health and Safety at Work Act 1974, including any subsequent amendments of legislation, the Reporting of Injuries, Diseases and Dangerous Occurrences Regulations (RIDDOR), the Control of Substances Hazardous to Health (COSHH); Hazard Analysis Critical Control Points (HACCP).

You should use the content to:

- describe the health and safety measures to be taken, to ensure personal safety and that of others when attending an emergency incident, with reference to the relevant health and safety legislation. **P6**

Grading tips

Ensure that you cover all the content.

This is an extension of P6 but instead of describing the health and safety measures you should:

- explain the need for measures to be taken, to ensure personal safety and that of others when attending an emergency incident, with reference to relevant health and safety legislation. **M3**

This is an extension of M3 but as well as explaining you should:

- evaluate the impact of health and safety legislation/regulations on services responding to an emergency incident. **D2**

Knowledge check

1. According to the Civil Contingencies Act, what is an 'emergency incident'?

2. How many grades of response are there for the police?

3. List four of the common objectives when responding to emergency incidents.

4. Which agency is responsible for setting the standard for the driving of emergency vehicles?

5. For what is the mnemonic CHALETS used?

6. List six of the roles and responsibilities of the police when dealing with an emergency incident.

7. List six of the roles and responsibilities of the fire service when dealing with an emergency incident.

8. List six of the roles and responsibilities of the ambulance service when dealing with an emergency incident.

9. What is the Highways Agency responsible for?

10. Who investigates accidents on the railway?

11. What is the HSE responsible for?

12. What are the objectives of crime scene investigation?

13. What details are contained within a Hazchem plate?

14. Which regulation prevents firefighters from standing on stools and householders' stepladders in order to fit smoke alarms?

15. What is the fundamental principle of the HASAWA 1974?

16. What does RIDDOR stand for?

17. What does COSHH stand for?

Preparation for assessment

Write an article for the emergency service responders that will:

1. Describe how emergency service incidents are graded by a selected public service control room. **P1**

2. Identify the initial actions, roles and responsibilities of the key services when attending at the scene of an emergency incident. **P2**

3. Explain the roles and responsibilities of the key services attending an emergency incident. **M1**

4. Evaluate the inter-agency cooperation of the emergency response services. **D1**

5. Describe the importance of responding safely to emergency incidents as an emergency response driver. **P3**

6. Describe the necessity for scene preservation and the service provisions of specialist units at emergency incidents as part of an incident investigation. **P4**

7. Explain how scene preservation and the service provision of specialist units contribute to an accident/incident investigation. **M2**

8. Identify the statutory and voluntary agencies who may work together at the scene of an emergency incident. **P5**

9. Describe the health and safety measures to be taken to ensure personal safety and that of others when attending an emergency incident, with reference to the relevant health and safety legislation. **P6**

10. Explain the need for measures to be taken to ensure personal safety and that of others when attending an emergency incident, with reference to relevant health and safety legislation. **M3**

11. Evaluate the impact of health and safety legislation/regulations on services responding to an emergency incident. **D2**

Grading criteria	Activity	Pg no.		
To achieve a pass grade the evidence must show that the learner is able to:			To achieve a merit grade the evidence must show that the learner is able to:	To achieve a distinction grade the evidence must show that the learner is able to:
P1 Describe how emergency service incidents are graded by a selected public service control room	15.1	46	**M1** Explain the roles and responsibilities of the key services attending an emergency incident	**D1** Evaluate the inter-agency cooperation of the emergency response services
P2 Identify the initial actions, roles and responsibilities of the key services when attending at the scene of an emergency incident	15.2	50		
P3 Describe the importance of responding safely to emergency incidents as an emergency response driver	15.2	50		
P4 Describe the necessity for scene preservation and the service provisions of specialist units at emergency incidents as part of an incident investigation	15.3	55	**M2** Explain how scene preservation and the service provision of specialist units contribute to an accident/incident investigation	
P5 Identify the statutory and voluntary agencies who may work together at the scene of an emergency incident	15.3	55		
P6 Describe the health and safety measures to be taken to ensure personal safety and that of others when attending an emergency incident, with reference to the relevant health and safety legislation	15.4	62	**M3** Explain the need for measures to be taken to ensure personal safety and that of others when attending an emergency incident, with reference to relevant health and safety legislation	**D2** Evaluate the impact of health and safety legislation/regulations on services responding to an emergency incident

Uniformed public services employment

Introduction

This unit is one of the most important units you will study on your BTEC National. It is designed to inform you of a wide variety of possible career options and help you decide which career options might be right for you. Even if you already have a clear idea of which service you want to join, you still need to know as much as you can about the other services. Increasingly, the services are working together in cooperation and partnership to deliver the best service to the public, and an understanding of all of the services will help you see how they can work together and impact upon each other. It is also important to understand the roles and responsibilities of the services, because they have a tremendous amount of power within society to affect people's lives and influence society and the government. They are often the nation's largest and most stable employers, and a career with them will normally be reasonably well paid, give numerous opportunities for promotion and be varied and challenging. For this reason, competition for employment opportunities in the services can be fierce, particularly for highly sought-after posts such as police officer, firefighter and certain roles in the armed services.

This unit will help you prepare for the time when you are applying to the public services and will help you make informed career choices. This in turn will make you more attractive to the public services, which are actively looking for people who are well informed and realistic about what life in a public service means.

After completing this unit you should be able to achieve the following outcomes:
- Understand the purpose, roles and responsibilities of a range of uniformed public services
- Understand a range of jobs and conditions of service within the uniformed public services
- Know the application and selection process for a given uniformed public service
- Understand the initial training and opportunities for career development within a given uniformed public service.

'Public service' is a broad term and means lots of different things to different people. What do you think the term 'public service' means? Come up with a definition that you can discuss with your colleagues.

Uniformed public services

This section examines the purpose, roles and responsibilities of a range of uniformed public services. In most societies there are organisations that provide professional services to the public and which are collectively called 'the public services'. In thinking about public service organisations you probably think about those that are uniformed, such as the police and the Army. However, there are many that do not involve wearing a uniform. Table 16.1 lists the uniformed and non-uniformed public services.

Uniformed	Non-uniformed
• Police service	• Probation service
• Fire service	• Social services
• Ambulance service	• Education service
• Army	• Local government
• Royal Navy	• Youth and community services
• Royal Marines	• Victim Support
• Mountain/cave rescue	• Civil service
• Royal Air Force	• MI5/MI6
• Coastguard	• Trade unions
• Prison service	• Refuse collection services
• Customs and Excise	
• National Health Service	

Table 16.1 Uniformed and non-uniformed public services

Funding

Most public services are funded by the government, with money from the taxes the public pays. Look at the public services listed in Table 16.1 and see if you can guess which ones are funded by the government and which ones are not.

Public services fall into two categories: statutory and non-statutory. Statutory public services are required to exist by law and are funded by the government. Non-statutory public services are not required to exist by law and are often charities or self-funded. See Table 16.2 for some examples of the two categories.

As you can see in Table 16.2, some of the services funded by the government do not involve wearing a uniform, such as the probation service, and some services not funded by the government do wear a uniform, such as the Salvation Army.

▼ The police, fire and ambulance services work best when they work together, without overlapping

Statutory public services	Non-statutory public services
Police service	Victim Support
Fire service	Help the Aged
Ambulance service	Trade unions
RAF	Alcoholics Anonymous
Royal Navy	Samaritans
Education service	NSPCC
NHS	Salvation Army
Probation service	Church groups

Table 16.2 Statutory and non-statutory public services

This unit focuses only on the uniformed public services, beginning with the emergency services: the police service, fire service and ambulance service. As you will be well aware by now, there are lots of different public services. Not all of them can be examined in a single unit. This unit will cover some of the most popular services; you will be encouraged to research the others independently.

The emergency services

Police service

The origins of modern law enforcement in the UK can be traced back to the 13th century, to the locally appointed magistrates and petty constables whose job

▲ The police are an important part of the local community

Consider this

The name Robert is often shortened to Bob or Bobby and this is why police officers are sometimes referred to as Bobbies – after their founder Sir Robert Peel.

was to maintain the peace and deal with those who broke the law. However, the modern police service in England and Wales was not formed until 1829. This was when the Metropolitan Police Act, created by the then Home Secretary Sir Robert Peel, was passed. A decade later, with the County Police Act, police services in counties outside the London metropolitan area were formed.

The roles and responsibilities of the police service have been changed by many other Acts since those early days, among them the Police and Criminal Evidence Act 1984, the Crime and Disorder Act 1998 and the Police Act 1997 and 2004.

■ Purpose and values of the police service

There are 43 police services in England and Wales, all of them sharing a common purpose and common values. These are to:

- uphold the law fairly and firmly
- pursue and bring to justice those who break the law
- keep the Queen's peace
- protect, help and reassure the community
- operate with integrity, common sense and sound judgement.

Beyond these overall aims, many police services also set local priorities, which largely depend on the needs of their particular area. Most services also have individual mission statements, which are summaries of the aims of the particular constabulary, and each will also have individual performance indicators that tell the public and government how well a particular police service is performing. The best way to examine this information is by looking at real examples of how the police services present this information.

On page 70 is a statement setting out the aims, priorities and mission of the Northampton police service.

As you can see, Northampton has a particular vision for policing in their area that includes information on their mission, priorities and resources. Most police services have something like this on their websites. You can access this information to find out more about which particular police service you would like to join. You can also use information like this to make comparisons between police service areas.

Consider this

Find the mission and priorities of three more police constabularies and compare them with the information from Northampton. Identify all the differences and similarities.

Making the Difference

Our Vision

A county in which communities feel safe and are secure

Our Mission

Policing in partnership to:

- Reduce and prevent crime
- Reduce and prevent anti-social behaviour and disorder
- Reduce fear of crime and disorder
- Increase public confidence
- Improve public safety
- Help communities to work together
- Bring offenders to justice

Our Values

We value people who make the difference by:

- Focusing on performance
- Acting with integrity
- Being honest, open and courteous to the public and to each other
- Displaying flexibility, initiative and commitment
- Appreciating and encouraging the contribution of others
- Respecting diversity

police

www.northants.police.uk

▲ **The mission statement of the Northamptonshire police service**   *Source*: Northamptonshire Police

■ Roles and responsibilities of the police

The police do a great deal more work than we are often aware of. Most of us think of police work as responding to emergency calls. This is true, but it doesn't cover half what the police are expected to do. Other duties include responding to non-emergency calls such as noise nuisance, abandoned vehicles and dealing with stray animals. But they are also involved with:

- completing a huge amount of paperwork
- improving community relations
- anti-terrorism work
- anti-smuggling work
- reducing the fear of crime by maintaining a visible presence on the streets
- working in partnership with other services to reduce crime
- crime prevention
- giving evidence in court
- crime investigation
- educational visits to schools and colleges
- firearms licensing
- the licensing of pubs and clubs
- regulating door supervisors
- referring victims of crime to support agencies
- overseeing the procedure for licensing betting offices
- underwater search
- missing persons' reports
- providing advice and information on personal safety and protection of property
- providing the government with information and statistics
- escorting of abnormal loads
- holding people in police custody
- responding to major incidents.

These are only some of the jobs that the police must do in order to fulfil the expectations of the public and the government.

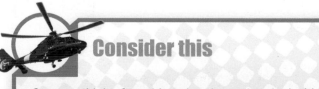

Consider this

Can you think of anything else the police deal with in the course of their work?

■ Accountability

The police are accountable for their performance to the public, the local police authority, central government and their inspectorate. This is covered in more detail on page 22 of *Uniformed Public Services Book 1*.

Positive	Negative
- Interesting and varied work.	- Unsocial hours/shift work interfering with personal and family life.
- Plenty of opportunities for career development and progression.	- Risk to personal safety.
- Work as part of a team and make friends.	- Unpleasant nature of some of the work, such as dealing with child abuse cases.
- Meet different people every day.	- Public attitudes towards the police are not always positive.
- Opportunity to change job roles throughout your career.	- Not just a 9–5 job – you must uphold the standards of the police service in your off-duty hours too.
- Good rates of pay compared with other services.	- Responsibility for people's safety is in your hands – you can't afford an 'off' day.
- Excellent pension and benefits.	
- Retire early (at 55).	
- Secure employment.	
- Ongoing training.	

Table 16.3 Positive and negative aspects of working in the police service

Consider this

Imagine that you are a police recruitment officer who is giving a talk to a local college about opportunities in the police service. The students ask you the following questions, and you must answer them as fully as you can. What would you say?

1 What is the purpose of the police?
2 What kind of priorities do the police set?
3 What kind of work do they do?
4 What are the good and bad things about being a police officer?

The history of the fire service in the UK can be traced back to the Great Fire of London in 1666. This fire blazed for three days and made over 200,000 people homeless. As a result, London was divided into quarters and each quarter was allocated firefighting equipment. This was one of the first organised attempts to prevent fire. The first formal fire brigade did not exist until 1824, when 80 men were recruited for the specific purpose of fighting fire in Edinburgh. The Fire Services Act 1947 is the legal basis for the existence of the fire service, although laws have been passed since then which have modified the role and responsibilities of the fire service such as the Fire and Rescue Services Act 2004. Today there are 50 separate fire brigades in England and Wales employing around 33,400 full-time firefighters and around 12,000 retained (part-time) firefighters.

■ Purpose and values of the fire service

Like the police service, the fire service is required to set aims, objectives and priorities. Since there is no national fire service to which you can go to find what these are, you must research individual fire brigades for their priorities and mission statements. The example below gives an indication of what some brigades are doing.

3. OUR VISION, MISSION AND VALUES

OUR VISION

We are committed to acknowledging the diversity of communities and agencies and supporting them by working together in partnership for a safer South Yorkshire by:

- Educating and encouraging people to take responsibility for their own safety
- Promoting risk reduction as a means of improving community safety, economic welfare, health and well-being
- Ensuring that there are no preventable emergencies

OUR MISSION

We are dedicated to building safer communities by:

- Reducing the risks that cause emergencies
- Dealing with emergencies when they happen
- Building public confidence in the fire and rescue service
- Working effectively with our local partners
- Continually developing our resources to meet changing needs

OUR VALUES

Service

We value service to the community by:

- Working with all groups to reduce risk
- Treating everyone fairly and with respect
- Being answerable to those we serve
- Striving for excellence in all that we do

People

We value our employees through:

- Fairness and respect
- Recognition of merit
- Honesty, integrity and mutual trust
- Personal Development
- Co-operative and inclusive working

Diversity

We value diversity in the Service and the community by:

- Treating everyone fairly and with respect
- Providing varying solutions for different needs
- Promoting equal opportunities in employment and progression within the Service
- Challenging prejudice and discrimination

Improvement

We value improvement at all levels of the Service through:

- Accepting responsibility for our performance
- Being open minded
- Considering criticism thoughtfully
- Learning from our experience
- Consulting others

www.syfire.gov.uk

▲ The South Yorkshire fire brigade mission statement

Source: South Yorkshire Fire and Rescue

Although these missions and values give an indication of what the fire service does at an organisational level they do not actually specify the tasks and roles the fire service may engage in. Some of these roles are detailed below.

■ Roles and responsibilities of the fire service

Apart from responding to emergency calls in the case of fire or serious road traffic incidents, there are a variety other roles and responsibilities the fire service is required to undertake, such as:

- promoting fire safety
- animal rescue
- hazardous materials incidents
- fire prevention
- disaster management
- fitting smoke detectors
- chemical spillages
- recovering objects
- educating children
- industrial accidents
- working in partnership with other services
- protecting the environment
- flooding incidents
- industrial fire training
- first aid
- releasing people trapped in lifts
- checking that business premises comply with fire regulations
- giving evidence in court
- preserving evidence at the scene of a deliberate fire (arson)
- fire safety advice in the home
- dealing with terrorist incidents.

▼ The fire service educates children about fire safety as part of its role

Consider this

Does the fire service have more roles and responsibilities than you thought?

List the five most important roles that the fire service fulfils, in your opinion.

Positive	Negative
• Secure employment. • Variety of work. • Retirement at 55. • Opportunity for progression and promotion. • Ongoing training. • Variety of work. • Saving lives.	• Unsocial hours/shift work. • Dangerous nature of the work. • Poor pay in relation to some other services. • Disturbing nature of some of the work, particularly when deaths are involved.

Table 16.4 Positive and negative aspects of working in the fire service

The armed services

The Army

The British Army has a long and distinguished history. It was formed by royal warrant on 26 January 1661. It is one of the few modern armies to be based on the 'regimental system', which makes it difficult to discuss the Army's history as a whole because each regiment has its own history and traditions. A soldier or an officer will normally serve in the same regiment throughout their career, a system which has the advantage of creating pride and loyalty in a regiment and which boosts fighting spirit and leads to a committed and motivated fighting force. Some regiments have had long histories, such as the Honourable Artillery Company, founded in 1537, the Royal Monmouthshire Engineers, founded in 1539, and the Coldstream Guards, founded in 1650, to name a few.

Of course the Army has faced many major reforms since 1661, particularly in the 19th and 20th centuries. After the Crimean War against the Russians there were major calls for army reform as many soldiers had died from disease and neglect and poor administration. Although the Crimean War was a successful endeavour for the British Army, the loss of many soldiers in non-battle conditions was disturbing and triggered the 'Cardwell Reforms', which improved conditions for those in the Army and changed the rules for commissioning officers. Other conflicts that changed the way the Army operated included the Boer War at the end of the 19th century. This brought about a major rethink in the Army's tactics and strategy, as it was not used to dealing with fast-moving and covert militia groups like the Boers. As a result the British Army that fought in the First World War (1914–18) was better trained than any previous one.

■ Mission and objectives of the Army

Like the police and the fire service there is legislation that sets out the parameters the Army must work within, such as the Army Act 1955 and the Armed Forces Discipline Act 2000. The Army is currently under strength in several areas, but has a total strength of around 100,000 and is the largest single UK employer.

The Army, along with the Royal Navy, Royal Air Force and Royal Marines, is part of the Ministry of Defence (MOD), which has a strategic mission that includes all aspects of the defence of the nation. This mission and the MOD's objectives are described opposite.

These objectives give you an idea of how the Army and the rest of the armed services see their role in terms of the wider issues of defence. However, they do not really describe what the Army actually does, day to day.

Ministry of Defence and Armed Forces

The Defence Vision

The key principles which provide the basis of work for Defence.

Defending the United Kingdom and its interests.
Strengthening international peace and stability.
A force for good in the world

We achieve this aim by working together on our core task to produce battle-winning people and equipment that are:

Fit for the challenge of today.

Ready for the tasks of tomorrow.

Capable of building for the future.

We have shown we succeed in what we do. We must continue to adapt to a more uncertain world. We will be flexible and creative, harnessing new technologies and ideas to make best use of our resources.

We will base our future direction on:

Providing strategy that matches new threats and instabilities

We face new challenges and unpredictable new conditions. Our strategy must evolve to reflect these new realities.

For the future this means:

Evolving strategy and military doctrine that is flexible and geared to changing conditions.

Behaving with speed, flexibility and creativity as an organisation – in the way we work and the way we respond to external events.

Holding fast, in the face of change, to our underpinning military traditions and commitment to public service.

Maintaining flexible force structures

As our strategy evolves, we will develop force structures to maintain battle-winning capabilities that are relevant and effective against emerging threats.

For the future this means:

Greater focus on capability rather than delivery platforms.

Developing pace of deployment and impact.

Increasing precision of effect.

Flexibility and agility in terms of platforms and equipment.

The highest standards of professionalism among men and women imbued with fighting spirit, well trained and properly equipped.

Reaching out into the wider world

We are major contributors to the business of government and to society as a whole. We will increasingly recognise and manage our contribution.

For the future this means:

Working closely with other Departments, with the private and voluntary sectors in the UK, and with our allies abroad, to integrate the military, diplomatic, economic and social components of crisis resolution.

Strengthening our links with the Civil Departments to implement the government's domestic agenda – making our contribution in the regions, and providing support in civil emergencies.

Playing a key role as part of wider society, for example in our contribution to training and skills and to health.

Helping the rest of government benefit from making wider use of our skills in project management and delivery.

Working in closer partnership with the private sector to deliver value for money.

Leading a high-performing organisation

The many demands on the MOD, including its role as military headquarters, require us to be first class in the way we lead and manage the business of defence.

For the future this means:

Clear leadership at all levels, focussed on delivering the vision.

Managers free to get on with tasks and held to account against clear objectives.

Demonstrably effective management of our resources.

Stripping out bureaucracy, with ways of working that are simple and "fit for purpose" and using common standards wherever possible.

Working flexibly, with project and task-based teams.

Investing in our people

We are world leaders in many aspects of how we manage and develop our people. We will build on this with strong leadership and focussed investment.

For the future this means:

Providing strong unified leadership, service and civilian personnel working together.

Benefiting from diversity by recruiting service and civilian personnel reflecting society as a whole and with the right skills for the task.

Balancing rewarding successful performance with robust management of poor performance.

Being a learning organisation, sharing knowledge, committed to developing our people.

▲ **The mission and objectives of the Ministry of Defence**

■ Roles and responsibilities of the Army

This is difficult to address because of the huge variety of individual roles within the Army. What the average soldier or officer does varies depending on the regiment they belong to. The main divisions of the Army are shown in Table 16.5, along with the roles they are likely to fulfil.

Army division	Roles
Household Cavalry and Royal Armoured Division	Armoured reconnaissance, ceremonial duties, mobile combat
Army Air Corps	Airborne combat, reconnaissance, directing artillery, moving troops and stores, airborne command
Royal Regiment of Artillery	Surveillance, target acquisition, armed defence of troops and equipment via projectile weaponry
Royal Corps of Engineers	Building bridges, destroying bridges, clearing and laying mines, surveys and map production, camp construction, power generation, airstrip building, ordnance destruction
Royal Corps of Signals	Communications
Intelligence Corps	Information gathering, spying, counter-intelligence
Royal Army Chaplain's Department	Support for soldiers and officers
Royal Logistics Corps	Provision and distribution of all equipment and stores to Army personnel
Royal Army Medical Corps	Wartime responsibility for sick and wounded of both sides in battlefield conditions and peacetime care of soldiers and their families' medical needs
Royal Electrical and Mechanical Engineers	Maintenance of all Army equipment to ensure it is safe and fit for purpose

Table 16.5 Army divisions and their roles

The British Army has a guide for the behaviour of all soldiers and officers regardless of which regiment they may be in, which promotes putting others before yourself, facing up to danger, high standards of discipline, loyalty to the service and respect for others. If you are unable to follow these rules then the Army is probably not the place for you.

◀ The Army requires high standards of discipline, loyalty and respect

Positive	Negative
• Varied and interesting role.	• Very disciplined environment.
• Wide variety of job opportunities.	• Lack of freedom to do as you please.
• Opportunities for advancement and promotion.	• Dangerous nature of work.
• Stable and secure employment.	• Very poor pay in comparison with other services.
• Opportunities for travel and living abroad.	• Postings abroad can harm personal relationships.
• Sense of belonging/ camaraderie.	• Promotion is difficult to get without a strong academic background.
• Early retirement.	
• Ongoing training.	
• Lots of opportunities for sports or developing new skills.	
• Food and lodgings provided.	
• Potential to make lots of friends.	

Table 16.6 Positive and negative aspects of working in the armed services

Other uniformed services

HM Revenue and Customs

Her Majesty's Revenue and Customs is one of the oldest public services and has developed greatly over time. However, its essential function has not substantially changed.

■ Roles and responsibilities of HM Revenue and Customs

Customs employs over 22,000 staff in the UK and its primary role is to collect taxes and duties from the public. These taxes help fund the running of our society, by helping to pay for the public services such as education, health care and the police. HMRC collects around £100 billion every year in taxes such as VAT and duties on tobacco, alcohol and petrol. It also protects the interests of British and international business by monitoring the import and export of goods, including the seizure of counterfeit goods, such as fake designer clothes or copied DVDs. Customs also has a large role

to play in the fight against crime, in that it detects and investigates individuals and companies who evade their taxes and works in partnership with other services to prevent the import of drugs into the UK; this is mainly done through the shipping ports and airports. It also works with other services to prevent the importation of offensive and illegal material such as child pornography and the trade in endangered plant and animal species.

Customs is a very successful service. In 2000–2001 it prevented drugs worth over £1.5 billion reaching the UK and intercepted hundreds of millions of pounds' worth of smuggled goods such as tobacco and alcohol, which otherwise would have lost the government many millions of pounds in taxes.

Positive	Negative
• Variety of work undertaken.	• Low rates of pay in comparison with other services, particularly at lower grades.
• Variety of entry levels depending on experience and qualifications.	• No automatic early retirement.
• Various sites round UK to be attached to.	• Financial aspects of the work may be routine and lack excitement.
• Safer than many other public service jobs.	

Table 16.7 Positive and negative aspects of working in HM Revenue and Customs

HM Prison Service

Prisons have a very long history in the UK. However, other methods of punishment have been used as alternatives to prison, such as hanging or transportation to convict colonies in America and Australia. Transportation to America ceased to be an option after the American War of Independence in 1776, and sending offenders to Australia was halted in 1857, although it was not officially abolished until 1868. These changes meant that more prisons needed to be built in this country. A rapid prison-building programme in the 1840s resulted in 54 new prisons being built, and many of them are still in service today. The prison service used to be run by local authorities, but the 1877 Prison Act brought all prisons under the control of central government, which is still the case today. The prison service currently employs 44,000 staff who deal with approximately 72,000 inmates in 138 prisons.

■ Roles and responsibilities of the prison service

The roles and responsibilities of the prison service are stated very clearly in its mission statement and strategic objectives:

HM Prison Service

Statement of Purpose

Her Majesty's Prison Service serves the public by keeping in custody those committed by the courts.

Our duty is to look after them with humanity and help them lead law-abiding and useful lives in custody and after release.

Our Vision
To provide the very best prison services so that we are the provider of choice.
To work towards this vision by securing the following key objectives.

Objectives
To protect the public and provide what commissioners want to purchase by:
– Holding prisoners securely
– Reducing the risk of prisoners re-offending
– Providing safe and well-ordered establishments in which we treat prisoners humanely, decently and lawfully.

In securing these objectives we adhere to the following principles:

Our Principles
In carrying out our work we:
– Work in close partnership with our commissioners and others in the Criminal Justice System to achieve common objectives
– Obtain best value from the resources available using research to ensure effective correctional practice
– Promote diversity, equality of opportunity and combat unlawful discrimination, and
– Ensure our staff have the right leadership, organisation, support and preparation to carry out their work effectively.

▲ **The prison service mission statement**

Source: HM Prison Service. Crown Copyright material reproduced with the permission of the Controller of Her Majesty's Stationery Office and the Queen's Printer for Scotland.

Of course these are the aims of the prison service overall, but what are the usual roles and responsibilities of an individual prison officer? The description below highlights the tasks that a prison officer may have to fulfil in the course of their duties:

- ensuring the security of the prison by conducting searches of prisoners and visitors and general security checks of property and locations
- maintaining order in the prison environment
- supervising prisoners and keeping a count of prisoners in the prison or the wing where an officer might work

- taking care of prisoners and their property
- promoting human rights
- administrative duties
- ensuring prisoners do not commit self-harm
- preventing bullying and victimisation of prisoners by other prisoners
- rehabilitation of prisoners
- writing reports on prisoners
- using appropriate restraint techniques
- transporting prisoners.

Positive	Negative
<ul><li>Early retirement.</li><li>Stable and secure employment.</li><li>Good opportunities for promotion.</li><li>Graduate fast-track scheme.</li><li>Rewarding job which is a service to the community.</li><li>Large variety of roles within the job.</li><li>A public service job which offers direct and sustained contact with the public.</li><li>Fast-track entry for experienced managers.</li><li>Opportunities for professional development and innovation.</li><li>Opportunities to develop teamwork skills.</li></ul>	<ul><li>Poor salary in comparison with other services.</li><li>Shift work.</li><li>Confined working environment.</li><li>Lack of opportunity to work outdoors.</li><li>Prison can be a tense and intimidating environment.</li><li>No guarantee of a posting of your choice.</li><li>Can be a dangerous environment.</li></ul>

Table 16.8 Positive and negative apects of working in the prison service

Many of the roles and responsibilities of the services in relation to specific duties such as peacekeeping or major incident response are covered in detail in other units, for example *Unit 8: International perspectives for the uniformed public services* and *Unit 14: The planning for and management of major incidents.*

roles of the armed forces; humanitarian work; disaster relief; conflict; working in prisons; transporting prisoners; patrolling coast; operating CCTV; working with local communities

- responsibilities – accountability (legal, professional and political), performance indicators (what they are, examples of, effect on work)
- public service work – range of emergency and routine work undertaken, daily work routine, administrative work, work with other public services, community work, implications of working in the public services on a personal level, positive and negative aspects of working in the services, examples of recent peace-keeping activities and humanitarian work, roles at major incidents, examples of activities in recent conflicts.

You must use this content to answer the question below.

1. Produce two fact sheets that describe the roles, purpose and responsibilities of two contrasting uniformed public services. **P1 M1 D1**

Assessment activity 16.1

In order to complete this assessment activity you are required to describe two uniformed public services. You must research the following content:

- type of services – emergency services (police, fire service, ambulance); armed forces (Army, Royal Navy, Royal Marines, Royal Air Force); other uniformed services (prison service, HM Revenue and Customs, HM Coastguard, private security services, e.g. local government)
- purpose – organisational objective, mission statements, legislation (e.g. Fire Service Act 1997/2002, Police Act 2004)
- roles – dealing with accidents and emergencies; routine work; peace-keeping activities; other roles, e.g. anti-terrorist and anti-smuggling roles; defence

Grading tips

P1 Choose two services you are familiar with or that are outlined in this chapter and describe their roles, purposes and responsibilities. They should be contrasting services, so consider one armed and one emergency service.

M1 This is a straightforward extension of P1. You simply have to explain in more detail the roles, purposes and responsibilities of two contrasting services.

D1 This is a further extension to P1 and M1. On one of the fact sheets you produce you should evaluate the roles, responsibilities and purposes of one service. This means weigh up how well it performs in its role and form sensible conclusions about its effectiveness.

This section is designed to help you find out about a range of different jobs within the services. It is important to remember that each service has many different job role opportunities which you can choose or be assigned to. This section cannot cover all of these, but it does provide a 'snapshot' of the type of work available in some of the uniformed services.

Jobs within the police service

There are many possible jobs in the police service, such as police officer, special constable and administrative officer, to name a few. In a well-organised service each role works to support the others, and they are all equally important to the operational effectiveness of the service. The three jobs we will examine and compare are:

- Police constable
- Civilian support staff
- Police community support officer.

Police constable

All police officers must spend two years on probation as a patrol constable before they can specialise in a particular area of police work. Many police officers choose to remain as patrol constables for their whole career. The role of patrol constable involves many of the following tasks:

- **Foot patrol** – This involves walking a specific route (or beat) to act as a visible uniformed presence. It can act as a deterrent to criminals who are operating in the area and reduces fear of crime in the general public. Although it is rare that a beat officer will come across a crime in progress, public opinion polls regularly show that people would like to see more officers on the beat.
- **Working in schools** – Patrol constables are often called upon by local schools to talk to children about issues as diverse as personal safety, making hoax 999 calls, drug awareness and paedophiles on Internet chat rooms. This means that they must be well-

informed about such issues and confident enough to speak about them. This kind of role can help build police–community relations in younger generations and is therefore very important. Some schools even have their own on-site constable in case trouble flares up at the school.

- **Assisting in the event of accidents, fights and fires** – Patrol officers are often called upon to attend unexpected incidents in which they might have to intervene in a public order incident, such as a pub fight or a domestic violence incident. They may also have to attend a local accident where a person has been injured and possibly administer first aid until assistance arrives.
- **Road safety initiatives** – Patrol constables may be called upon to participate in road safety initiatives. This may include visiting schools to educate children on the dangers of traffic, or it may include taking part in initiatives such as exhaust emissions testing, documents checks, and roadside car safety checks such as tyre depth.
- **House-to-house enquiries** – During the investigation of serious crimes, such as murder or abduction, officers are often called upon to go door-to-door on a particular estate to gather information that householders may have about a crime that has taken place in their area. This can be time-consuming but is a necessary task and a valuable investigation technique.
- **Policing major public events** – Patrol officers are often asked to ensure public safety at events such as football matches and public demonstrations such as political rallies. When large crowds gather there is always the risk of fights breaking out or people being hurt in crushes. Police officers plan for contingencies at such events to make sure everyone is safe.
- **Giving evidence in court** – Police patrol officers are often called upon to give evidence in court. They may have information relevant to a crime or an incident that will affect the outcome of the trial.
- **Reducing crime initiatives** – Police patrol officers also take part in very specific crime-reduction

Police constable role	Duties
Dog handler	Dog handlers and their dogs work as a team. The dogs assist with catching criminals, searching buildings and policing large crowds, such as those at football matches. They are often trained to find drugs or explosives.
Traffic police	All forces have officers deployed on road policing. Part of their duties involves tackling vehicle crime. They ensure road safety by enforcing traffic laws such as those relating to speeding and drink driving. They also deal with road accidents and help road users.
Criminal Investigation Department (CID)	Officers engaged in detective work account for about one in eight of all police staff. They receive intensive training to enable them to work effectively in this field. The day-to-day work of detectives is busy and demanding. Their core role is to investigate serious crime and to act upon intelligence which can lead to the arrest and prosecution of hardened or 'career' criminals.
Special Branch	Special Branch officers combat terrorism. They work at airports and seaports, providing armed bodyguards for politicians and public figures and investigating firearms and explosives offences that may be connected to national security matters.
Firearms units	These are specialist teams trained in the use of firearms who assist with dangerous operations.
Drugs Squad	The growth in the misuse of drugs in the United Kingdom is a major cause for concern. These specialist officers work with operational officers and other agencies to target drug dealers and tackle the drugs problem. They play a very important role in combating this area of organised crime
Fraud Squad	We all bear the cost of fraud in our insurance premiums or in the higher cost of products. The police service has a specialised Fraud Squad, run jointly by the Metropolitan Police and the City of London Police. Other forces also have Fraud Squads and they assist each other in investigating fraud. Fraud Squad officers also work with the Serious Fraud Office, a government department set up to investigate large-scale fraud.
Mounted units	Police horses work under the guidance of very skilled riders and play a vital role at events where there are large crowds, such as football matches, race meetings and demonstrations. They are also used to provide high visibility policing at a local level, often in parkland and open spaces.

Table 16.9 Police constable roles

operations that target problem crimes such as underage drinking or youth nuisance behaviour which may be causing problems in a particular area. They also offer crime-reduction information on protecting your property and neighbourhood watch.

Once the probation period is over a police constable can apply for a role other than that of a patrol officer.

Civilian support staff

The civilian support staff employed by the police service play a very important role in ensuring the police service runs smoothly and that uniformed officers are not so tied up in administrative duties that they cannot police the streets.

The variety of support roles for civilians includes crime researcher/analyst, a role involving gathering crime intelligence and analysing it for patterns which can then be addressed by uniformed officers. Researchers/analysts also gather information on police force effectiveness in order to ensure that the force is meeting its Home Office targets. More common support roles involving contact with the public are call handlers and front-counter personnel. These are usually the first people the public will come into contact with when reporting a crime or contacting the police. They handle general non-emergency telephone enquiries as well as 999 calls and prioritise the response of the uniformed officers. The front-of-house staff deal with general enquiries by the public as well as dealing with people who are called to attend the police station for other reasons, such as surrendering themselves for arrest. They are the public face of the police and need to be very aware of creating a good impression in order to improve and build upon police community relations. One of the best-known civilians in the police service is of course the traffic warden, whose job is to police parking and static traffic violations. Traffic wardens help maintain a smooth flow of traffic and help to ensure that illegal parking is punished, as such behaviour could create danger for other motorists and for pedestrians.

■ Police Community Support Officer

A police community support officer (PCSO) is a civilian who acts as a visible presence on the streets of local areas where anti-social behaviour is a problem. They perform some of the same duties as a patrol constable in that they reduce fear of crime among the public in such troubled areas. Their role is relatively new and may involve any or all of the following duties:

- dealing with anti-social behaviour, such as graffiti, truancy, litter and youth nuisance
- supporting victims of crime
- protecting the public from security threats
- assisting with house-to-house enquiries
- detaining a suspect until a police constable arrives
- directing traffic and removing vehicles.

PCSOs complement the work of the traditional police constable by focusing on lower-level crime, so that the police can respond more effectively to more serious crime. Support officers are uniformed, and many police services have introduced a uniform that is very similar to the uniform of a police constable. This is to give the role credibility with the public.

Consider this

Do you think one police role in particular is more important than others? Explain your reasons.

There is also a range of part-time opportunities in the public services, such as Special Police Constable, TA soldier and retained firefighter. These are covered in more detail in *Unit 3: Citizenship, contemporary society and the public services*, Book 1, pages 101–102.

Assessment activity 16.2

This assessment examines types of different roles within the public services. Research the following content:

- different operational jobs (e.g. ambulance service, patient transport services, technician and paramedic, Royal Navy, operator mechanics, engineering technicians and writers)
- civilian support roles (e.g. police control room operators and scenes of crime officers; community support officers; management and administrative roles)
- part-time opportunities (e.g. special constables, retained firefighters, Royal Navy Reserve, Territorial Army)
- jobs undertaken by the private sector.

Use your research to answer the following question:

1. Describe the type of work done in three different jobs within a named uniformed public service. **P2 M2**

Grading tips

P2 For this activity you need to describe three different jobs that you can do within a public service, such as police constable, PCSO and support worker.

M2 This is an extension of P2 but you are required to explain in more detail the three roles you have chosen.

Conditions of service

You need to know about the conditions of service in order to make a reasoned career choice about which service would suit you best. They include:

- starting salary
- hours and holidays
- benefits
- retirement age
- length of service
- postings
- shift patterns
- staff development.

Table 16.10 shows a comparison of the conditions of service in several public services.

	Police Service *Constable*	Fire Service *Firefighter*	NHS *Paramedic*	Prison Service *Prison Officer*	The Army/Navy *Soldier/Rating*
Starting salary	Approx £20,000	£19,918 as a trainee	£18–24,000	£17,744	£12,577
Holidays	23 days for first 5 years	28 days	20–25 days	25 days on entry	30 days per year
Retirement age	60–65 depending on rank from 2006, however, can retire on full pension after 30 years' service at any age.	55 years old	65 years old	55 if employed before 1987 otherwise 60	Eligible for full pension 22 years after joining
Length of service	No set length	No set length	No set length	No set length	Career length is 18 years. Can leave early during training or with sufficient notice
Postings	Anywhere within a police constabulary area	Any fire station in brigade area	Anywhere within the ambulance service area	Any prison in England and Wales	Home and abroad at any British or Allied military base
Shift patterns	Varies between forces	2-day shifts of 9 hours followed by 2 x 15-hour night shifts followed by 4 days off	Rotation shift pattern including nights, weekends and holidays	Various – day/evening/night/weekend	Variable depending on regiment, location and situation
Hours	40 hours per week	42 per week including lunch breaks	39 per week	39 hours per week	Depends on operational needs
Training	Ongoing	Ongoing	Ongoing	Ongoing	Ongoing
Pension	Yes	Yes	Yes	Yes	Yes

Table 16.10 Examples of conditions of service

Assessment activity 16.3

This activity requires you to examine the conditions of service within a public service. Research the following content:

- conditions of service – starting salary, holiday entitlement, benefits (e.g. gym use, private medical insurance), retirement age, pension arrangements, sick pay, maternity/paternity provisions, minimum length of service, postings, shift patterns, contracted hours, access to training and education.

Use your research to answer the following question:

1. Produce a written report that describes the current conditions of service for a given job within a uniformed public service. **P3**

Grading tips

P3 This is a very straightforward question. Pick a service of your choice and describe the conditions of services, such as pay, holidays and shift patterns.

Entry requirements specify the minimum personal and professional achievements that you should have before applying to a public service. The more specialised and difficult the role, the more entry requirements will be asked for. If you do not meet the entry requirements for your chosen public service, you will have to consider what you can do to develop your skills and abilities to meet or even exceed the requirements. Of course in some cases it may just be a case of waiting until you are old enough to join. Even so, you could be doing things that make you more attractive to a public service, such as getting additional qualifications at college or taking up some voluntary work in the community.

Whenever you consider applying to a public service you should remember that there are many other people who want that particular job, and these may be people with more experience and qualifications than you. As you can imagine this can make it difficult to succeed, but the key is good preparation. If you have researched your chosen career and you have made the most of the opportunities you have been given in your life so far, you will have a distinct advantage over the competition.

▲ **Figure 16.1 Some common entry requirements for the public services**

The public services have a variety of entry requirements you may have to meet before you can apply. Figure 16.1 highlights some of the most common ones.

The police service

Working for the police is a rewarding and challenging career, but it requires a very special kind of person to ensure that the roles and responsibilities which were described to you earlier are fulfilled to a high standard. Many people are not suited to a career in this service, no matter how much they may want to join.

Just because you meet these essential requirements doesn't mean you will be a good police officer. In addition to these you need to possess the following skills and qualities:

- self-confidence
- teamwork skills
- interest in the community
- ability to work on your own initiative
- excellent communication skills
- problem-solving ability
- tact and diplomacy.

The application process

If you meet all of the entry requirements and you think you would make a good police officer then the next stage of the process is to get an application form. This can be obtained from your local constabulary recruiting department or from the police recruitment website at www.policecouldyou.co.uk . Some constabularies require you to send in a CV so that they can assess you for suitability before they send you an application form, but this can vary from force to force so it is always wise to check first. Once you receive an application form you will usually have to give the following personal details:

- name
- address
- date of birth

Category	Requirement
Age	You must be 18 years old to apply, but if you are successful you will not be appointed until you are 18 ½.
Height	There is no height requirement for this service.
Health	You are required to undergo a physical examination, so you should be in a good physical and mental state of health. The police service may reject applicants who are obese, diabetic, asthmatic, have a history of mental health difficulties or who have any other condition that may affect their ability to perform the duties required.
Fitness	You do not need to be super-fit, but you will be expected to show a good level of fitness which will include stamina, agility and strength which will be assessed in a job-related fitness test. (This test is detailed in *Unit 7: Physical preparation and fitness for the uniformed services*, Book 1, page 249.)
Qualifications	The police service does not require any formal qualifications, but you must demonstrate a good standard of English which will be tested during your application procedure. However, it is important to remember that although you may not need any formal qualifications to join, they will certainly help you appear more attractive as a potential new employee and help with your promotion prospects.
Eyesight	The current vision requirements are not less than 6/36 unaided in each eye (this is the second line down on an optician's chart) and 6/6 vision (the seventh line down on an optician's chart) when using both eyes. However, you may be aided by glasses or contact lenses. You should also be able to distinguish primary colours, which rules out individuals with some forms of colour blindness.
Nationality	You must be a British citizen, a member of the Commonwealth or EU and have no restrictions placed on your residence in the UK.
Criminal convictions	You should declare all criminal convictions in your application. Having a criminal record will not necessarily prevent you from becoming a police officer as many convictions are judged on an individual basis, but there are some offences which will automatically rule you out. These are offences such as: murder, manslaughter, rape, kidnapping, terrorism, hijacking and death by reckless driving. In general you will be excluded if you have served a prison sentence or if you have committed crimes of violence.

Table 16.11 Police officer entry requirements

- contact details
- forces you wish to apply for (only applies if you are using the Internet form)
- 'Do you wish to apply for the High Potential Development Scheme?' (a scheme for graduates who have the potential to be promoted relatively quickly)
- nationality
- convictions and cautions
- tattoos
- health and eyesight
- business interests
- financial position
- previous addresses
- details about your immediate family
- employment details and references
- education, qualifications and training.

In addition, there is a competence assessment that asks you about situations you have been involved in and how you reacted, including equality and diversity situations:

- Why do you want to be a police officer?
- What do you expect the job to be like?
- How have you prepared for your job application?
- An equal opportunities questionnaire
- A personal statement.

Completing the form takes time and effort. If you complete it incorrectly or it shows you in a poor light, you will be weeded out in what is called a 'paper sift'. A paper sift is a way of getting rid of unsuitable applications and it is used by many public services as well as many other employers. It involves checking application forms and weeding out any that are incomplete, do not show a reasonable standard of English or where the form demonstrates that an individual is clearly unsuitable for the job or doesn't meet the entry requirements.

■ Hints and tips to complete your police application form

1. Read the form thoroughly and ensure you understand every question.
2. Read the guidance notes thoroughly. They give you specific advice on what you need to do.
3. Photocopy the form several times so that you can practise filling it in and get it checked through before you complete the original.
4. Be honest. If you are not you are likely to be found out and you will ruin your chances of having the career you want.
5. Be meticulous about your spelling and grammar.
6. Ensure the things you write do not breach the principles of equality and diversity.
7. Take guidance from your local careers office or your college lecturers on how best to present yourself.

Use the appropriate style of writing. If it says use black ink and block capitals, then this is what you must do. In addition, your handwriting should be clear and legible.

The police recruitment procedure is becoming increasingly standardised across all 43 police services in England and Wales. This means that the procedure for becoming a police officer will be more or less the same wherever you apply. However you should still check for regional variations with your local force.

Personal statements

When you are completing your police application form, or indeed any application form, the most difficult part is often the personal statement or the supporting information that is required. You should pay particular attention to this, as it is your opportunity to tell the service of your choice why they should take you on as a new recruit. It should be relevant and specific to the requirements of the job you are applying for. Examples of good practice in giving answers can sometimes be found on public service websites such as www. policecouldyou.co.uk.

Take it further

Write a 200-word personal statement that summarises the achievements in your life so far.

Police selection procedure

The list below assumes you are successful at every stage of the procedure.

1. On receipt of a full application form your details will be checked to make sure you meet the entry requirements.
2. If you meet the requirements your application form will have a competency-based questionnaire review.
3. If you are successful at the competency-based questionnaire review your medical form will be forwarded to the occupational health unit.
4. If your form is approved by the occupational health unit you will attend a recruit assessment centre.
5. If you are successful at the assessment centre you have to complete a medical questionnaire confirmed by your GP and forwarded to the occupational health unit.
6. Background checks and references will be taken up.
7. You will attend for a medical examination.
8. You will attend for the physical fitness test.
9. A joining date will be agreed.

Police assessment centre

One of the most important parts of the police application procedure takes place at the assessment centre, which each constabulary runs for its potential recruits. The assessment centre will have a variety of exercises such as:

- written communication exercises such as memos, reports or letters, which are marked on spelling, grammar, appropriateness and respect for diversity
- interactive role plays such as dealing with difficult members of the public in a customer service situation
- formal interview for the position of constable, which includes a certain number of set questions
- Police Initial Recruitment Test (PIRT), which is a series of questions designed to check your maths and verbal logical reasoning.

Assessment activity 16.4

This activity requires you to know about the current entry requirements for a service. In order to answer the question you should research the following content:

- entry requirements – educational, physical, medical and other requirements
- application forms – types of forms and their requirements on completing forms; personal statements and supporting information
- curriculum vitae – different formats, essential information, good and bad practice.

1. Research, prepare and deliver a PowerPoint presentation with supporting notes which describes the current entry requirements and the selection stages for a given uniformed public service. **P4**

2. Your presentation should also explain the process of applying for a given job within a uniformed public service. **M3**

Grading tips

P4 You should choose a service and describe its current entry requirements and then detail the stages in the selection procedure.

M3 Using the same job you looked at in P4 you need to explain how you would apply for this job role.

Curriculum vitae (CV)

You may be asked to produce a CV at some point in your application for any service, and it is important that your CV is up to date and relevant to your application. It used to be the case that a CV was just a list of your personal information, but the presentation of CVs has moved on and you should be aware of this. The two examples below show CVs with identical information: the first one is an example of how not to do it and the second one is an example of good practice.

CV Example 1 – Bad Practice

Name: David Smith jnr
Address: 32 East Way Close, Botheringham, B32 7AJ
Telephone Number: 01742 112112
E-maoil: daveyboy@lovemachine.co.uk

Date of Birth: 1/1/1989
Marital status: Single, but have a girlfreind
Driving Lisense: I do not drive, but I am taking lessons
School: Botheringham Compreensive I passed 5 GCSE's
Maths E
Endlish F
Geography C
PE A
French F
I have also completed a Btec Fitst Diploma in Public services at Botheringham College
Work experiences: I have woked in a pizza shop and done a paper round. I also do some roofing with my dad and help at a local youth club

References:
David Smith Snr   Fat Garrys Piza shop
Botheringham Roofing Co   101 high Street
Botherningham   Botheringham

CV Example 2 – Good Practice

Curriculum Vitae
David Smith
A hard-working and energetic young man, well able to cope with working in a high-pressure environment under specific time constraints. Excellent interpersonal skills and a high level of experience in working with the public in a variety of situations. Excels in a variety of sports and has a high level of commitment to working with the community.

Contact Details:
Address: 32 East Way Close, Botheringham, B32 7AJ
Telephone: 01742 112112 (Home) 07967 11231123 (Mobile)
E-mail: d.smith@both-coll.ac.uk
Date of Birth: 1/1/89

Educational Achievements:
1998 – 2003   Botheringham Comprehensive School, Main Street, Botheringham, B23 4EW
GCSEs: Physical Education A
Geography C   English F
Maths E   French F
I also achieved 100% attendance certificates for every year I attended Botheringham Comprehensive and I won The Arthur Wenden Award for excellence in sporting achievement in 2001, 2002 and 2004.
2005 – 2006   Botheringham College of Further Education, Lower Vale, Botheringham, B45 4TY
BTEC First Diploma in Public Services (6 units)
The Public Services   Distinction
Public Service Skills   Distinction
Public Service Fitness   Distinction
Crime and Its Effects   Merit
Expedition Skills   Merit
Workplace Welfare   Distinction

Career Achievements:
Sept 2003 – June 2004   Newspaper Delivery Operative
This position involved the delivery of early morning and evening newspapers on a set route. I developed my time management skills and self-discipline fulfilling this role, as I had to be very conscious of making sure I delivered all of the goods regardless of external conditions such as the weather.
July 2004 – May 2005   Pizza Chef
Working to fulfil food orders with speed and efficiency. I interacted with the public on an ongoing basis, providing a friendly and reliable front-of-house service as well as observing health and hygiene regulations with diligence.
June 2004 – Sept 2006   Builder's Labourer
In this position I worked as part of an interconnected team of roofers and builders, adhering to strict deadlines and producing high-quality work. My teamwork skills were enhanced and I developed an appreciation of how people working together can achieve more than individuals working alone.
Sept 2005 – Present   Volunteer Youth Worker
I volunteer three evenings a week to help at a youth club in my local area. This involves coordinating and running sporting events for young people aged 11–14, improving their sporting skills and ensuring that health and safety guidelines are followed. I enjoy this type of work very much and like to think that I act as a positive role model for the young people I train.

Additional Information:
I have played football and cricket for the county under 18's teams and I enjoy a variety of other sporting and adventurous activities such as skiing, climbing and canoeing. I like to go to the cinema, particularly to see science fiction films and socialise with my friends. I have recently started to attend ju-jitsu classes and I hope this will enhance my physical coordination and sense of self-discipline even further. I am looking for a career opportunity where I can work with people in a community environment as I feel that this is what my skills and inclination best suit me for.

References
Ms Alison Court, Lecturer in Public Services
Botheringham College of FE
Lower Vale, Botheringham, B45 4TY

Mr A J Singh, Youth Services Manager
Botheringham Youth Club
Murray Road, Botheringham, B17 9LU

Consider this

How do the two CVs compare? Consider their differences and similarities.

Assessment activity 16.5

For this activity you need to accurately:

- complete the application form for the service of your choice
- produce a CV for the service of your choice. **P5**

Grading tips

P5 You need to get an application form for your chosen service (many of these can be downloaded or printed from the Internet) and complete it accurately. You need to answer the questions fully and sensibly, ensuring your spelling and grammar are good. Remember that a poor application form or CV will not get you to the next stage of the procedure.

Additional recruitment information

Table 16.12 highlights some common factors you might have to deal with during any public service application and selection procedure.

Psychometric tests	These are tests designed to assess your capabilities in maths, English, problem solving, spatial awareness and mental agility. Not all services use them but many do; they give the service in question a reasonably accurate picture of your abilities.
Fitness tests	These are self-explanatory and you will find several of them detailed in *Unit 7* of Book 1. They show the service of your choice that you are fit enough to complete the duties required of you.
Simulations	Role plays and simulations are becoming more common in public service selection as they give an idea of how people react when put in difficult situations. They can be used to assess the potential recruit's interpersonal skills and problem solving ability.
Presentations	Many services require you to give a presentation of around 10 minutes on a particular public service topic. It highlights your ability to speak in public and communicate information effectively to others, which as you can imagine is a key skill in the public services.
Types of interview	There are many kinds of interview that you might be faced with in applying to a public service. These might include formal interviews, group interviews, and panel interviews. It is your responsibility to find out what you are likely to face and prepare for it.
Dress code	Generally you should always be smart and professional at interview, unless you are attending for a fitness test or other task which requires specific dress. This means suits for both men and women.

Table 16.12 Additional recruitment factors

■ Psychometric testing

Psychometric tests are used to measure the characteristics of people, such as intelligence, ability and personality. They are used as a screening process to ensure that the applicant is suitable for the job. The public services make extensive use of psychometric testing as part of their interview procedure. This may take the form of the Police Initial Recruit Test (PIRT) or the British Army Recruitment Board (BARB) and may involve tests such as:

- verbal checking
- spatial awareness
- decision making
- numerical reasoning
- observation
- spelling/dictation
- writing skills.

Psychometric tests can generally be broken down into two main areas:

Psychometric testing	
Ability and aptitude tests	**Personality tests**
These focus on what a person can currently do and the potential they may have. They may include: • psychomotor tests • general ability tests • specific ability tests.	These assess what a person is actually like. They may include: • motivation scales • personal interest inventories • personality scales.

Aptitude and personality tests can be very intimidating, but they are actually considered a great deal fairer than a traditional interview because they automatically treat people as equals, without the influence of stereotypes or prejudice. Psychometric testing can be culturally biased however and great care must be taken to ensure the test itself is fit for purpose. Testing also does not provide an employer with a face-to-face picture of a candidate and for this reason you are unlikely to face psychometric testing alone; it is much more likely to occur before a formal interview as a method of weeding out unsuitable or poorly qualified candidates.

Format	Detail
Formal	This is a structured interview in which you are likely to be asked a set series of questions in a formal or rigid environment. It is likely that more than one person will interview you and you may be asked to produce a presentation or report as part of the procedure.
Informal	More relaxed and in a less formal setting than in a formal interview. May be only one or two individuals conducting the interview rather than a panel.
Full day	Some interviews can last anything up to 10 hours. These can be exhausting and it is likely that you will interact with the others who are competing for the job.
Multi-day	These are common in the public services and you may have to be interviewed on three or more days over several weeks.
Panel	Many interviews are conducted by a panel of up to six or seven individuals. Each individual may assess you on different aspects of your performance and then discuss their findings with the others to form a picture of you as a whole.
Individual	Sometimes a single individual may interview you, although this is not considered to be good practice because they have no second opinion or expertise to reinforce or challenge the conclusions they draw.

Table 16.13 Types of interview

Planning for interview

It is amazing how many people do not prepare adequately for an interview and are then disappointed when they don't get the job they want. A burning desire to be a police officer *isn't* enough! You must be able to prove that you are more suitable for the job than any of the other 100 applicants, and that is a tall order. However, there are many things you can do to maximise your chances.

- **Take care with personal appearance** – You must dress appropriately; this will usually mean a suit for both men and women. Jewellery and make-up must be subtle and discreet and you should be free from any facial piercings such as eyebrow, nose or lips. Men should consider removing earrings. Your clothing should be clean and pressed and you should get a friend or family member to check you over before you set off. Your shoes should be polished and your clothing should aim to give a message about you and your ability to perform the job. You should ensure that you are clean and tidy and project an air of confidence and professionalism.

- **Be punctual** – There is no excuse for being late. It gives the impression that you are unreliable. Instead, aim to arrive around 10 minutes early. If necessary, practise your journey beforehand to ensure you have your timings right.

- **Be gracious to other candidates** – Part of the assessment process in public service interviews revolves around your interaction with others. If you are unpleasant or uncooperative to your competition you will be seen as lacking the interpersonal skills needed for working in a close-knit team or with the public.

- **Do your research** – It does you no credit if you turn up to an interview without knowing the first thing about the public service in question. If you are completing a public service qualification you will have an advantage, but don't become complacent. Research your chosen public service, be familiar with its structure and principles, and ensure you have read its annual reports and its literature. If you want the job, be prepared to learn everything you can about the local, national and international issues which affect it.

- **Be confident, not dominant** – If you try and dominate an interview it screams 'NOTICE ME!!' Your interviewer will notice you, but for all the wrong reasons. You should project an image of a confident team player, not a dominant leader.

- **Be genuine** – Public service interviewers are usually officers of many years' standing and they will have seen hundreds of hopeful candidates just like you. Don't think that flattery or humour will sway them in their choice and don't be tempted to exaggerate or lie about your skills and abilities. Recruiting officers read people very well and the last thing you want is to be considered false or fraudulent. It is appropriate to laugh politely at a joke made by your recruiter but

▲ A smart personal appearance is essential at an interview

inappropriate to roll about on the floor claiming it's the best joke you've ever heard.

- **Don't get rattled** – Interviews are tremendously nerve-racking! Make sure you stay calm and in control. This means not fidgeting, paying close attention to questions and making sure you understand the question before you answer. When people are nervous they tend to babble and may say inappropriate things. Watch for this! The interviewer expects a certain amount of nervousness, but someone who appears very edgy will give the impression of not coping well in stressful situations – clearly not a desirable quality in the public services.

Remember!

- Interview skills are of crucial importance throughout a public service career.
- Interviews are conducted for a variety of reasons, such as appraisal, leaving jobs, getting a new job etc.
- You have to work hard at interviews if you are to succeed.
- You must research the job role and the organisation thoroughly.
- You must pay attention to the issue of equal opportunities.
- You must listen carefully to the questions you are asked and make sure you answer them.

■ Interview questions

Most interview questions are fairly standard in employment interviews. You can expect to be asked in some form or other any or all of the following questions:

- Why do you want this job?
- What skills can you bring to the job?
- Describe how your previous experience makes you suitable.
- What do you hope to gain from the job?
- What do you know about the job?
- Do you know about current developments affecting the job?
- Are you able to work as an individual and a team member?
- What are your long-term career goals?
- What training and education do you have which would enable you to tackle this job effectively?
- What are your views on equal opportunities?

In addition to these questions you may be asked to take part in role-play scenarios designed to test your practical coping skills in a variety of circumstances which are likely to be unfamiliar to you. The responses you give to the questions and scenarios are crucial in the interview procedure and you must be ready to deal with unexpected questions. Consider the following examples.

Interview question 1

The police are trying to recruit more ethnic minority officers into the ranks. What is your view on this?

Poor answer	Good answer
People should get into the police on the basis of their own ability. If ethnic minority people can't get in any other way than because of their colour it's not fair is it? They should not be given any special treatment.	Its important that the police service is representative of the communities it serves. This means having an inclusive recruitment procedure, which encourages all sections of the community to apply. Without this the service could be seen as racially exclusive, which doesn't help the police to develop an understanding of cultural awareness and doesn't improve community relations. The Macpherson report highlighted many potential steps forward in building community relations and eliminating racism and I think this is a positive recommendation to come from that report.

Interview question 2

Why do you want to be a police officer?

Poor answer	Good answer
I wanted to be a policeman since I was a lad. I always watch *The Bill* and I've really got into *CSI* lately. Besides, it's good money, isn't it?	It's a decision I've thought long and hard about because I know that it is a stressful and potentially dangerous job. I've done a great deal of voluntary community work and I find it immensely rewarding to give something back to the community. I'd like to think that the job I do makes a difference to the community and the individuals within it. I also like the idea of a job that combines this with the challenge of learning and developing skills on an ongoing basis.

Interview question 3

The regiment you are hoping to join is currently serving with the UN as peacekeepers in Kosovo. What do you know about this situation?

Poor answer	Good answer
Is Kosovo abroad? Is it about that Al Keyda bloke?	I know that peacekeeping is one of the primary roles of the British Army today. I think that it is crucial that the UN and NATO are able to deploy forces to protect civilians and offer humanitarian aid in situations of conflict across the world. The British Army play a key role in this, particularly in Kosovo, where they serve in KFOR and SFOR.

You need to be answering the question they are really asking you. This means you should be able to see through the language used to phrase their question and see the real question beneath it. For example, consider the three interview questions above.

Question	Real question being asked
The police are trying to recruit more ethnic minority officers into the ranks. What is your view on this?	Do you support equal opportunities? Are you racist? Have you been bothered enough to research this issue?
Why do you want to be a police officer?	Do you have any idea what the job is really about? Are you more bothered about the money and security than the job itself?
The regiment you are hoping to join is currently serving with the UN as peacekeepers in Kosovo. What do you know about the situation?	Do you understand what it means to be a modern soldier? Do you keep up to date with global political issues that affect us? Have you been bothered to do your research?

Some of the questions asked by interviewers require a little more analysis before you rush into an answer – you must be sure you know what each question is designed to find out before you answer it.

Once you have been successful in the application and selection procedure you must remember you are only at the beginning of a public service career that will hopefully last many years and be very rewarding. It is highly unlikely that you will want to do the same thing for the next 30 years or so, and the public services offer a variety of opportunities to change your role regularly and move through the ranks. We will now investigate what happens during your initial training in a public service and what you might choose to do after you have completed your probationary period.

Initial training and career development opportunities

Most public services have a period of basic training for new recruits. This is designed to equip them with the skills and abilities essential for successful completion of their initial duties. This is often followed by a probationary period where a new recruit has the opportunity to put these skills into practice in a supportive environment until they are fully qualified members of a public service. These periods of initial training and probation vary between services and are often dependent on the complexity of the job you would be required to do. Table 16.14 shows you the differences.

Public service	Initial training	Probationary period
Police	15 weeks	2 years
Fire Service	16 weeks	1 year
Royal Navy	8 weeks	Depends on specialisation. Could be up to 6 years to train as a nuclear engineer.

Table 16.14 Initial training and probationary periods in the public services

Royal Navy training

Initial training for Royal Navy ratings is conducted at HMS *Raleigh* and lasts eight weeks. It involves intensive study and testing, and requires you to take in a great deal of information in a relatively short time.

The process is as follows:

■ Week 1

You need to complete an enrolment form, which commits you to spend the next four weeks at HMS *Raleigh*. After four weeks, if the service is not for you, then you may leave. Medical and dental checks are conducted to ensure you are in a good state of health to perform your duties. You are taught how to take care of your kit and equipment. In addition you begin to learn naval drill and work on increasing your fitness.

■ Weeks 2–8

This is when training begins in earnest, and it continues throughout the seven weeks. It involves the following activities:

- **Parade training drill** – This involves learning how to perform naval drill, which is slightly different from Army and police drill. Learning drill is a team task and it promotes teamwork, coordination and discipline.
- **Education** – You have to sit the basic English and maths tests for the navy and be taught how to keep a ship seaworthy and safe.
- **Kit inspection** – This involves keeping your kit clean and tidy. Ships are very cramped environments and space is at a premium, so it is very important that each rating learns how to respect others by maintaining kit.
- **Firefighting and first-aid training** – These are important skills in a naval environment and you will be taught the basics of both.

▲ A good level of fitness is essential for Royal Navy ratings training at HMS *Raleigh*

- **Ship's damage control** – It is important that ratings understand the design of the ships they will serve on. This is because they may be called upon to repair damage caused by enemy weapons. This includes becoming familiar with the repair equipment used on board your ship.

■ Physical training

Fitness tests must be completed before passing into the Royal Navy. These are conducted in the eight-week basic training period and are as follows:

- **Raleigh fitness test** – A 2.4-kilometre run (to be completed within a set time), a 300-metre shuttle run, press-ups and sit-ups.
- **Swimming** – This involves swimming 40 metres in naval overalls, followed by treading water for three minutes. You will also practise life-raft drills dressed in a life jacket and survival suit.
- **Outward-bound activities** – This involves an adventure-training weekend where you will learn how to use a map and compass, complete practical teamwork exercises and an expedition (with backpack) across Dartmoor.

- **Military training** – You will learn how to carry out drills and firings.

The common reasons that recruits fail to complete basic training include:

- injuries
- personal problems
- difficulty with culture of the service
- wrong perception of the service
- poor fitness
- failing an assessment.

Ranks in the Royal Navy

As we have already discussed, you may decide you have the potential to progress further in your career and decide that you wish to consider promotion. It should be noted that starting at the bottom as a rating will mean it will take you much longer to progress up the career ladder. Only 20% of officers start as naval ratings; the majority of officers have higher educational qualifications such as a degree and enter the service as officers.

The promotional structure in the navy is as follows:

- Able Rate – the starting point
- Leading Rate – the Royal Navy suggests that an able rate who is capable should be able to become a leading rate by the age of about 22
- Petty Officer – a capable leading rate who works hard and shows an aptitude for leadership should be able to make petty officer by the age of around 27
- Chief Petty Officer – the average age of a member of the service who reaches this rank, having started as an able rate, is early to mid-30s
- Warrant Officer
- Sub-lieutenant
- Lieutenant
- Lieutenant Commander
- Commander
- Captain

Case study: Joining the Royal Navy

Aysha is 17 and just about to complete her First Diploma in Public Services. She wants to join the navy but is unsure whether to join now or get more qualifications so that she can join as an officer. She needs some career advice and she has asked you to help her.

1. **Do you think Aysha should join the navy as a rating or as an officer?**

2. **What preparation should she do to help her during her eight-week basic training?**

3. **If Aysha joins as a rating how long would it take her to get to the rank of chief petty officer?**

4. **What can Aysha expect from her basic training?**

Police officer training

The two-year probationer training programme is made up of a number of stages. Each stage is equally important and all of them must be completed if a recruit is going to become a fully fledged police officer.

- *Stage 1 (2 weeks minimum)* – You will be introduced to policing to:
  - gain a basic understanding of the role of a police officer
  - learn how to deliver the best service to the public.
- *Stage 2 (15 weeks)* – You will study the law and learn the core skills needed to deal effectively and professionally with a range of duties the police are expected to attend to.
- *Stage 3 (2 weeks)* – You will:
  - be prepared for accompanied patrol
  - learn about local procedures, force priorities and the communities you will serve.
- *Stage 4 (10 weeks)* – You will work with a trained tutor constable as you put everything you have learned into practice on patrol under his or her guidance.
- *Stage 5 (2 weeks)* – You will:
  - be assessed for suitability for independent police patrol
  - learn more about local procedures and local policing plans for your own constabulary.
- *Stage 6 (remainder of probation including a further 30 days' minimum training)* – You will complete the rest of your probation with your own constabulary, with a minimum of 30 days dedicated to further training.

Your performance will be assessed in terms of competence, skills and knowledge and if you are found to have been successful in your probationer training after this two-year period you will be confirmed as a regular police officer.

All police officers must complete these two years on probation regardless of their qualifications or ambition. After the two years are completed, a recruit can seriously consider how they would like to progress in the service. The promotional structure for the police service is as follows:

- Police Constable
- Police Sergeant
- Inspector
- Chief Inspector
- Superintendent
- Chief Superintendent
- Assistant Chief Constable
- Deputy Chief Constable
- Chief Constable

Assessment activity 16.6

Produce an A1 poster which describes the initial training programme for a given uniformed public service. **P6**

Grading tips

P6 Choose a uniformed public service and describe how a new recruit would move through initial training. Cover the stages and what they would do at each stage.

Career progression in the police service

Promotion in the police service is not easy, automatic or dependent on length of service. Officers are promoted according to their individual performance, skills and abilities, and they must pass further exams and interviews. These exams are Objective Structured Performance Related Examinations (OSPRE) and they come in two parts: part 1 tests the officer's knowledge of the law; part 2 tests their management and supervisory skills. This is important because as an officer moves through the ranks they also take on more and more management responsibility.

Consider this

Do you think that a two-year probation period for all police officers is a good idea? Explain your reasons.

Fire service training

The basic training of a firefighter begins with 80 working days (16 weeks) at the fire service training school, which involves learning the skills in the use of firefighting equipment, fire safety legislation, rescue techniques, first aid and fire extinction. There is also a strong emphasis on maintaining the high standards of fitness needed in the service. The initial training of firefighters is very intensive and trainees are expected to undertake revision and study in their own time as well as in class.

The one-year training probationary period of a firefighter is conducted at a fire station in the area they have chosen to join. This is effectively a year of on-the-job training, where a recruit's performance is continually assessed for ability and competence. However, a firefighter is not considered fully qualified until they have completed two more years of active service in an operational fire station.

Promotion in the fire service

Currently there are no advanced routes into the fire service as there are in the police and the Royal Navy. All recruits join as a firefighter and all have an equal chance of promotion to senior positions. The ranks in the fire service are:

- Firefighter
- Leading Firefighter
- Sub Officer
- Station Officer
- Assistant Divisional Officer
- Divisional Officer
- Senior Divisional Officer
- Assistant Chief Fire Officer
- Deputy Chief Fire Officer
- Chief Fire Officer

In theory it is possible to reach the rank of station officer with five years' experience, but generally it will take much longer than this. Promotions above this level do not crop up very often and you may be required to move brigades if you want to advance your career further.

Assessment activity 16.7

As part of an assessed discussion, describe what opportunities are available for career development within a given public service. **P7**

Grading tips

P7 As part of your discussion make sure you include content such as: promotion or career specialisation, including details of training and examinations; rank structure; competition for promotion or specialisation; minimum service required; personal skills and qualities required; main roles and responsibilities of supervision, e.g. leading paramedics, leading firefighters, police sergeants, non-commissioned officers or specialist staff.

By the end of this unit you should have enough information to be able to seriously consider the uniformed public service you want to join and your own suitability for it. As much as you may want to join a service, you may not have the personal and professional qualities they require. It is best to assess yourself very honestly before you undertake the application process.

Assessment activity 16.8

1. As part of an interview with your tutor, comment on your own suitability to complete basic training and for your career development within a chosen uniformed public service. **M4**

2. As part of the same interview, evaluate both the potential and the limitations for your own career development within your chosen uniformed public service. **D2**

Grading tips

M4 **D2** This interview should be a frank assessment of your own skills and abilities in relation to fulfilling a public services role. You need to be as honest as you can about your chances of making it through the selection procedure and what your options are for future career development.

Knowledge check

1. What is a PCSO?
2. What roles do the police service have?
3. What is the starting pay for a naval rating?
4. How many days' holiday does an Army soldier get?
5. What does CV stand for?
6. What are psychometric tests?
7. What should you wear for a public services interview?
8. Describe the basic training of a naval rating.
9. What is the rank structure of the fire service?
10. Why do some recruits fail basic training?

Preparation for assessment

You have just completed basic training in one of the uniformed public services and your old public services lecturer has asked you to come and speak with the following year's learners about your experiences. You will give a presentation to them which covers the following questions:

1. Describe the roles, purpose and responsibilities of two contrasting uniformed public services. **P1**

2. Explain the role, purpose and responsibilities of two contrasting uniformed public services. **M1**

3. Describe the type of work done in three different jobs within a named uniformed public service. **P2**

4. Describe the current conditions of service for a given job within a uniformed public service. **P3**

5. Explain in detail the work of a job within a uniformed public service. **M2**

6. Evaluate the role, purpose and responsibilities of a uniformed public service. **D1**

7. Describe the current entry requirements and the selection stages for a given uniformed public service. **P4**

8. Complete an application form and curriculum vitae accurately for a given job within a uniformed public service. **P5**

9. Explain the process of applying for a given job within a uniformed public service. **M3**

10. Describe the initial training programme for a given uniformed public service. **P6**

11. Describe what opportunities are available for career development within a given public service. **P7**

12. Comment on their own suitability to complete basic training and for their career development within a chosen uniformed public service. **M4**

13. Evaluate both the potential and the limitations for their own career development within their chosen uniformed public service. **D2**

Grading criteria	Activity	Pg no.		
To achieve a pass grade the evidence must show that the learner is able to:			To achieve a merit grade the evidence must show that the learner is able to:	To achieve a distinction grade the evidence must show that the learner is able to:
P1 Describe the roles, purpose and responsibilities of two contrasting uniformed public services	16.1	79	**M1** Explain the role, purpose and responsibilities of two contrasting uniformed public services	**D1** Evaluate the role, purpose and responsibilities of a uniformed public service
P2 Describe the type of work done in three different jobs within a named uniformed public service	16.2	82	**M2** Explain in detail the work of a job within a uniformed public service	
P3 Describe the current conditions of service for a given job within a uniformed public service	16.3	83		
P4 Describe the current entry requirements and the selection stages for a given uniformed public service	16.4	87	**M3** Explain the process of applying for a given job within a uniformed public service	
P5 Complete an application form and curriculum vitae accurately for a given job within a uniformed public service	16.5	89		
P6 Describe the initial training programme for a given uniformed public service	16.6	97	**M4** Comment on their own suitability to complete basic training and for their career development within a chosen uniformed public service.	**D2** Evaluate both the potential and the limitations for their own career development within their chosen uniformed public service.
P7 Describe what opportunities are available for career development within a given public service.	16.7 16.8	98		

Understanding the criminal justice system and police powers

Introduction

This unit will provide you with an overview of police powers and an insight into the criminal justice system. It links very closely with *Unit 22*, which also covers the legal system in detail. The powers that the police have can change from year to year depending on when new legislation is introduced by the government. It is important to remember to check for any recent changes to the law when reading this unit.

The unit focuses on the powers that police officers have regarding issues such as arrest, stop and search, and detention and questioning. It also examines the rights of suspects when they are being arrested and questioned. The police must be accountable for their behaviour and their professional performance. We would not have much respect for a police service which ill-treated us or failed to uphold the principles of justice. It is also important to remember that police officers are public servants and must treat the public with courtesy and respect, regardless of a person's ethnic background, religion or political beliefs. If police powers were not monitored how would the public know if the police were abusing them?

After completing this unit you should be able to achieve the following outcomes:

- Understand the requirements of a lawful arrest and the regulations regarding detention of suspected offenders
- Understand the regulations regarding the search of people and premises
- Understand pre-trial procedure in criminal courts
- Know how the criminal trial process works in both magistrates' and Crown courts.

The police have a great deal of power over the general public. What would happen if they abused this power? Find a newspaper report that deals with a breach of police power. What power was breached and how could this potentially affect the reputation of the police service?

Lawful arrest and detention regulations

This section deals with how the police and the public can make arrests and the laws and rules that govern the process. It also covers what happens after a person has been arrested, in terms of how long they can stay in custody and what rights they have.

Citizen's arrest

All citizens of the UK have the legal right to arrest another person. This is given to the public by section 24 of the Police and Criminal Evidence (PACE) Act 1984, but it actually dates back far before this. However, there are clear rules as to when citizens can and cannot make an arrest. You cannot make an arrest just because you suspect someone is guilty of a crime; it doesn't matter how strong your suspicions are, they alone are not enough. And if you make an arrest that is incorrect, you might find yourself in trouble with the police.

There are three sets of circumstances for a valid citizen's arrest:

- Arrest for an 'indictable offence' under the Police and Criminal Evidence Act 1984.
- Arrest of persons committing, or about to commit, a Breach of the Peace under common law.
- Use of reasonable force to prevent crime or arrest offenders or persons unlawfully at large under the Criminal Law Act 1967.

Case study: Citizen's arrest

In 2006, chip-shop owner Nicholas Tyers and his son Lee made a citizen's arrest of a 12-year-old boy who had spat a chip at one of his customers and smashed a window. The boy was picked up by Mr Tyers and his son in their car and driven to their shop, where the police were called. The boy complained about his treatment and both Mr Tyers and his son were charged with the offence of kidnap, which carries a maximum jail sentence of life imprisonment. The case was dismissed at Hull Crown court in January 2007 after the judge argued that since the boy was only held for between 2 and 6 minutes, the evidence did not support the charge. Mr Tyers and his family had to wait six months for the charges to be dismissed, during which time he lost his business and his son Lee, who was a serving Royal Marine, could not join his unit in Afghanistan.

No charges were ever brought against the 12-year-old boy for the original offence.

1. Do you think Mr Tyers should ever have been charged with an offence in the first place? Explain your answer.

2. What does this case highlight about the problems with making a citizen's arrest?

3. Are citizen's arrests still needed in the UK?

4. What would you have done in Mr Tyers' circumstances?

The powers of citizen's arrest are still really important in the UK as they form the basis of the powers of arrest which belong to Police Community Support Officers (PCSOs).

There are several differences between police arrests and citizen's arrests:

1. You cannot make a citizen's arrest if you believe a crime is about to be committed, only if one is *being* committed or *has been* committed. Only the police can arrest if they believe a crime is *about to be* committed.

2. Citizens can only arrest another person for 'arrestable' offences; these are more serious offences. The police can arrest for any offence.

Citizen's arrests are not carried out often by the general public and should not be carried out at all if there is a risk of violence involved. The safest thing to do is call the police and allow them to do their job.

Key terms

PACE Police and Criminal Evidence Act 1984

Reasonable suspicion

Reasonable suspicion is a very easily explained term – it means that police officers have to have reasonable grounds to suspect you have been, currently are, or will be involved in a criminal act. If a police officer stops, searches or detains anybody they cannot do so without first having reasonable suspicion. The difficult question police officers have to face is what actually is reasonable suspicion? It could be an individual moving along a line of cars peering through the windows, or an individual running off when spoken to, or someone who cannot account for why they are out alone in the early hours of the morning. It is important to remember that there may be perfectly reasonable explanations for all of these actions.

There are some cases where the police do not need to have reasonable suspicion, but these will be examined later in this unit under the topic of stop and search.

Arrest with a warrant

The police apply to a magistrates' court for a warrant to arrest a suspect. The warrant can be issued under the Magistrates' Courts Act 1980 and must contain the name of the suspect and the offence they are alleged to have committed. The decision to issue a warrant or not rests solely with the magistrate; if the magistrate issues a warrant the police officer may then make the arrest, even if they have to use reasonable force to enter premises where they think the suspect might be.

Arrest without a warrant

In reality many arrests are carried out without a warrant, either because the police are called to the scene of a crime and must act rapidly or they do not know who is about to be arrested before they deal with an incident and therefore could not get a warrant. Section 24 of **PACE** sets out general powers of arrest, which may be exercised by the police as well as the public.

▼ **The police can carry out an arrest when certain conditions are satisfied, such as a breach of the peace**

The concept of an 'arrestable' offence is an important one. So what is an arrestable offence? Arrestable offences are those which fall into the following categories:

- The sentence is fixed by law, e.g. murder.
- Any crime for which an adult may be sentenced to imprisonment for a term of five years or more.
- Any offence which parliament has declared to be arrestable.

Offences which are not arrestable and for which an officer does not have a warrant are dealt with under section 25 of PACE (see below), which states that if an officer has reasonable grounds to suspect that any non-arrestable offence has been committed they may still arrest if any of the general arrest conditions are satisfied.

These are the key factors the police use when deciding whether to arrest.

Conditions	May arrest if:
Identity	- The name of the person is unknown. - The officer doubts whether the name provided is accurate.
Address for service of a summons	- The person fails to provide an address. - The officer doubts whether the address is valid for a summons to be issued.
Preventative measures	- The person may cause injury to self or others. - The person is suffering from physical injury. - The person is causing damage to property. - The person is offending public decency. - The person is causing obstruction of the highway.
Protection	- The person is a threat to the public or particular individuals who may be vulnerable.

Table 17.1 General Arrest Conditions S25 PACE

The police can arrest in other instances, such as breach of the peace, and if there are public order issues such as at riots and violent demonstrations

Assessment activity 17.1

This activity requires you to examine conditions of arrest in order to answer the following question.

1. Produce a 200-word report which outlines the difference between arrest with and without a warrant. **P1**

2. Analyse the requirements of lawful arrest and detention. **M1**

3. Evaluate the powers of arrest, detention and search. **D1**

Grading tips

P1 Remember that an outline does not require a great deal of detail – your answer should be brief and concise and examine the primary differences between the types of arrest.

M1 This involves analysing the requirements of lawful arrest and detention. Remember that an analysis is a detailed examination of an issue, with sensible conclusions.

D1 This requires you to 'evaluate'. This is a careful examination of the advantages and disadvantages of the police powers of arrest, detention and search and generating sensible and logical conclusions.

Time limits and extensions

The police have to conform to the law when a person is arrested, which means that the person cannot be held indefinitely at the police station. The police must follow strict timelines and the suspect must be released or charges made at the end of the time limit. Generally speaking the police can hold a person for up to 24 hours without charging them with an offence. In serious cases, where more time is needed by the police to question

▲ A person held in police detention still has certain rights, though the right to be silent has been eroded

the suspect or gather additional information, the police themselves can extend the time limit for another 12 hours, making a possible total of 36 hours of police custody.

However, the courts can also extend the time a person spends is held without charge. The police can apply to the courts to get the custody period extended to a maximum of 96 hours. In terrorism cases, the courts can extend the time period to a maximum of 28 days, after which the police must either charge or release.

Consider this

Is allowing the police a maximum of 28 days without charging someone reasonable? Human rights campaigners argue that this period is too long and that if the police have sufficient evidence in the first place they wouldn't need to detain people for this length of time. What are your views?

Rights of a detained person

Once a person is detained at the police station they should be informed of their legal rights. There are three main rights that a detained person is entitled to:

- the right to speak privately with a solicitor who will be provided free of charge at any time while they are being detained
- the right to notify someone that they have been arrested
- the right to read the codes of practice about how detainees are treated.

The right to silence is the right to say nothing when asked questions by the police without later penalty. This right was severely eroded by the Criminal Justice and Public Order Act 1994, which changed the law so that if a person chose to remain silent at interview they could later find themselves in difficulty in court for not raising information which they knew earlier, such as:

- failure to mention a fact when questioned under caution before charge which is relied on in your defence

- failure on being charged with an offence or informed of likely prosecution, to mention a fact which it would have been reasonable for you to mention at the time.

Fingerprints, DNA and other samples

Once a person has been arrested the police are entitled to take their photograph, their fingerprints and a DNA sample if they have been arrested for an offence that carries a possible prison sentence. Since the majority of crimes in this country have the potential to have a prison sentence attached to them, the police actually take DNA, photo, and fingerprint samples from virtually all of the individuals they arrest.

▲ The police usually take fingerprints when an individual is arrested

Consider this

In essence, suspects can still remain silent if they wish, but it will harm their defence if they do. Some would question whether this is really a right to silence or a way to punish suspects who say nothing. What is your view on this?

Assessment activity 17.2

This assessment requires you to produce a leaflet on arrest and detention which answers the following questions.

1. Describe the rights of a detained person. **P2**
2. Evaluate the powers of arrest, detention and search. **D1**

Grading tips

P2 These are very straightforward criteria; you simply have to describe in your own words the rights a person has while detained in police custody.

Case study: The national DNA database

Before 2001 all DNA samples taken from individuals who were not charged or found not guilty had to be destroyed. This was changed by the Criminal Justice and Police Act 2001, which allowed all samples to be retained on a national database of offenders. The UK's database is the largest of any country; by the end of 2005 it held over 3.4 million DNA profiles. This amounts to 5.2 per cent of the total population of the UK. Responses to the existence of the database have been mixed, with human rights groups protesting that innocent people are having their records retained against their wishes and government agencies arguing that the invasion of privacy experienced by those people who are on the database is outweighed by the benefits it brings in tracking down offenders.

1. **Should we have a national DNA database at all? What are the pros and cons of the database?**
2. **Should innocent people have the right to have their DNA sample destroyed?**
3. **Should everyone in the country be registered on it?**
4. **How might this lead to an abuse of human rights?**

Police interviews

Police interviews are very tightly regulated by PACE (Section 66, Schedule 1), specifically the following codes of practice:

- **Code of Practice C:** detention, treatment and questioning of persons by police officers
- **Code of Practice H:** detention, treatment and questioning by police officers of persons under Section 41 of, and Schedule 8 to, the Terrorism Act 2000.

It is important that police interviews are tightly regulated so that the tapes can be used as evidence in court to secure a conviction and also so that the police are protected against claims that suspects were bullied, beaten, tricked or coerced into confessing to a crime. In the past, PACE statements were often handwritten by the police officers conducting the interview. This led to problems, as it was relatively easy to change the statements and the officers' honesty and integrity came into question.

A police interview is a process whereby a person who may have information regarding a crime is questioned about what they know. Police interviews with suspects are usually conducted at a police station. The suspect must be informed as to what offence they are being questioned about and reminded that they have the option of free legal advice. During each 24-hour period that the suspect is held at the police station, they have the right to a continuous 8-hour rest period in which they are not questioned. They are also entitled to rest breaks and refreshment breaks approximately every two hours or at mealtimes.

Consider this

If suspects are entitled to a continuous 8-hour rest period, that means there are potentially 16 hours in which they can be questioned. Do you think this would be appropriate? How would you feel after being questioned for up to 16 hours? Is it likely that the police would actually do this?

■ Appropriate adult

An appropriate adult is someone over the age of 18 (usually a parent or guardian) who sits in on an interview with anyone who is 16 years old or under. Appropriate adults also sit in on interviews with individuals who have mental health difficulties or who are deemed to be mentally vulnerable. The appropriate adult can also be a social worker or volunteer, and they help the suspect understand what is happening during the process of interview.

Legislation

There are some very important pieces of legislation which govern the powers of the police. The Police and Criminal Evidence Act 1984 was one of the most important of these. It establishes a balance of power between what the police can do in the course of their duties and the individual's citizen's rights to go about their business free from interference by the police. This has already been covered in some detail throughout this section. One of the most controversial new laws which provide the police with powers is the Serious Organised Crime and Police Act 2005 (SOCPA). This law created a serious organised crime squad, which was intended to deal with the most serious crimes in our society, such as human trafficking, which are often conducted by underworld gangs. However the law has become incredibly controversial in its approach to human rights and the powers it provides to the police. Read the article on the following page from the *Observer*:

A law the Stasi would have loved

By Henry Porter

The Serious Organised Crime and Police Act is the most pernicious piece of legislation yet introduced by this government. Before too many tears are shed over David Blunkett's departure, we should not forget that, as Home Secretary, he was the author of a vast extension to police powers, some of which have yet to come into force. After 1 January, there will be almost no offence where the police cannot make an arrest and insist on taking DNA and photographs.

That is the legacy of the man who slunk from office after a second scandal. I feel a little sympathy for the faults that made him commit those mistakes, but none for the disdain for individual rights displayed in the Serious Organised Crime and Police Act, a piece of legislation that will profoundly alter the relationship between the police and the public.

The attack on liberty from Blunkett and Mr Blair has been so broad that it has been difficult to keep track of the measures being pushed through parliament. The proposals come thick and fast. They are widely drafted and often disguised in a bill which appears to address one or other of the public's major fears about terrorism and organised or violent crime.

As any Home Office lawyer could have predicted, the measures in the act that gained most attention were the establishment of a Serious Organised Crime Agency and the proposal that demonstrations should not be allowed within one kilometre of parliament. For the British people to be denied access to their own parliament seemed odious enough, but beneath the surface of this act lurks a greater change which has nothing to do with either organised crime or security.

The new arrest procedures contained in the bill were slipped through parliament with barely a whisper. Tony Edwards, a solicitor with London firm TV Edwards, regards it as the most serious extension of police powers in decades. Few who know what these powers mean disagree.

Under the 1984 Police and Criminal Evidence Act, a balance was struck between police powers and the individual's rights. There was a clear distinction between non-arrestable offences, arrestable offences and serious arrestable offences. Everyone knew where they stood and the public was protected from officious or malevolently motivated police constables.

From 1 January, there will be no such distinction. Every offence will be arrestable. That means motoring infringements, dropping litter, swearing and behaving loudly in a demonstration will very likely end in arrest.

There are specific tests of necessity a police officer must satisfy, yet at the end of the list come two paragraphs which give the officer complete freedom. The first stipulates that an arrest may be carried out to allow the prompt and 'effective investigation of the offence or of the conduct of the person in question'. The second says that an arrest may take place 'to prevent any prosecution of the offence from being hindered by the disappearance of the person in question'.

If the officer feels he cannot satisfy the first requirement, he will certainly take refuge in the second. Arrest is a certainty, however minor the offence.

Now comes the sinister part. For all but a truly minor crime, the officer is empowered, using force, if necessary, to take a sample of the suspect's DNA from his mouth, to photograph and fingerprint him and, finally, to take impressions of his footwear. Remember, at this stage, the suspect is just that – a suspect. He has not been found guilty by a court and, under British law, is therefore presumed innocent. And yet he has been forced to submit to a humiliating process as though he were about to enter prison.

This goes against the tradition of Britain's regard for liberty and the sense that the public is largely well-meaning and well-behaved. As important is the effect it will have on the police who, according to the white paper last year, requested this simplification with the unbelievable claim that officers found it difficult to make distinctions between non-arrestable and arrestable offences.

Most solicitors who deal with the police on a daily basis are convinced that these new powers criminalise the public. Because every offence becomes arrestable, it is unlikely that someone held by the police will be able to make a case for an unlawful arrest. The sentence in the act which allows 'prompt and effective investigation of the offence or the conduct of the person in question' is a catch-all which means the police officer may say that he was reasonably investigating someone's behaviour.

East Germany's Stasi would have been content to operate under such a provision.

So, respect for the public and law-abiding citizens who make trifling mistakes is replaced by suspicion and contempt – unsurprisingly, the twin characteristics which have informed Blair and Blunkett's attack on liberty. Arresting someone, photographing and forcibly taking samples from them places an individual in an entirely different relationship with the state from the one most of us have known.

Naturally, there will be a vast increase in the number of DNA samples taken from suspects. The current rate of new samples runs at between 8,000 and 10,000 a week. Liberty, the human-rights organisation, already reports that one-third of DNA samples are taken from Afro-Caribbean males.

For a lawyer, the Prime Minister has astonishingly little regard for the immutable principles of British justice. Blunkett has been his Dr Strangelove in this campaign, and one of their main strategies was to introduce controls and harsher penalties by stealth. It is hardly any wonder that the prison population is heading towards 80,000 (it was 60,000 when Labour came to power) while the crime rate is actually going down.

Bills such as those covering anti-terror measures, violent crime and the introduction of identity cards all seek to extend control over the general population and lock up more people.

Asbos are a good example of how a loosely drafted law can become a potent but also unjust weapon. Because the penalty for breaking an Asbo is five years, people are being jailed for longer periods than laid down for the original crime they may have committed. Often, no crime is involved. An order may simply specify that a couple should stop rowing, as we saw last week, or that a man may not sit in the front passenger seat of a car, an order imposed by Birmingham magistrates' court. Even if no crime has been committed, breaching the Asbo can lead to imprisonment.

One little-remarked-upon measure in the Serious Organised Crime and Police Act allows accountable public bodies to seek Asbos against individuals, while in the Violent Crime Reduction Bill, a variant allows police to issue a dispersal order (with no court involved) to people who are not doing anything wrong but who might at some future date, in a police officer's opinion, be involved in illegal activity. If they break it, they risk imprisonment. Imagine how that could be used to stifle the right to demonstrate.

Blair is, without doubt, the most authoritarian leader we have had in the last century. In assuming powers beyond those taken by any other peacetime Prime Minister, he is attacking rights which have stood for hundreds of years. We can only hope that last week's rebellion on the anti-terrorism bill is a sign of things to come. MPs of all hues now have a grave responsibility. They are the stewards of our democracy and they should damn well start behaving like it.

1. What human rights concerns does the author of this article have about SOCPA?
2. Do the police need the new extension to their powers? Explain why.
3. Does this piece of law change the relationship the individual has with the state and the police?
4. What are the advantages of SOCPA for the police and the government?

Source. *Observer*, Sunday 6 November, 2005. © Henry Porter 2008.
Reproduced by kind permission of the author.

Searching people and premises

This section requires you to be familiar with the powers the police have when undertaking a search and what the public can do if they believe they have had their person or their property searched unlawfully.

Stop and search

A stop and search is when a police officer stops you in a public place as you are going about your business and searches your person and any bags or items you might be carrying. The police can stop and search any member of the public at any time as long as they abide by the law and codes of practice. You can also be stopped and just questioned. This is simply called a 'stop'.

'Stop and search' can happen for a variety of reasons, but generally it will be one or more of the following:

- There has been serious crime nearby and police want to check whether you were involved.

▲ The police have the power to 'stop and search' any member of the public

- On public transport such as the London Underground, police may stop and search as part of the anti-terrorist campaign.
- You look like a suspect that police want to arrest or talk to about a previous crime.
- The police suspect you may be carrying something illegal such as drugs, knives or firearms.
- They think you may be carrying stolen property.

A police officer will normally ask some simple questions about who you are, where you are going and what items you are carrying. If they are satisfied with the answers they may decide not to search you at all, but if your answers give them suspicion that you may have committed or be about to commit a crime, then they can search you. A public search will normally take place in the street and you will be asked to turn out your pockets, open your bags and take off items such as coats, scarves and gloves to allow the police to ensure you are not carrying anything illegal. The police must provide you with a written record of your stop and search.

Search after arrest is slightly different as the police can search you for reasons other than those given above. They can search you if:

- they believe you may be a danger to yourself or others
- they believe you may be carrying an item which might help you escape
- they think you may have evidence of a crime on you
- they need to do a check on what belongings you have brought to the police station.

Whenever possible, searches must be done as soon as possible after arrest or there may be a risk to the safety of officers and the public and evidence may be destroyed.

Remember!

If the police ask a member of the public to remove an item of religious dress such as a head or face covering, then the search must be conducted somewhere private where the public cannot see.

Consider this

According to 2006 Home Office research, black people are six times more likely to be stopped and searched than white people, and Asian people twice as likely to be stopped and searched. What do you think this shows?

Assessment activity 17.3

This assessment activity requires you to examine the policy and practice of police searches of people and premises in order to answer the following question:

1. Research, prepare and present a PowerPoint presentation which outlines the powers the police have to search people and premises. **P3 M2**

Grading tips

P3 An outline is simply a concise overview of police search powers.

M2 This is an extension of P3. Rather than providing a simple outline you must provide more detail in the form of an explanation of the powers the police have to search people and premises.

Vehicle stops

These are very similar to a stop and search, but a vehicle is involved rather than a person. A police officer can stop a vehicle at any time and ask to see documents, such as a driving licence, and ask you questions about where you are going. He or she will be looking for exactly the same things as in an ordinary stop and search such as drugs, weapons or stolen property. Interestingly, the police can search your vehicle without your permission and without your presence, but they must leave you a form saying what they have done and why, and you are entitled to claim for compensation if they damage your vehicle while searching it.

Searching premises

As with searches of people and vehicles, the police can enter and search your house or premises for lots of different reasons. The police do not always need a search warrant to enter and search your premises but they always need to have a good reason for doing so. The police must be careful how they conduct a search because if the search is conducted improperly they will not be able to use as evidence anything they find – the court will not allow it.

There are three main ways in which your premises or house can be searched. They are outlined in Table 17.2.

Search	Description
Search with your consent	The police can search your premises if you give them permission to do so. The permission should be in writing and you should have been told why the search is happening and the fact that the police can take items that they consider to be evidence.
Search of premises under a magistrate's warrant	Magistrates can issue police with a warrant to enter a premises in order to search for evidence of serious offences. This means that the police can enter a premises and search it even without the consent of the owner. The material is likely to be of substantial value – whether by itself or together with other material – to the investigation of the offence.
Entry and search without a warrant	The police can also enter a property without either the owner's consent or a warrant. They are given powers under various acts of law such as: • Gaming Act 1968 • Misuse of Drugs Act 1971 • Firearms Act 1968 However, PACE is one of the most important pieces of law. It allows the police to enter and search a property for the following reasons: • To arrest someone • To recapture a person who has escaped from lawful custody • To arrest a child or young person who has been remanded or committed to local authority accommodation • To save life or limb or prevent serious damage to property

Table 17.2 Police rights to search premises

Unlawful entry and searches

Individuals who feel that they or their property have been searched unlawfully have the option to complain to the Independent Police Complaints Commission (IPCC). Complaints must be made within one year of the incident and must refer to particular officers rather than being just a general complaint against the whole constabulary or a particular policy. These complaints are usually dealt with in one of two ways: local resolution and investigation. Local resolution is where the complainant has the opportunity to speak with the officers concerned and hear an explanation of their behaviour or receive an apology if appropriate. Investigations happen when the police misconduct is much more serious, such as in a police shooting or allegations of police racism or homophobia. The IPCC conducts an investigation into the conduct of the officers concerned and if the complaint is upheld the officers can face disciplinary proceedings or even criminal charges. Searching property without proper authority also leaves the police open to being sued in a civil court and they may have to provide compensation to the victim of their actions.

Both this section and the next one have very strong links with *Unit 22: Understanding aspects of the legal system and law making process*, and information will be cross-referenced where required. This section examines what happens in the criminal justice system before a trial commences.

Pre-trial procedure

All court cases proceed in the first instance to the magistrates' court, but the offence may be dealt with eventually by another court. Which court an offence will ultimately be tried in depends on the type of offence.

Categories of offences

All criminal offences can be divided into three categories: summary, indictable or triable either way.

■ Summary offences

These are only dealt with in a magistrates' court. Generally these offences are considered less serious and are punishable by a maximum of 6 months' imprisonment and/or a £5000 fine.
- Minor assaults
- Driving without insurance
- Indecent exposure
- Assault on a police officer
- Taking without owner's consent (TWOC)

■ Indictable offences

These offences appear in magistrates' court firstly, but are then automatically committed for trial in the Crown court. Generally these are the most serious offences and they are punishable by the penalty prescribed by law, which could be anything up to life imprisonment for certain offences.
- Murder
- Manslaughter
- Rape
- Blackmail
- Aggravated burglary

■ Triable either way

These offences can be tried in either the magistrates' court or the Crown court, depending on what the prosecution thinks is appropriate, what the defendant wishes and the nature of the case involved, i.e. the value of stolen property or the extent of injuries. These tend to be middle-range crimes.
- Indecent assault
- Making off without payment
- Obtaining services by deception
- Going equipped for stealing
- Handling stolen goods
- Possession of a controlled drug

Assessment activity 17.4

This assessment activity requires you to participate in a small group discussion which covers the following question.

1. Describe the pre-trial procedure in criminal courts in a given situation. **P4**

Grading tips

P4 This task again asks only for an outline, so you must provide a simple and concise overview of how a summary, indictable or triable-either-way offence is dealt with prior to trial.

Bail

It is important for the custody officer to decide whether the defendant should stay in custody or be released on bail after they have been charged (although people can be bailed before charge if the police wish to gather more evidence). Bail means that the person is free until the next stage in the process of their case. The laws relating to how bail is given and dealt with are laid out in the Bail Act 1976 and the Criminal Justice and Public Order Act 1994.

A custody officer may refuse bail if they suspect the person:

- will not return to custody
- will commit further offences
- will interfere with witnesses or evidence
- needs custody for his or her own protection.

The police may also impose conditions on the bail that they give, such as:

- surrender of passport
- report to the police station at regular intervals.

If the police refuse bail to a suspect they must present him or her at the magistrates' court as soon as possible. If the magistrate cannot deal with the whole case at that time, then the magistrate makes a further decision on whether to grant bail or remand in custody until the matter can be resolved. According to Martin (2000) five out of six defendants are given police bail; only one out of six is decided in magistrates' court. In the UK money is not paid for bail.

Case study: Bail

You are a custody officer at a large town centre police station. You must decide on the following bail issue. A 21-year-old crack addict has been brought in on a burglary charge. He has been positively identified by the owners of the property he was trying to burgle. The suspect had an existing warrant for his arrest for failing to attend court on a similar charge. In addition the householder had made threats against the suspect's life if he is released.

1. **What factors must you consider in general when evaluating the bail application?**

2. **What are the particular risk factors involved in this case?**

3. **What would your decision be?**

4. **Which pieces of law currently govern the process of bail?**

As you will see from Unit 22 there are two main areas of law where individuals may require access to legal advice and representation: civil law and criminal law. These are governed by the Legal Services Commission (LSC), which operates the legal aid schemes in England and Wales. The LSC runs a legal aid scheme for both civil and criminal matters:

- Civil – The Community Legal Service
- Criminal – The Criminal Defence Service

■ The Community Legal Service (CLS)

This service exists to provide assistance in matters of civil law such as providing advice on civil matters, resolving or settling disputes involving legal rights and help in enforcing legal decisions involving compensation. It does not cover some of the most commonly used areas of civil law such as:

- allegations of negligence
- conveyancing
- wills
- company/business laws
- boundary disputes.

The money for the CLS is provided by the Community Legal Service Fund (CLSF). The main difference between this system and the old system is that the budget of the CLSF is capped; once it is gone it is gone. People may be refused assistance, whereas in the other scheme there was no cap on the funding available.

■ The Criminal Defence Service (CDS)

The CDS came into being in April 2001. Its job is to ensure that those involved in criminal proceedings have access to advice, assistance and representation. The CDS provides for free duty solicitor access at police stations. The solicitor is available on a 24-hour rota to assist those who are being charged, questioned or placed in police custody. Although this initial assistance is free it must be in the interests of justice for further representation to continue to be free. The level of funding in criminal cases is not capped and is demand-led. Only solicitors' firms who have a contract with the LSC are able to offer state-funded criminal defence. This defence falls into three categories:

- **Advice and assistance** – This is the provision of advice and assistance from a solicitor. It covers aspects of criminal defence such as general advice, preparing a written legal case and getting legal opinions from barristers. It does not cover representation in court.

- **Advocacy assistance** – This form of help covers the cost of preparing a case and the initial representation in a magistrates' court and Crown court. This form of assistance is not means tested, but it is merits tested. This means that the provision of defence must be in the interests of justice.

- **Representation** – Representation covers the cost of a solicitor to prepare the case and represent defendants in court. It may also cover the cost of a barrister in Crown court and the cost of appeals.

Remember!

- The system of legal aid was changed by the Access to Justice Act 1999.
- Civil Legal aid is now the responsibility of the Community Legal Service (CLS).
- Civil legal aid has capped funding.
- Criminal Legal Aid is the responsibility of the Criminal Defence Service (CDS).
- Criminal legal aid is free in the initial stages and then is merit tested.

■ The Crown Prosecution Service (CPS)

The CPS was created by the Prosecution of Offences Act 1985 and became fully operational the following year. It was initially proposed in the Phillips Report in 1981, which was a review of the criminal procedure of the time. The Phillips Report stated that it was undesirable for the police to both investigate and prosecute crime due to issues of bias and differing practices in police force areas.

The CPS operates between the police and the courts, as shown in Figure 17.1.

Police	→	CPS	→	Courts

▲ **Figure 17.1 The CPS takes the prosecution from the police to the courts**

The police are responsible for arresting and detaining a suspect and preparing a case file for the CPS. The CPS decides the charge, then takes over the prosecution from that point and reviews the case files in order to check that the evidence presented justifies the charge given. If it does not, then the reviewing lawyer may discontinue proceedings or charge the offender with a lesser offence. This power to discontinue or downgrade prosecutions was intended to save money by not proceeding with cases that couldn't be proved, but in practice what it did was cause tension and alienation between the CPS and the police. In addition to this role the CPS prepares cases for court, prosecutes cases in magistrates' court and instructs counsel in Crown court.

The decision the CPS makes on whether to prosecute is based on two main 'tests', which when used together are known as the code for Crown prosecutors:

- **The Evidential Test** – Is there enough evidence that the case is likely to succeed? If there isn't then the CPS is likely to discontinue a case. This happens in about 12 per cent of cases where the police have charged a defendant.

- **The Public Interest Test** – If the CPS's reviewing lawyer thinks that there is enough evidence for the case to have a reasonable chance of success he or she will then consider whether a prosecution is in the public interest, i.e. will it benefit the public for a prosecution to be continued? The factors which influence the CPS decision on the public interest test are laid out in a document called 'The Code for Crown Prosecutors'.

The present Director of Public Prosecutions is Sir Ken Macdonald QC and he is head of the CPS. The CPS employs almost 9000 people with one-third of those being lawyers and the rest legal officers and administrative staff. They deal with 1.3 million cases a year in the magistrates' court and approximately 115,000 in the Crown court.

▶ **Sir Ken Macdonald QC is the head of the CPS**

Other agencies such as the Environment Agency and the local council can initiate a prosecution. It is also important to note that individuals can initiate a private prosecution, beginning the process themselves, with the CPS making a decision at a later stage as to whether or not to take over the prosecution (if it has merit) or discontinue it (if it does not). Private prosecutions are conducted when a member of the public feels very strongly about an issue but the CPS or the police won't take the case forward. A good example of this is the case of *Joy v Rees-Davies*. In 1974 PC Joy pulled over a motorist who had gone through a stop sign. The motorist then refused to undergo a breath test when asked to do so at the scene. The motorist turned out to be a Member of Parliament and PC Joy's senior officers did not wish to pursue the case. PC Joy considered this to be unjust and so brought his own prosecution, which led to the eventual conviction and fining of the MP.

Plea bargaining

Plea bargaining is a way to speed up court proceedings. It involves a defendant pleading guilty to a lesser charge than the one they were originally dealing with. It is an extremely common method of securing convictions in the USA, but the UK has no official plea bargain system.

Case study: Private Prosecution – *Whitehouse v Lemon* [1979] 2 WLR 281

Mary Whitehouse was a well-known public moral campaigner who was involved for many years with ensuring that the media did not cause offence via blasphemy (blasphemy is when a person shows disrespect to God or a deity). She also campaigned to get rid of video 'nasties' and pornography from the media. In 1976 a poem by James Kirkup called 'The Love that Dares to Speak its Name' was published in the *Gay Times*. The poem outlines acts of homosexuality being committed on the dead body of Christ as he is taken from the crucifix. Mrs Whitehouse brought a private prosecution for blasphemous libel against the *Gay Times* and its publisher, Denis Lemon. The prosecution was successful and Mr Lemon was sentenced to a 9-month suspended sentence and a £500 fine, and the *Gay Times* was fined £1000.

1. **Do you think that the media have a responsibility to uphold high moral standards?**

2. **Should individual citizens have the right to prosecute broadcasters or artists whose work they find offensive?**

3. **What are the rights of the artist to have their work heard or seen?**

▲ Mary Whitehouse in the 1970s

4. **Consider the information you received about** *Joy v Rees-Davies* **and** *Whitehouse v Lemon***. Why is it important for the public to have the right to prosecute?**

This section requires you to know how the criminal trial process works in the UK. This is largely covered in *Unit 22* (pages 218–251) and therefore will not be repeated here. It is also important that you use both this unit and *Unit 22* for your assessments, since they are so closely linked.

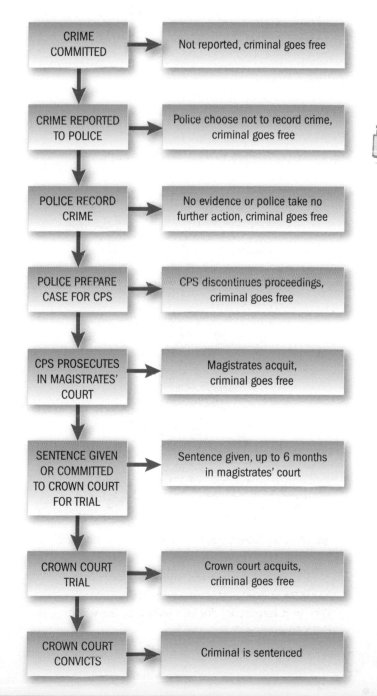

Figure 17.2 The criminal trial process

Assessment activity 17.5

In this assessment you are required to examine the information on courts in this unit and Unit 22 to answer the following questions, in the form of a report.

1. Describe how the criminal trial process works in both the magistrates' and Crown courts, using one example each of a summary and an indictable offence. **P5 M3**

Grading tips

P5 This task requires you to cross-reference the courts' information in Unit 22 with the categories of offences information in this unit. For example you could choose a summary offence of assault and explain how the magistrates' court would process the case and an indictable offence such as murder and discuss how both the magistrates' and Crown courts work together to deal with it.

M3 This is a straightforward extension of P5 but you must make sure you also compare (identify similarities and differences) between the pre-trial and trial process in the courts.

Assessment activity 17.6

This assessment again rests very heavily on content discussed in Unit 22. You should make a point of cross-referencing the information in order to answer the following questions, in the form of an informative and eye-catching large poster.

1. Describe the powers of the courts in sentencing offenders and the routes and grounds for appeal in criminal cases in a given situation using one example of a summary and one example of an indictable offence. **P6** **M4** **D2**

Knowledge check

1. What does PACE stand for?
2. What is a citizen's arrest?
3. What is the time limit on keeping a member of the public detained?
4. Describe the rights of a detained person.
5. What can a person do if they have been searched unlawfully?
6. What is bail?
7. List the three categories of offences.
8. What is the role of the CPS?
9. What is legal aid?
10. What does SOCPA stand for?

Grading tips

P6 A poster is a good medium for this assessment, as you have the opportunity to use labelled diagrams of the courts and their appeal procedures. Again choose one summary and one indictable offence and describe how courts can sentence them and their routes of appeal.

M4 This is an extension of P6 but you are required to select a single court to focus on.

D2 You should ensure your poster contains an evaluation of the criminal court process in order to achieve D2.

Preparation for assessment

You are a PCSO who needs to know more about police powers in order to apply to become a regular police officer. Your supervisor recommends you produce a study guide for yourself which covers the following questions:

1. Outline the difference between arrest with and without a warrant. **P1**

2. Describe the rights of a detained person. **P2**

3. Analyse the requirements of lawful arrest and detention. **M1**

4. Outline the powers the police have to search people and premises **P3**

5. Explain the powers the police have to search people and premises. **M2**

6. Evaluate the powers of arrest, detention and search. **D1**

7. Describe the pre-trial procedure in criminal courts in a given situation. **P4**

8. Describe how the criminal trial process works in both the magistrates' and Crown courts, using one example each of a summary and an indictable offence. **P5**

9. Compare the pre-trial and trial process in given situations in the magistrates' and Crown courts, using one example of a summary and an indictable offence. **M3**

10. Describe the powers of the courts in sentencing offenders and the routes and grounds for appeal in criminal cases in a given situation, using one example of a summary and an indictable offence. **P6**

11. Explain a selected criminal court's sentencing powers and the grounds for appeal in a given situation, using one example of a summary and an indictable offence. **M4**

12. Evaluate the criminal court process. **D2**

Grading criteria	Activity	Pg no.	To achieve a merit grade the evidence must show that the learner is able to:	To achieve a distinction grade the evidence must show that the learner is able to:
To achieve a pass grade the evidence must show that the learner is able to:				
P1 Outline the difference between arrest with and without a warrant	17.1	106	**M1** Analyse the requirements of lawful arrest and detention	**D1** Evaluate the powers of arrest, detention and search
P2 Describe the rights of a detained person	17.2	108		
P3 Outline the powers the police have to search people and premises	17.3	113	**M2** Explain the powers the police have to search people and premises	
P4 Describe the pre-trial procedure in criminal courts in a given situation	17.4	115	**M3** Compare the pre-trial and trial process in given situations in the magistrates' and Crown courts, using one example of a summary and an indictable offence	**D2** Evaluate the criminal court process.
P5 Describe how the criminal trial process works in both the magistrates' and Crown courts, using one example each of a summary and an indictable offence	17.5	119		
P6 Describe the powers of the courts in sentencing offenders and the routes and grounds for appeal in criminal cases in a given situation, using one example of a summary and an indictable offence.	17.6	120	**M4** Explain a selected criminal court's sentencing powers and the grounds for appeal in a given situation, using one example of a summary and an indictable offence.	

Understanding behaviour in public sector employment

Introduction

The public sector offers a diverse range of employment opportunities that require individuals to adapt their everyday behaviour. Working within a disciplined and structured environment is a challenge and can be a source of stress. Understanding how and why certain behaviour happens can help you to understand your own reactions as well as the reactions of others.

This unit covers several important issues, such as the psychological approaches to behaviour and how they can benefit a public service organisation and benefit you, as an employee dealing with a pressurised job role. Another key topic you will look at is communication. Uniformed public servants are often in the public eye and they must use communication very clearly to advise or warn the public and also to coordinate public service operations and teams in order to provide a more effective service. Linked to this is the idea of managing and dealing with conflict effectively. This does not just mean conflict which you might be called upon to deal with in the course of your duties. It also means conflict with colleagues, friends and family members. Learning how to deal with conflict is a key transferable skill that you can use in many areas of your life.

After completing this unit you should be able to achieve the following outcomes:

- Know about different approaches to psychology and their benefits to public services
- Understand the different types of communication behaviour
- Understand the possible areas of conflict between individual and group behaviour
- Know the different ways of overcoming possible conflicts between groups and individuals through the use of effective conflict management techniques.

This section examines how approaching psychology from different viewpoints can help us understand human behaviour and how this understanding can be used to benefit a public service organisation.

Approaches to psychology

There are many approaches to psychology that could be examined. This unit will focus on the following theories, in order to provide a broad cross-section of the knowledge you need:

- humanism
- psychodynamic approach
- cognitive psychology
- free will vs determinism
- 'nature vs nurture'.

Humanism

The humanistic approach emerged in the 1950s and 1960s from the work of Abraham Maslow and Carl Rogers. It believes that individuals are responsible for choosing their own behaviour rather than simply responding to environmental or unconscious forces which act upon them. In essence humans have a free will and make their own choices about how to behave.

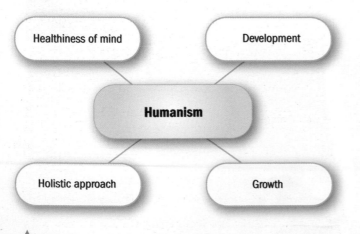

Figure 18.1 The humanist model of psychology

We all need fulfilling personal relationships

■ Self-actualisation and positive regard

Carl Rogers suggested that humans have two basic needs. The first is 'self-actualisation'. This is striving for personal development and the aim of achieving your full potential – being all that you can be. Rogers saw the other need as the requirement for positive regard. This is the love, respect, trust and affection of others, which you might find in personal relationships such as friendships, romance and family. These are the factors that motivate individuals and may influence behaviour choices.

Rogers saw individuals very differently from psychoanalysts and behaviourists. He saw an individual as a whole person not as a group of component parts. He didn't believe, as psycholanalysts do, that an individual has automatic tendencies towards destructiveness and neurosis. Instead he emphasised the essential healthiness of the mind, having a natural tendency to grow and develop rather than repress and destroy.

■ Person Centred Therapy

Rogers developed a treatment for psychological problems called Person Centred Therapy (PCT). It differs from psychoanalytic therapy in that the therapist is encouraged to engage in the problems of the client and use their own personal qualities to understand the world, as the client perceives it. In essence the therapist does not keep the same professional distance as other types of treatment. They actually question and challenge in order to understand and help a person make changes in their life.

Evaluation of the humanistic approach

It is hard to see humanism as a coherent approach to psychology. It is best described as a way of thinking instead.

Many of its concepts are difficult to test scientifically. They are vague and difficult to define and there is a lack of research to support the ideas. It doesn't provide an explanation of how personality develops.

It has been labelled by some as self-centred and self-indulgent. They argue that it focuses too much on the individual's feelings and needs rather than what may be really happening.

PCT relies on the individual discussing how they feel with a therapist. However, many individuals may not be discussing what they really feel, but what the therapist wants to hear. In addition, some people may not know how they feel about a situation at all.

Remember!

- Humanism developed in the mid-20th century from the work of Maslow and Rogers.
- It treats the person as a whole, recognising and respecting individuality.
- It argues that individuals have a natural tendency for growth and development. Individuals develop difficulties when this growth and development is halted by external forces.
- It led to Person Centred Therapy, from which most forms of counselling have developed.
- It is more a way of thinking than a hard and fast scientific approach to psychology.

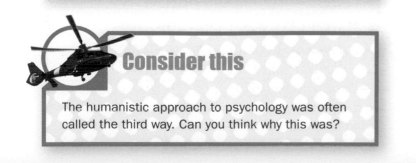

Consider this

The humanistic approach to psychology was often called the third way. Can you think why this was?

▲ Sigmund Freud is known as the father of psychoanalysis

Psychodynamic approach

This approach to the study of human thought and behaviour is based on the work of Sigmund Freud (1856–1939). Freud pioneered the use of a psychological therapy called psychoanalysis. It is still widely used today in helping people identify the causes of their psychological problems and suggesting ways in which these can be overcome. Freud's theory suggests that the majority of our behaviour is influenced by factors we are not consciously aware of.

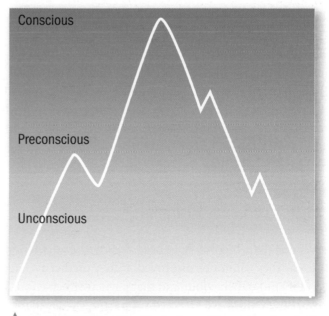

▲ Figure 18.2 The Freudian iceberg: the unconscious is the largest part of the mind

The conscious, preconscious and unconscious

The **conscious** is the part of your mind that is currently aware of itself. It knows you are reading this book. It knows when you are due in class, and it knows your circumstances and feelings right at this moment.

The **preconscious** mind is the short-term storehouse for memories and thoughts. It contains information, ideas and beliefs that are not currently on your mind or are temporarily forgotten, but can be recalled easily when they are needed. This might include information such as names, phone numbers, addresses or the answers to your last assignment.

The **unconscious** mind, according to Freud, is the most substantial part of this equation; it contains emotional experiences, ideas and memories that are 'repressed' by the individual. Repression is the process whereby information or significant experiences are buried deep in the mind and the individual concerned will not even be aware of their existence. Freud theorised that the content of the unconscious exerts an influence over the actions and behaviour of the individual even though the individual may be unaware of it. Sometimes the unconscious mind tries to tell us things through dreams. Psychoanalytic theory also greatly stresses the importance of early childhood experience on the eventual mental state of adults. For Freud, problems in adolescence and adulthood were directly traceable to events occurring in early childhood.

The psychodynamic approach to the study of psychology has been tremendously influential, from its creation at the end of the 19th and beginning of the 20th century to the present day. It has contributed substantially to fields of study such as gender, development, aggression, sleep and motivation. Freud believed that humans are driven by instincts, of which sexuality and aggression are of paramount importance.

Evaluation of the psychodynamic approach

Psychoanalytic theories have been regarded as unscientific because they cannot be disproved. If they predict a certain kind of behaviour and that particular behaviour occurs then they have gathered supporting evidence for their theory. If, however, the behaviour does not occur, then the individual is repressing the instinct to perform that behaviour and the psychoanalysts have still gained evidence to support their theory. In essence, regardless of what behaviour is displayed psychoanalysis can't be wrong!

In 1952 Hans Eysenck heavily criticised Freud's theory when he pointed out that the recovery rates for patients undergoing psychoanalytic treatments was virtually the same as patients who underwent spontaneous remission, i.e. they got better on their own. Eysenck further noted that the patients opting to undergo psychoanalysis were often young, wealthy and intelligent and therefore the type of patients most likely to recover anyway. This brings into question whether psychoanalysis can help people to deal with their day-to-day behavioural issues.

In order to be effective, a traditional course of psychoanalysis happens several times a week for several years. This is clearly extremely expensive and puts it out of the reach of the majority of the population. It also raises the spectre of unscrupulous therapists who may be incorrectly or inadequately trained in psychoanalytic techniques, causing further psychological damage to the patient or simply 'milking them' for thousands of pounds.

Take it further

What are your views on Freud's impression of the mind as an iceberg? Keep a dream diary for one week. At the end of the week, use a Freudian-based dream interpretation dictionary to see what your unconscious mind is trying to tell you.

Remember!

- The inspiration of psychodynamic theories is the work of Sigmund Freud.
- Freud's psychoanalytic approach has had a substantial impact on the evolution of psychology from the beginning of the 20th century.
- Freud believed that only a small fraction of the mind is directly accessible. He called this the 'conscious'.
- The rest of the mind is not immediately accessible. It consists of the preconscious, which holds information we might need at a moment's notice and the unconscious, where we repress information we would rather not deal with.
- The unconscious has a large impact on our behaviour, even if we are unaware of it.

Cognitive psychology

Unlike the other perspectives we have examined, cognitive psychology does not have a spokesperson or pioneer who engineered its development, such as Freud for psychoanalysis or Rogers for humanism.

The origins of cognitive psychology lie in the focus on topics such as human performance, attention and memory. It is also linked to developments in computer science and linguistics. Cognitive psychology is concerned with the mental processes within an individual and the consequences of these processes on behaviour. It focuses on aspects of the individual such as perception, motor control, memory, language and decision-making. Cognitive psychology relies upon scientific methodology and empirical results to support its case.

The dominant view in cognitive psychology is that the brain is an information-processing system. This view is linked to computer science and communications theory and likens the brain to a computer into which information is input and behaviour is output. This has led to an over-reliance on laboratory experiments as a method of providing evidence for the theory, as the case study below highlights.

Cognitive psychology proposes that learning is simply a process of recognition; the learner perceives new relationships amongst the parts of a problem. The essence of the approach is that how a person thinks will largely affect how they feel and behave. Cognitive psychology is interested in the mental processes which occur between the stimulus and response.

Cognitive psychology has become strongly associated with computer science and the study of artificial intelligence. It explores whether computers are capable of problem solving in similar ways to humans and examines the parallels between the human brain and the computer. Cognitive psychology, like other approaches we have examined, has had a substantial impact upon developments in the field; it has also spawned a range of cognitive behavioural treatments for mental health difficulties.

Case study: Tolman's cognitive behaviourism

Working in the early part of the 20th century, Tolman examined the process by which learning takes place. The experiments were conducted with laboratory rats that had to find their way through a maze. The rats were split into three groups:

- Group 1 received food every time they made their way successfully through the maze.
- Group 2 never received food.
- Group 3 received food only after ten days had gone by.

The results of the study were relatively predictable: Group 1 navigated the maze most effectively; Group 2 were the least effective; and Group 3 made improvements after day 10. It is interesting to note that cognitive experiments such as this are often extrapolated to humans and form parts of theories designed to explain human behaviour.

1. **Can cognitive experiments on animals be used to predict how humans would behave in the same circumstances?**

2. **Do all animals behave in the same ways when presented with the same circumstances?**

3. **What are the potential benefits of these animal studies?**

4. **Do you think humans can be trained to do a task faster if they are promised a reward?**

5. **Is a laboratory a suitable place to observe 'natural' behaviour?**

Evaluation of the cognitive approach

One of the main criticisms levelled at the cognitive approach is that the use of lab experiments on humans decontextualises their behaviour and thought processes. By taking an individual out of a natural setting and placing them in an artificial environment, their thought processes may be changed.

The cognitive approach also neglects individual differences to some extent. It generalises across all humans in terms of how they perceive, receive, process, store, retrieve and use information.

The likening of the human mind to a computer neglects culture, history and interaction with others and the environment. It doesn't address issues of group cognition, the process of remembering or learning things in groups. Instead it only emphasises the individual mental processes without reference to others.

Some of the experiments conducted by cognitive psychologists are questionable in their aim. For instance a cognitive psychologist may wish to study short-term memory and provide a list of words for subjects to memorise. However, this is not a normal procedure for people who remember things through imagery. If psychologists use unrealistic experiments they will receive flawed data.

Remember!

- Cognitive psychology is not a cohesive theory and has no particular spokesperson.
- It developed from the 1950s onwards as a result of performance testing on humans and developments in computer science.
- Cognitive psychology draws parallels between the human brain and computers, seeing them both as information-processing systems.
- It studies the mental processes involved in perception, motor control and memory, etc.
- It is particularly concerned with how we perceive, receive, process, store, retrieve and use information.

Free will vs determinism

Free will is the idea that an individual has the freedom to choose how they will act and develop, whereas determinism puts forward the idea that everything that you do is already predetermined.

Free will embraces the concept of freedom of choice and responsibility for your actions. It maintains that people's actions are not solely determined by their genetic or environmental circumstances. Determinism on the other hand puts forward the idea that a person's behaviour and actions are a direct result of their genetic inheritance and their past experiences, which come together to form a predicable course of action which cannot be changed or avoided.

In order to have free will a person must have an array of choices available to them and not be pressured or forced to make any particular decision. As individuals, many people support the view that they are free to choose what they do and they are the ones who must take responsibility for poor decisions. In fact, our criminal justice system is based on the fact that citizens have free will and can choose the course of their actions. If a person had no choice but to commit a crime, how can society have the right to punish them?

Consider this

What are the implications for our criminal justice system if the principle of determinism is true? Could we hold people responsible for their actions when effectively they had no choice?

This perceived lack of responsibility in determinism is one of the major problems with examining it in relation to behaviour. If a person is not responsible for their actions because of their genes or because of how they have been treated in their environment, and the people who treated them badly are not responsible for their behaviour and so on, you get a spiral of non-responsibility. Effectively nothing is anybody's fault or responsibility. However, it is very important to note that to put free will on one side of the debate and determinism on the other over-simplifies the situation.

The debate on free will and determinism is not really part of psychology at all. It actually belongs to psychology's parent discipline, philosophy. It usually finds its way into the subject of psychology via the 'nature vs nurture' debate, which revolves around whether a person's behaviour is caused by genetics or by their environment.

'Nature vs nurture'

This viewpoint examines whether behaviour is caused by our genetic make-up or our environment. It is usually used in discussions about crime and criminals, with one side arguing that criminals are born bad and the other side arguing that individuals are drawn to crime because of their environment. However, as with most theories, the reality is a little more complicated.

■ Nature

The nature side of the debate concentrates on the genetic inheritance we are given by our parents and the role of these genes in the personality and intellectual development of an individual. This view enjoyed great popularity in the early part of the 20th century and it was heavily influenced by the work of biologists such as Charles Darwin, whose research highlighted the importance of heredity in the ability to survive and be biologically successful. **Genetic determinism** (nature) argues that our personality and intellectual characteristics are inherited from our parents; this would include the tendency to commit crime or other forms of anti-social behaviour. The evidence for this side of the debate lies in the results of scientifically controlled experiments such as twin studies and family studies, which examine crime and delinquent behaviour in groups of genetically related individuals. Some of these are described below.

Twin studies

Identical twins (also called monozygotic or MZ twins) share exactly the same genes. Pairs of twins have been studied to test whether if one becomes a criminal, the other is also likely to be criminal; this is called 'concordance'. In essence if one identical twin commits crime, the other would be more likely to commit crime. Also, the concordance for non-identical twins should be lower as they only have about half their genes in common. There does seem to be some evidence to support this, such as studies of Goldman and

▼ Studies of identical twins have been used to support genetic determinism

Cottesman (1995), which showed that if a twin committed a crime, the likelihood of the other twin committing a crime was higher amongst identical twins than amongst non-identical twins. However, other researchers have pointed out that most identical twins also share the same environment and argue that this plays a more important role in the commission of crime.

Family studies

If crime is a product of genetic determinism then it should show concordance in related individuals. In essence, crime should 'run in the family'. This form of study has a long history. Dugdale (1875) inspected a prison in the USA and realised that six of the prisoners were related. He eventually traced hundreds of relatives in an attempt to assess the patterns of criminality in this family, who were nicknamed 'The Jukes'. There is more modern evidence which highlights that criminal parents are more likely to have children who become involved in criminal behaviour than parents who are law abiding. Farrington (1991) carried out a 30-year longitudinal study (i.e. following a group of subjects over many years) of working-class boys to examine if, when and why they became delinquent. It was found that 6 per cent of families were responsible for 50 per cent of the criminal acts reported. This appears to indicate that crime does have some kind of familial link, and geneticists argue that this is a result of the genetic transmission of genes that cause anti-social behaviour and crime.

Consider this

What is your view on the Nature or Genetic Determinism argument? Are you responsible for your own behaviour or is it your genes?

■ Nurture

The nurture side of the argument is equally compelling. The idea behind these perspectives is that our personal experiences are the main influences on our behaviour. For example, the Farrington study described above identifies that many crimes are committed by just a few families, which seems to indicate that there may be a genetic link. But it also highlighted that some of the primary factors associated with crime amongst working-class boys are:

- **Low family income** – Although poverty does not in itself cause crime, the economic deprivation which goes along with it may lead to individuals wanting a standard of life they cannot afford. This may in turn lead them to get this standard of life through illegitimate means – crime.
- **Poor child-rearing techniques** – Not all parents are effective in their child-rearing role. If parents do not care or do not show an interest in the behaviour of their children, then the children may be more likely to become delinquent. Equally, if children are raised in a violent home or with inconsistent discipline they may be less likely to have a clear understanding of social boundaries and be more likely to transgress them.
- **Large families** – Farrington discovered that families with many children were more likely to have some delinquent children. This may be because large families are very demanding and children may not always get the attention and guidance they need.
- **Low educational achievement** – Education is the key to economic success and low educational achievement can mean poverty or unemployment in adult life.

These factors would seem to support the notion that criminal behaviour is a product of an individual's environment rather than an inherited tendency. Sutherland's Differential Association Theory (1939) also supports the environmental view. He argues that, as with any other form of behaviour, criminality is learned. The socialisation of children by their parents and their interaction with their peer group is of paramount importance in examining why individuals become criminals.

Conclusion to 'nature vs nurture' debate

The debate surrounding nature/nurture is unlikely to be resolved any time soon. The evidence that each side of the argument produces often does not show the full picture of crime and leaves many questions unanswered.

The current debate centres not around nature or nurture alone, but how these two different perspectives could be combined to explain criminal behaviour. This of course would have tremendous use in public services such as the police, courts, prison and probation.

Remember!

- Nature is the argument that criminals are born.
- Nurture is the argument that criminals are made.
- There is evidence on both sides of the debate.
- The real relationship between nature and nurture is still unknown.

Theory into practice

Saara and Sureya are non-identical twins who are raised in the same home environment, with their younger brother Parvis and mother and father. When the twins are 16 their younger brother, who is 14, begins to get into trouble at school. This trouble eventually becomes more serious and Parvis is sent to a young offender institution at the age of 15. The twins' father also had a history of petty crime in his youth, but is a responsible and upstanding citizen now. The twins' mother has never been involved in crime.

- How would supporters of the nature argument explain how Parvis became involved in breaking the law? What about supporters of the nurture argument?
- What is the likelihood that the twins will engage in criminal activity?
- How might Saara and Sureya differ in concordance from identical twins?
- Would the twins' mother be likely to become criminal?

Assessment activity 18.1

In this assessment you are required to examine the approaches to psychology in order to address the following task:

1. Produce a written report which describes the approaches to psychology with one example of each type. **P2**

Grading tips

P2 In your own words describe the approaches to psychology which have been outlined, such as humanist and cognitive.

Consider this

If crime is linked to genetic inheritance, how might this affect:

- The way criminals are sentenced?
- The way crime is prevented?
- What impact would it have on the services?

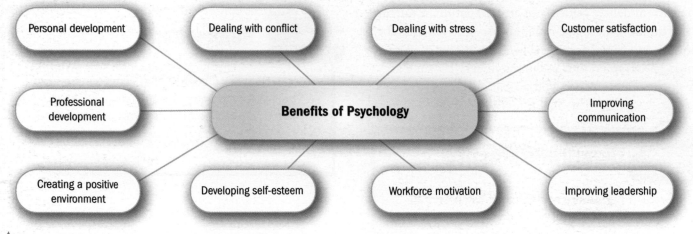

▲ Figure 18.3 Psychology can have many benefits for public service workers

Benefits of psychology

There are lots of reasons to use psychology within large organisations such as the public services, including financial benefits and motivation. These uses benefit both the individual themselves, small teams and the organisation as a whole. We will now examine these benefits in more detail.

Dealing with stress

Public service work, whether uniformed (such as the police, firefighters or nurses) or non-uniformed (such as teachers, lecturers and probation officers), comes with a certain amount of stress attached to the job. This stress may be caused by:

- low pay compared to the private sector
- dealing with a potentially hostile client group
- working in rigidly hierarchical employment structures that ensure the individuals at the lowest rung on the ladder must implement policies and initiatives they have had no input in developing
- the risk of physical assault and verbal abuse
- the demands of the government to constantly work harder with fewer resources.

Top this off with mountains of paperwork and long hours which cause disruption to personal relationships and you have a recipe for a workforce prone to stress-related illnesses and psychological problems.

Psychology can be used by the particular organisation concerned to try to reduce the impact of these stresses on the workforce. This may take the form of actively reducing the stress by ensuring limited working hours or providing mechanisms to help the workforce deal with stress more effectively, such as sports facilities or in-house counselling.

Millions of pounds are lost every year due to staff absences from stress. It is in the interests of an organisation to realise that lowering levels of stress will make them more efficient, not less. The organisation and the individual can use their knowledge of psychology to reduce stress and increase motivation and efficiency by identifying psychological and physiological stressors such as:

- **Noise levels** – Continuously high noise levels have been linked to ulcers and high blood pressure (Evans *et al*, 1995). This understanding can inform employers on how to reduce high noise levels in order to make a better working environment for public service employees in order to improve efficiency and motivation.
- **Levels of light** – Generally the better the levels of light the better the work performance. Psychology in this instance can be incorporated into the design of buildings so that light levels are bright enough to motivate and encourage enhanced work performance.

▲ **The effects of workplace stress are damaging for employees and employers**

- **Temperature** – Both extremes of high and low temperature cause stress and inability to perform work. The Health and Safety at Work Act acknowledges the importance of a good working temperature, but optimum working temperatures can be evaluated and examined by psychologists who can save organisations a great deal of money by helping to maximise the productivity of employees.

- **Space** – Lack of personal space, overcrowding and lack of privacy cause stress in individuals. Unfortunately this is often a feature that many public service workers deal with, and indeed many other workers, including office workers, also suffer in the same way. Discoveries in this field by psychologists can be incorporated into the design of buildings and the structuring of offices to help workers feel more comfortable in their environment.

- **Shift work** – Again a very common feature in public service life. Sparks and Cooper (1997) found that

the longer the hours worked the less productive an individual is and the more likely they are to suffer from stress-related illness. Tepas *et al* (1985) found that divorce was 50 per cent more common amongst night shift workers than others. Having knowledge such as this can help employers change shift patterns to a less damaging format and offer support mechanisms for employees who find it difficult to adjust.

It is important to note that many public service workers actually thrive on stress factors such as these because they add variety and excitement to the nature of the work. Although there is no doubt that public service life can be stressful at times it is also personally rewarding and professionally fulfilling.

However, even simple changes can mean that the individual, team and organisation will be more motivated to succeed and will therefore be more financially productive or efficient.

Case study: Psychology's role in improving the workplace

A study entitled 'Environmental Satisfaction in Open-Plan Environments: Effects of Workstation Size, Partition Height and Windows' by Charles and Veitch (2002) examined some of the characteristics of open-plan offices to see if they made any difference to the productivity and general satisfaction of employees. The study examined the individuals' workstation areas (their desk and surrounding environment), their partition height (which indicates how much privacy they have) and the presence of windows near to the person's work environment. It found that the larger the person's workspace the better they felt about performing their role. The presence of a window close by also improved a person's satisfaction with their environment and the more privacy they had the better they felt about working in the environment.

1. If you were a psychologist how would you use the results of this study to improve the working areas in a police station?

2. Why do you think that the amount of space a person has to work in matters to them?

3. Why might the presence of a window make people feel better about their work environment?

4. Why is privacy in the workplace important? Consider this in a public service office particularly.

Improving communication

Psychologists have spent a great deal of time researching communications in organisations and between individuals. It forms a large part of a later section of this unit – see section 18.2 on page 139.

Workforce motivation

Psychological studies have focused greatly on the issue of motivation, analysing how and why individuals can be motivated to perform better and be more positive. You will find more information on this in *Unit 2: Team leadership in the uniformed public services* and *Unit 4: Team development in public services.*

Creating a positive environment

Customers, clients and staff need a positive environment in which to interact and perform their respective roles. A negative environment harms productivity. For example, if a police station reception was dirty and intimidating fewer people would be inclined to go in to report a crime. Equally, if the offices of a building are dirty and intimidating there may be increased absenteeism by staff who dislike the environment. Psychological studies have found optimum conditions which are likely to be conducive to the productivity and comfort of all, and they are able to highlight the benefits of good working conditions. This information can help with the physical design of buildings and with training for managers on how to deal with members of staff.

Professional development

Psychology has a role to play in the effectiveness of appraisal systems, which have a direct impact on the professional development undertaken by an individual. Appraisals outline an individual's strengths and areas that require development and training. Effective appraisal systems may mean the difference between promotion and standing still within an organisation.

Dealing with conflict

Dealing with conflict is a daily part of the professional life of most individuals. However, this is more pronounced in the lives of public service workers who may deal with conflict from:

- the public
- colleagues
- superiors
- the government
- media
- pressure groups
- family.

Psychology can provide people with useful tools to avoid, minimise and resolve conflict. This is because they will have a larger range of coping techniques and a deeper understanding of what motivates others to act the way they do. They will also understand themselves better and control their response to difficult situations. This is discussed in more detail later in this chapter.

Personal development

The humanistic approach to psychology argued by Maslow and Rogers puts an individual's need for self-development and self-actualisation at the forefront of psychological theory. People have a natural urge to try and reach their full potential. An understanding of psychology can help them to be aware of and overcome barriers to this self-fulfilment and achieve their goals more quickly and efficiently.

Improving leadership

Confident and effective leadership skills are of vital importance in a public service organisation and many people at various ranks have these skills. Unfortunately some do not and this is where problems can occur. Psychology can help good leaders become better and help poor leaders understand and overcome the challenges they face. Effective and ineffective leadership is discussed in detail in *Unit 2: Team leadership in the public services*, but consider the case study on the following page.

Developing self-esteem

An understanding of psychology can be used by organisational managers to improve the self-esteem of their employees. Equally, individuals themselves can use psychology to promote their own self-esteem. Self-esteem and self-confidence are important components in performing stressful and difficult jobs effectively.

Customer satisfaction

Although it is not often seen this way, the public services have a customer base of 60 million individuals – the entire UK population. In addition they service numerous other thousands of individuals abroad in delivering humanitarian aid and engaging in UN-backed military action such as, recently, in the Balkans, Afghanistan and Iraq. Like any other organisation, the public services must keep their customers satisfied with their performance or the government would be forced to change, reform or even replace the functions that the public services currently call their own. Psychology can offer techniques on how to deal with customers effectively and sensitively, regardless of how angry, upset, grief stricken or drunk they may be. This is vital in training officers to deal with the public courteously and respectfully.

People approach everyday situations very differently from each other. For example, one person's approach to a violent situation may defuse it, while another person's approach may escalate it. For example if you refer to the case study below (page 142) on using psychology to deal with conflict, you will see that if WPC Dev and PC Jensen had approached the situation in an aggressive manner they might have arrested a man with a head injury for being drunk when in actual fact his head injury could have caused his bizarre behaviour and he might have been a victim of a violent crime. Taking a more considered approach would have calmed the situation, ensuring that the man received medical treatment and calmed the angry shopkeeper, making a better and safer situation for all parties. This shows the usefulness in having a considered understanding of how psychology can enhance the professional role of public service officers. It is a useful skill to be able to assess how your colleagues and your potential customers (the general public) approach situations from a psychological standpoint.

Case study: Using psychology to improve leadership

Penny is the leader of a tightly knit and highly effective team of workers who are widely respected within the educational organisation they inhabit. Penny's team sits within a larger management structure headed by Rhys, who is Penny's line manager. Rhys has poor relations with Penny's team largely because he accords them no professional respect, constantly criticises them and ensures Penny does a great deal of the work that is actually within his remit to do.

Penny is justifiably proud of her team and the achievements they have earned and she understands their resentment, as she has also had to deal with unfounded criticism from Rhys. Penny suspects that Rhys feels threatened by the success of the team and is trying to consolidate his own leadership position by putting others down.

1. **How could an understanding of psychology help Penny understand and deal with Rhys' behaviour?**

2. **How could an understanding of psychology be used by Rhys himself to understand his actions?**

3. **What aspects of psychology could Penny use to motivate her disgruntled team?**

4. **How could psychology improve the flow of communication between all concerned?**

5. **What aspects of psychology could help Penny deal with the conflicts she faces?**

Assessment activity 18.2

In this assessment you are required to show how understanding the approaches to psychology can benefit the public service and the impact this will have on public service employees.

1. Research, prepare and present a PowerPoint presentation that describes the benefits of understanding the approaches to psychology within the public services. **P3**

2. Produce some supporting notes that assess how the different approaches to psychology will have an effect on employees in any public service employment. **M2**

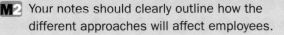

Grading tips

P3 These are straightforward criteria. Describe in your own words the benefits that understanding the approaches to psychology can bring to an organisation in terms of improved efficiency and a motivated workforce.

M2 Your notes should clearly outline how the different approaches will affect employees.

Another aspect of human behaviour, which is particularly relevant for individuals wishing to have a career in the public services, is the field of communication. Communication is an integral part of all our lives and a critical factor in most areas of employment, especially when the job involves substantial contact with the public and teamwork situations with colleagues – both of which occur almost all the time in public service work.

Communication is a very complex process, although most people don't give a thought to the complexities involved in it simply because they communicate all the time and don't notice it as it happens. We use all of our senses when we communicate with others:

- sight
- hearing
- touch
- taste
- smell.

Communication is not just about being understood. It is a mechanism to both give and receive messages, which we need in order to interpret the situation and environment around us and act accordingly. When we communicate with others we do not simply speak to them. In fact, studies suggest that what we say is far less important than how we say it: the tone of voice we use, our facial expressions and body language.

Types of communication behaviour

Our senses are involved in giving and receiving communication all the time, although we may often not be directly conscious of it. We will examine four main styles of communication:

- aggressive
- avoidance
- submissive
- assertive.

We will then examine the benefits of effective communication to the public services.

Aggressive

Communicators who use an aggressive style may be generally disliked because they intimidate others. It may be that their body language is threatening, they are loud, dominant and abrupt in verbal communication, and they may often interrupt and shout over others, which indicates very poor listening skills.

As a public service employee it is likely that you will encounter this communication from members of the general public as you conduct your duties. Less frequently you may encounter it in a colleague or a boss. This form of behaviour can be considered bullying and should never be accepted. However, the best way to deal with it is rarely to respond in kind. Responding to aggression with aggression simply leads to a worse situation for all concerned. In addition, you should never behave in an aggressive manner to the public, even on occasions where you may be called upon to restrain someone or otherwise stop certain behaviours. A good public service officer will maintain a calm temperament and take action based on the situation rather than on feelings of anger or resentment.

Aggressive communicators may have very low self-esteem and feel unable to control a situation without showing anger and aggression. By doing so they put their own rights above the rights of anyone else and avoid responsibility for the way they behave. Aggressive managers may give destructive feedback to employees, which harms their confidence and work performance. They also tend to create confrontational situations or initiate conflict to suit themselves. This can have a detrimental effect on the workforce and the organisation itself.

Advantages	Disadvantages
• You will be heard. • You may get what you want.	• You will be feared not respected. • You may cause aggression in others. • You may be personally and professionally disliked. • May cost job prospects. • You may be labelled a bully. • You are likely to be a poor manager.

Table 18.1 Advantages and disadvantages of aggressive communicators

Avoidance

Avoidance is a technique that people can use to avoid or evade conflict, communication and responsibility. It involves things such as not responding to requests, not attending meetings, and planning situations to ensure that nothing is asked or requested of you. A person who uses this technique is unlikely to become involved in conflict or even recognise that there is a problem because to do so would require effort on their part.

Managers who avoid conflict are letting down their employees. They are unlikely to provide any feedback on performance, engage with the appraisal process or help with staff development. Equally they are unlikely to take the concerns or complaints of employees seriously, which can lead to a reduction in staff morale and efficiency.

Advantages	Disadvantages
• You will avoid confrontation. • Your workload will be reduced.	• You will not be professionally respected. • You may lose your job. • You are unlikely to be given a position of responsibility.

Table 18.2 Advantages and disadvantages of avoidance

Submissive

Submissive communicators generally defer to the opinions of those with more power and can be very hesitant in putting across their own message. A submissive approach to communication is unlikely to command authority and respect, making it an inappropriate choice for the majority of public service work.

Many people use submissive communication in their daily lives without being aware of it. It may appear when you are speaking to your tutor or your boss at work. It may even be apparent when you communicate with your friends and parents. Submissive communicators have body language designed to make them appear smaller, and may avoid eye contact. This style is in direct opposition to aggressive communicators, who may stare and whose body language is designed to make them appear larger. Often submissive communicators want to keep the peace and find it very hard to say no, as they prefer to please people by allowing them to have their own way.

Submissive managers are rare, but they can be found. They are not very effective in resolving conflict between staff members or the public as they want to please everyone rather than address the issues at hand. Submissive managers often create more conflict because of their strategy of telling individuals what they want to hear rather than the truth. This may mean giving individuals positive feedback when their performance doesn't warrant it.

Advantages	Disadvantages
• You may be able to keep out of trouble and away from conflict. • It requires less effort and commitment. • It is effective if you want to avoid drawing attention to yourself.	• You will not be respected. • You may be ignored. • You are unlikely to be placed in positions of leadership or responsibility. • You may be considered weak. • You may get so frustrated that you have an aggressive outburst.

Table 18.3 Advantages and disadvantages of submissive communication

Assertive

Assertive communication strikes a balance between all the styles we have examined. It ensures communication is direct and clear, but still has room for other aspects of communication such as sympathy, empathy and negotiation. Body language may be relaxed but alert, and eye contact is maintained but it does not generate a feeling of tension in the other person. It has the capacity to calm a tense situation and it commands authority through respect, not fear.

A key component of assertive communication is confidence. A genuinely confident person does not need to shout and scream to make a point; nor do they agree with others for the sake of a quiet life. An assertive manager is able to deal with conflict effectively by communication and negotiation. They are able to provide constructive feedback on the performance of employees and their honesty can help dcfusc conflicts.

Advantages	Disadvantages
• You will be heard and are more likely to be respected. • Actions are more likely to come from your message. • You are more likely to be put in positions of responsibility and leadership. • You can respect yourself. • You will develop confidence. • You will be less stressed.	• Requires you to be firm and polite even when others are not. • Requires energy and commitment. • Can be mistaken for aggression by some people.

Table 18.4 Advantages and disadvantages of assertive communication

Remember!

- There are various styles of communication.
- Good communicators ensure that they can adapt their style to the situation.
- The most productive form of communication in the public services is assertive communication.
- Aggressive communication styles can be considered bullying and usually show an individual has little confidence.
- A submissive communicator is unlikely to be given positions of responsibility and leadership.

The benefits of understanding communication

There are many benefits to understanding communication. If communication in your organisation is clear and direct:

- there will be less chance of misunderstandings and mistakes, which can be very expensive to correct
- your organisation should perform more efficiently, which adds to efficiency and saves money
- employees are happier and more motivated because they know exactly what they have to do and why
- customers of your organisation will be happier since they will receive a better service from the employees
- your organisation can achieve its overall aims and objectives with more success.

Assessment activity 18.3

This assessment activity requires you to show your understanding of communication behaviour and its impact on the public services. Produce a short 10-minute role-play that answers the following questions.

1. Describe different types of communication behaviour and their benefits in the public services. **P1**

2. Analyse how communication behaviour can affect colleagues and members of the public when working in any area of public service employment. **M1**

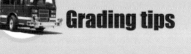

Grading tips

P1 A role-play is a good way for you to practically demonstrate each type of communication behaviour. Be sure to cover the four types: aggressive, avoidance, submissive and assertive.

M1 You should explain in detail how each type of communication behaviour can affect other people.

Understanding conflict is a very important part of public service life. It is likely that you will be exposed to conflict throughout your career, whichever public service you choose to work in. There are many types of conflict you may encounter, such as:

- conflict between individuals
- conflict between an individual and a group
- public demonstrations
- conflict between teams and departments.

Consider this

What types of conflict have you experienced from the list (left)? Do you find dealing with one sort of conflict easier than dealing with another? Explain your answer.

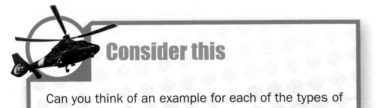

Consider this

Can you think of an example for each of the types of conflict listed above?

An understanding of psychology can help a public service officer deal with situations where there is the potential for conflict. Consider the case study below.

Areas of conflict

Conflict can occur for many reasons. Since we are all unique individuals the reasons why we feel conflict will be equally unique. A situation in which you may feel at home may cause someone else to feel uncomfortable. It is important to remember that the key to being good at managing conflict is understanding that not everyone feels the same way about it.

There are some common reasons why conflict might occur. These are detailed below with examples.

Case study: Using psychology to deal with conflict

PC Jensen and WPC Dev have been called out in response to calls from the public about a disturbance in a local shopping centre. When they arrive on the scene they find a man in a state of disarray, shouting abuse to passers-by and bleeding heavily from a head wound. One of the local shopkeepers has left his shop and is behaving very aggressively towards the injured man, who he believes to be drunk. Neither of the police officers can smell alcohol on the injured man and attempt to resolve the situation.

1. **How could the police officers use psychology to diffuse the situation?**

2. **Considering your own knowledge of psychology, what explanation would you give to the officers as to why the man who is shouting abuse might be behaving this way?**

3. **How do you think psychology would explain the actions of the shopkeeper?**

4. **If you were one of the police officers in this situation, what would your first action be?**

5. **How important in resolving conflict is an understanding of psychology and the reasons that people behave the way they do?**

Not fitting in or feeling isolated at work

There are some people who have the confidence and ability to fit into every social situation they face and there are those who do not and may feel very awkward and isolated. Equally there are teams that welcome new people and encourage them to be part of their structure and there are teams that dislike newcomers. In these situations conflict can occur if the individual feels they are being deliberately isolated or the team feels that a member is not worthy of joining them. This can lead to reduced motivation and performance for both the individual and the team, which can have an impact on the efficiency of the organisation as a whole. On some occasions an individual can be left isolated for reasons which are outside their control, such as race, gender and disability. Although discrimination is outlawed it is still a reality for many people in the workplace. This may include behaviour such as sexual harassment or assault, racist name-calling or prevention of advancement.

Management and staff conflicts

This is very common and will happen in most workplaces at some point in time. The conflicts usually arise out of contractual issues such as:

- pay
- leave
- pensions
- working hours
- shift patterns
- changes to duties or job roles.

When staff and management are in conflict then productivity is likely to be lowered, as employees are less motivated to work hard for an employer they see as being unfair. The employees might band together and take collective action against their employer in the form of working to rule and strikes. This usually involves the organisation's union. Examples of this include the Fire Brigade strikes in 2004 and the postal worker strikes in 2007.

Public demonstrations

Sometimes the general public fall into conflict with local or central government on issues which directly affect them. The right of the public to peacefully protest is a fundamental right they should be accorded. After all, the government is elected to serve the people. If the people are unhappy they should have the right to make this known.

▲ The police can experience a conflict of interests at public demonstrations

There have been public demonstrations on a whole host of issues such as:

- war
- abortion
- homosexuality
- school closures
- changes to terror laws
- tax.

In some countries the right of the public to protest is severely restricted or even banned and they have no way legal way of expressing their grievances to the government. The public services are in a difficult position here because they are required to police and in some cases restrict the right to protest, even though they may actually agree with what the protestors are fighting for.

Assessment activity 18.4

This assessment activity requires you to demonstrate an understanding of how and why conflict occurs in order to address the following question:

1. Produce an A3 poster which describes the type of and reasons for conflict in the public services. **P4**

Grading tips

P4 Make sure your poster is professional and informative and clearly describes different types of conflict and why it can occur.

Knowing how to resolve conflict once it has arisen is a key aspect of any work where you have to deal with the public and with colleagues. Conflict management and prevention techniques are transferable skills that you can use in your personal as well as your professional life.

Conflict management techniques

Conflict management techniques are tactics and strategies you can use to prevent and resolve conflict. They are practical solutions you can use in your interaction with the public and colleagues. They may not always be successful, but you will get better with practice. There are two main ways of managing conflict you need to be aware of: prevention and reducing escalation.

Prevention of conflict

This means identifying a problem that might be occurring early enough for it to be resolved quickly and easily. A skilled public service officer or manager will be able to spot situations that have the potential to become confrontational and will put in place techniques to resolve it. If you are in an organisation, this might include strategies such as teambuilding. Teambuilding is supposed to enable teams to work together in a different setting in order for them to understand how the others work best. Or, if you are a police officer working with the public, simply moving someone along might be enough to avoid a violent conflict with another person.

Reducing escalation

This is another important technique which involves calming a situation which is already occurring. This can be done in many ways such as your tone of voice, eye contact, body language and humour. Acting assertively can calm a situation down and allow the people concerned to refocus on what they want to gain from the situation. Remember that factors such as alcohol, drugs and attitude may prevent you from reducing the conflict – in essence some situations may be beyond your control.

Styles of conflict management

Styles of conflict management are also very important in how conflict is dealt with. *Unit 2: Team leadership in the uniformed public services* and *Unit 4: Team development in public services* examine this in more detail.

In terms of practical techniques you can use to prevent or reduce conflict, these fall into two main categories: formal and informal. As a general rule you would only move on to the formal mechanisms when the informal mechanisms have had little or no effect or when the conflict was so serious that a formal response was the only sensible solution.

Informal actions

■ Mentoring

Mentoring is the process of pairing up a more experienced member of staff with a less experienced one in order to assist and help the inexperienced member of staff to become proficient and confident in their role. This is often used in the police service, where probationers are allocated to a more experienced police officer during their training. Mentoring can help a new member of staff resolve conflict as they can look to their mentor for advice and guidance. A method of mutual mentoring is called the 'buddy' system. This is where a pair of individuals help and assist each other in the execution of their duties, the idea being that if one person is struggling with a conflict or difficulty the other one will know how to help and vice versa. Many public service officers or public sector workers also have a role model. This is a person they look up to and respect and may try to emulate.

■ Sharing best practice

This is an informal technique that most organisations use to improve their performance and increase their efficiency. It involves looking at an individual or a departmental team who are excellent in their job role and cascading what they do to other parts of the organisation, so everyone can learn from their example or adapt their practice to improve performance.

■ Socialisation and humour

These are some of the most useful tools in resolving conflict. A team that bonds well socially and enjoys a shared sense of humour is likely to be able to resolve conflicts much more easily than a team that doesn't. Humour is a tremendously important tool for diffusing conflict, but care must be taken not to use it inappropriately because then it can make the situation far worse.

■ Acts of gratitude and kindness

Maintaining a good atmosphere is key in reducing conflict. Simple gestures such as saying thank you and showing appreciation for the work people do can reduce tensions and help people feel much more motivated.

Formal actions

■ Codes of behaviour

Organisations often produce formal codes of conduct for their employees that relate to behaviour such as personal conduct, timekeeping, uniforms, absences and performance, to name just a few. These codes of conduct often have a disciplinary policy attached to them in the form of sanctions. Sanctions are methods of punishment that are used when the code of conduct is broken. Sanctions can either be formal, such as downgrading, loss of pay or job, or informal, such as an interview with a manager or being placed on unwelcome duties. The idea of a code of behaviour with sanctions is that if everyone knows the standards of behaviour that are expected from them then conflict will be kept to a minimum.

■ Retraining

This is when a member of staff has poor job performance or has been on other duties for a significant length of time and needs to retrain to become more efficient in their role. It is also used to good effect in conflict management, as you can train all employees in how to deal with conflict and equality and diversity issues.

■ Internal mediators and advisors

These are trained people within an organisation who are used to diffuse or resolve conflict as unbiased outsiders. They can be very effective as they do not favour one side or the other; they are simply there to help resolve a problem.

■ Record keeping

Another method of resolving conflict is to keep records of individuals' behaviour. For example, if a manager and employee are in disagreement over an issue of punctuality it would help if the manager had a record of lateness to which they could refer. Written records are useful tools in resolving conflict as they provide evidence for one side or the other which may put the issue to rest.

Assessment activity 18.5

In this assessment activity you must demonstrate that you know the ways that conflict can be prevented and resolved in order to answer the following questions:

1. Produce a written report that describes ways of overcoming conflict between groups and individuals.

   P5

2. Your report should also compare the effectiveness of two different methods of overcoming conflict between individuals working in any area of public service employment.

   M3

3. Your report should further include an evaluation of two methods of resolving conflict in any public service employment.

   D1

Grading tips

P5 This is a straightforward description of how conflict can be overcome.

M3 This is a comparison. You should choose two different methods of overcoming conflict, such as humour and record keeping, and compare how effective they are.

D1 An evaluation is where you make a reasoned conclusion about how effective two methods of resolving conflict are.

Knowledge check

1. Which psychological theory is Carl Rogers associated with?

2. Who developed the pyschoanalytic theory?

3. What are the benefits of understanding psychology to individuals?

4. Describe the key features of aggressive communication.

5. How does assertive communication differ from submissive?

6. What types of conflict are the public services likely to encounter?

7. What are the most common reasons for conflict?

8. Describe two informal actions someone could take that might reduce or prevent conflict.

9. What is the buddy system?

10. What is a mentor?

Preparation for assessment

As part of your training as a new member of the Territorial Army you are taught about how understanding behaviour is a crucial part of doing the role well. You realise this is a weak area for you and decide to draw up a revision booklet that will help you remember all the key aspects of human behaviour such as conflict, communication and approaches to psychology. Your booklet should answer the following questions:

1. Describe different types of communication behaviour and their benefits in the public services. **P1**

2. Analyse how communication behaviour can affect colleagues and members of the public when working in any area of public service employment. **M1**

3. Describe approaches to psychology with one example of each type. **P2**

4. Describe the benefits of understanding approaches to psychology within the public services. **P3**

5. Assess how the different approaches to psychology will have an effect on employees in any public service employment. **M2**

6. Describe the types of and reasons for conflict in the public services. **P4**

7. Describe ways of overcoming conflict between groups and individuals. **P5**

8. Compare the effectiveness of two different methods of overcoming conflict between individuals working in any area of public service employment. **M3**

9. Evaluate two methods of resolving conflict in any public service employment. **D1**

Grading criteria	Activity	Pg no.		
To achieve a pass grade the evidence must show that the learner is able to:			To achieve a merit grade the evidence must show that the learner is able to:	To achieve a distinction grade the evidence must show that the learner is able to:
P1 Describe different types of communication behaviour and their benefits in the public services	18.3	141	**M1** Analyse how communication behaviour can affect colleagues and members of the public when working in any area of public service employment	
P2 Describe approaches to psychology with one example of each type	18.1	133		
P3 Describe the benefits of understanding approaches to psychology within the public services	18.2	138	**M2** Assess how the different approaches to psychology will have an effect on employees in any public service employment	**D1** Evaluate two methods of resolving conflict in any public service employment.
P4 Describe the types of and reasons for conflict in the public services	18.4	143	**M3** Compare the effectiveness of two different methods of overcoming conflict between individuals working in any area of public service employment.	
P5 Describe ways of overcoming conflict between groups and individuals.	18.5	145		

Communication and technology in the uniformed public services

Introduction

This unit investigates the equipment and skills used to communicate within the uniformed public services. During the unit you should develop and practise skills that will be of value in the context of public service work and further study. This includes specific formalised written communication used in this specialist area of work, and will give you an idea of the different ways the uniformed public services communicate on a day-to-day basis.

This unit explores the different forms of communication transmission and radio communication, and you should have the opportunity to practise these, using the techniques and skills developed throughout the unit. You will explore how the uniformed public services use different types of technological systems to support them in their difficult job. Particular focus is placed on the different types of equipment used by the uniformed public services and the benefits gained by the uniformed public services through using such equipment. This will help you to understand the types of equipment used and identify the skills required in the public services. You will also develop some of these skills for yourself during the practical elements of the unit.

This unit offers you the opportunity to demonstrate and build upon the key skills of communication and ICT. You will need to work closely with others to perform some of the practical tasks and problem solving exercises.

After completing this unit you should be able to achieve the following outcomes:
- Understand formal written communication used in the public services
- Understand different types of communication systems
- Know how to use the radio procedure of a uniformed public service
- Know the different types of technological systems used by the uniformed public services.

Thinking points

The unit is essential in developing your communication skills. Communication is an essential component when working in a uniformed public service team and all the services will use a range of communication methods. This means that potential uniformed public service workers need to understand the various formal and informal forms of written communication, along with the different types of communication systems such as radios and the more recent communication systems such as Bluetooth and the Internet.

Consider the ways you might communicate with others and consider the situations when certain modes of communication would be more appropriate.

- For example, if you came across a road traffic incident would you text someone for assistance? You should be able to put the theory of the unit into practice both in and out of an educational setting. This means that you should have the opportunity to explore and reinforce these skills in a variety of situations.

Communication skills are critical as uniformed public services employees often work in situations that rely on others to carry out their individual roles effectively. This is often in dangerous situations, such as responding and dealing with a major incident, when multiple services will be involved. In order to communicate effectively you need to be able to use various types of equipment effectively, such as correct radio procedures and understand the need for specialist equipment.

- Think about how you would communicate with several uniformed services at the same time, and coordinate them effectively.
- Think about how you would search for survivors if you came across a factory building that had collapsed due to an explosion.

Formal written communications

Each branch of the public services has developed its own, very specific, procedures for written communication in the form of: content, format and language. These are often updated on a regular basis so it is important that you are aware of this when completing your own research. Always check that you are looking at the most recent information. Another problem facing you, and this book, is that much of the information surrounding these documents is confidential. However there are constants and similarities and these are covered below.

Letters

The vast majority of letters sent inside the public services will be of a formal nature. Letters which relay official information such as orders or schedules should always be of a formal nature. The language of formal letters is straight to the point and the information is often numbered. Demi formal letters are used when communicating on a person-to-person basis, for example an official letter thanking someone for a job well done or for hospitality shown on a visit. Here is an example of a formal letter set out in the standard format used by the Army.

RESTRICTED (i)

S/TGB/121 (iv)

2L1
AN Army Barracks
Soldierville (ii)
Armyshire

AN Army Barracks ext 222

5 Sep 2007 (iii)

Internal Information (v)
Captain BE Alert

Training Ammunition

Reference our telephone conversation of 4 Sep 2007.

1 The allotment of training ammunition for 51 mm mortars has been delayed until 20 Sep 2007

2 Your unit will now use Field Firing Range 2 on 22 Sep 2007 instead of Field Firing Range 1 on 16 Sep 2007 (vi)

Capt IAM Ready

Captain IAM Ready

Distribution
External: (vii)
Internal: (viii)
Captain BE Alert
Action: (ix)
QM
Wpn Trg Offr
Information: (x)
2iC
RSM

▲ **Example of a formal letter as used in the Army**

■ Explaining the letter

   i. Security classification

   ii. Recipient's address

   iii. Date

   iv. Reference code

   v. Sender

   vi. Information which is being communicated. Note the brevity of the language.

   vii. External recipients (none in this case)

   viii. Internal recipients

   ix. Who will action the letter, in this case the Quarter Master and Weapons Training Officer. Note the use of abbreviations.

   x. Who will receive a copy of this letter for information, in this case the 2nd in command and the Regimental Sergeant Major.

Obviously each public service will have a slightly different format for a formal letter, but with all letters the following aspects are very important.

■ Accuracy

Spelling should always be checked for accuracy. Equally as important is punctuation. 'I'm mad you left in a hurry' is very different from 'I'm mad, you left in a hurry'. In the first example the writer is angry at being left in the lurch. In the second example a third party ran away because the writer is insane!

The facts should be accurate. Any opinions stated should be clearly identified as such. For example: 'It is the opinion of this group that...'. Deductions should be justified and backed up with facts.

■ Language

The language used should be clear and unambiguous. The reader should not be left to ponder the meaning, as mistakes in the public services can be costly or even fatal. Communications should be brief, giving the reader the information needed in the shortest and clearest possible way. Abbreviations specific to each public service may be used.

■ Format

The writer should follow the set procedures for the format of each different type of communication, for example letters, memos or reports. All written communications should be dated and if relevant also include a time. During battle or times of national crisis this becomes essential. Pages should be numbered. If a document is dropped it is easier to organise it again and stops any mistakes occurring. When reference is made to another document, the title, author and date of that publication should be noted for cross-referencing. Longer documents, especially reports, often have appendices. These contain the detailed evidence used to support the findings and more often than not come in the form of data presented by means of charts and graphs. They are placed at the back of the document but are referenced at the relevant points, for example 'see Appendix 1.2'.

■ Identification

Each document should clearly identify the sender and/or the group they represent. It is often the case that a reference code is also used. Communications should also clearly state their destination.

The security classification or status of the document should be written clearly and centrally, often at the top of the first page. The Army for example uses: Top Secret, Secret, Confidential and Restricted, with each of these classifications having a defined audience.

Copies should be made and given to the relevant people using their correct rank or title, or simply filed.

Theory into practice

Collect examples of letters written by the Army, Royal Navy, Royal Marines, Royal Air Force, police, fire and ambulance services and Customs and Excise and compare the formats.

What similarities and differences are there?

Memos

Memos are most often sent internally within organisations, for example between stations within a regional Fire Brigade. They are a concise document that conveys essential information quickly by passing on information or updating staff of new initiatives

MEMO

To: Ann Entity

From: Dee Boss

Date: 30th November 2007

Subject: Guidelines on the use of pepper spray

Owing to a series of complaints regarding illness and negative side effects caused by the use of pepper spray in the apprehension of suspects, the constabulary has decided that with immediate effect pepper spray should not be used by police officers until further research has been conducted on the possible long-term effects.

▲ **An example of a police service memo**

or procedures. Each of the public services has its own standard format. These come in the form of pre-printed (often self-carbonating) memo pads for handwritten memos, or preset formatted templates for word processing. In today's electronic age, however, e-mail is rapidly taking over and is being used more and more by the public services, as it is a quicker and often more reliable method of communicating.

Memos can be laid out differently but they will generally have the following information on them:

1. Name of recipient/s
2. Name of sender/s
3. Date
4. Subject of memo
5. Body of text/instruction
6. Action expected of recipient/s

Memos can be written in the first or third person. Most memos within the public services will be written in the third person as it maintains formality and emphasises the main points between the sender and the recipients. Memos should be single-spaced, with an extra space between paragraphs. Longer memos may need sub-headings in the body of text. The memo should describe the key information concisely by stating what is required within a couple of sentences and then stating the action required by the recipient.

Consider this

Why is it important for language to be brief and clear?

Reports

Reports are often used to communicate the findings of specific investigations or to review the current state of affairs of public services in areas such as finance, procedures or performance issues. They are formal word processed documents and may include tables, charts and graphics. For example a report may be written on the findings of an investigation into the reaction times of the ambulance service. Reports are always presented in a formal manner and follow a similar format whatever the public service. In brief this is:

- a statement detailing the purpose of the investigation
- the details of the persons carrying out the investigation
- the name of the person(s) responsible for writing the report
- the date of both the investigation and publication of the report
- the status of the report, for example a final report, a draft report

- a summary of the main findings
- a detailed description of the findings
- proposals including a timeline
- appendices (often in the form of data, charts or graphs).

■ Annual reports

An annual report is a document which a public service will present to stakeholders. It will take the form of a sleek, colourful and professionally presented document.

Consider this

Choose three contrasting public services and list the possible stakeholders.

Theory into practice

A police service Annual Report is likely to include:

- **service structure** – a breakdown of the key personnel within the organisation (chief constable, etc.)
- **strategic aims** – this is an overall statement of purpose
- **strategic priorities** – these are the key priorities that the service has identified to action and be measured against
- **performance indicators** – this is a review of the success of the service against previous or continuing strategic priorities
- **policing performance** – this is a review of what it is doing generally in the local area
- **policing plan** – this can include long-term and short-term plans for the future of policing in that constabulary
- **financial statements** – this includes how much money is allocated to them and how it is spent, such as on police officers and tackling certain crimes through initiatives.

■ HM Inspection reports

All the public services are subjected to HM Inspections, which are conducted on behalf of the government on appointment by the queen. They are independent of both the government and the public service itself. They provide independent scrutiny, and will provide a report on their findings, including a grade for the public service and necessary actions needed before a subsequent inspection.

■ Audit reports

Audits can be conducted either internally by a finance team or externally by independent auditors. The public services are audited by the Audit Commission, which conducts an independent review and examination of all records and activities of the service to assess the adequacy of system controls, to ensure compliance with established policies and operational procedures, and to recommend necessary changes in controls, policies, or procedures.

The Audit Commission, which is an independent public body, will produce reports which highlight whether public money is being spent economically, efficiently, and effectively within the public services. The reports are aimed to help promote good practice within public services and improve the way money is spent.

The first three reports mentioned in this chapter should be made available to the public so that they can read the reports themselves.

■ Incident reports

There are many types of reports that have a predetermined structure and can be completed easily by a member of the public services or public on a day to day basis; these include the reporting of hate crime or non-urgent incidents to the police. The forms are either paper-based or electronic and are completed by filling in the blank sections.

POLICE INCIDENT REPORT

This form is to notify police of non-urgent matters in your local area such as anti-social behaviour.

Today's date................................

Date of incident .... Time of incident ....

Location of incident

....

Nature/Details of incident:
....
....
....
....
....
....

Was the matter reported to the police? **Yes / No**
If yes then please give reference number ....

The police may wish to discuss the matter further, please supply your contact details in order for us to respond to your complaint/concerns.

Name: ....
Address: ....
Telephone: ....

Would you be happy for the police to contact you? **Yes / No**

Once completed please drop the form into your local police station

▲ **Example of a Police Incident Report form**

Internet

The Internet is a worldwide, publicly accessible computer network. It consists of a series of millions of domestic, academic, business, and government networks, which together carry various information and services, such as web pages, e-mails and file sharing.

The World Wide Web (WWW) is the main service accessible via the Internet, which is linked together by a series of browsers, hyperlinks and URLs. The forms of communication found on the WWW – such as web sites, online newsletters and bulletin boards – will often contain news and information which is up-to-date. Like other forms of communication it can be changed and updated easily.

Advantages	Disadvantages
It is an immediate form of communication	Paper publications are more professional
Unlimited by space or time as your message is available 24 hours a day and seven days a week.	Electronic information can be lost easily
	Internet viruses can be costly if they corrupt software and hardware.
Allows an organisation to be accessible by millions of people all across the world.	People don't read the pages
	Little legal regulation of electronic information
Low cost to distribute information	It is replacing more traditional forms of communication such as face-to-face interaction

Table 20.1 Some advantages and disadvantages of the Internet

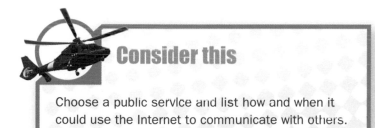

Consider this

Choose a public service and list how and when it could use the Internet to communicate with others.

E-mail

Electronic mail (e-mail) is the term given to the storage, composing, sending, forwarding and receiving of electronic messages. Organisations such as public services will have computer systems that have an internal e-mail service and the ability to receive and send messages externally. E-mail based communication is the most widely used written medium in any organisation.

The layout of an e-mail is very similar to a memo and to a large extent people will use e-mails when requesting information or giving instructions to others.

■ A basic e-mail will have the following information:

- **From:** the e-mail address or person's name (created automatically)

- **To:** the e-mail address/es or name (a person's name can be selected in most internal e-mails instead of writing the full e-mail address)
- **Date:** the time and date of the message will be created automatically when the message is sent
- **Subject:** a brief summary of the contents of the message.

The message will then follow and the rules on memos should be observed apart from the fact that most e-mails will be informal and in the first person.

▼ **The Internet is an essential technological tool**

Advantages	Disadvantages
Distance is no barrier	Very time consuming – people can spend 20%–50% of a working day using and sorting out e-mails
People can talk via e-mail through instant messenger services and Internet forums	The context and meaning of a message can be lost easily when e-mailing, as it is less formal
Messages are sent instantaneously at any time of the day – faster and more efficient	E-mails when overused can lead to an excess and duplication of information
Can distribute information to a large number of people at the same time for little cost, compared to the post	People can become bombarded with 'Spam' which is unsolicited bulk e-mail
It is easy to track and determine whether it has been received	
Most e-mail accounts are checked daily	
Environmentally friendly as it is paper free	

Table 20.2 Some advantages and disadvantages of e-mails compared to memos

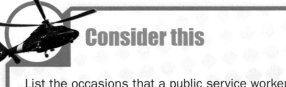

Consider this

List the occasions that a public service worker should send a memo instead of an e-mail.

Intranet

Intranets are private restricted electronic networks that are contained within an organisation. They are generally used to provide and share information internally within an organisation via the computer system's web space. It is very similar to the Internet, but it is only available to a certain group of people – for example, the employees within a hospital, but not the patients. This is done in order to ensure that confidential information is not made available to everyone with Internet access. In most cases you will have to log on to a computer within that organisation to use an Intranet, in order to ensure that it stays secure. All Intranets are different and are designed to meet the internal needs. Some employees may use it more than others but all employees should be able to access the information they need to help them do their jobs efficiently and effectively.

The kind of information that is shared and provided is likely to include the organisation's policies and procedures, key announcements, minutes from meetings or information about anything which has changed or is new. They are cheap, fast, and reliable and an ideal way of creating a non paper-based information centre. Intranets have been a neglected area in the past but there is now a great demand and requirement for employees to have easy access to information that they need for their work. For example, an army soldier should be able to access the Intranet easily and fill out and send a form electronically for additional leave, without directly requesting it.

Advantages	Disadvantages
All employees have access to the organisation's information	Need to know what information is available to them
The data is centralised and easy to access	Not all employees can easily use computers
Employees are empowered and have more control and independence	The system needs to be managed and updated 24 hours a day
Creates a safe environment for people to share information	The cost to train all people to use or update the Intranet
Helps employees to keep up to date with decisions and initiatives	
Helps to get the whole organisation involved with strategic planning	
Helps the organisation to be transparent	

Table 20.3 Advantages and disadvantages of Intranets

Other written communication

There are many different forms of written communication within any public service, and they also differ from service to service. This chapter has so far highlighted the most generic and common forms, but here are a few more examples.

Journals

Journals are a collection of printed work and records and they are similar in format to a magazine, but journals usually provide more scholarly or professional information, and they will use appropriate technical vocabulary. They are often used as a way for experts and researchers in a particular area to publish and share their findings with one another and the public, and are often referred to as periodicals. Journals are often published by an association or institution and contain articles relevant to their subject area.

Here are some examples of journals related to policing:
- *British Journal of Criminology*
- *Jane's Police Review* – the UK's best selling policing magazine
- *Police Professional* – journal of the UK Police Service
- *Police Magazine* – the magazine of the Police Federation of England and Wales.

PSIs and PSOs

Prison Service Instructions (PSIs) and Prison Service Orders (PSOs) outline the various rules, regulations and guidelines by which prisons are run. They shape the framework within which the whole prison service fulfils its obligations as a public authority. They are updated regularly so prison workers need to be aware of them and check for changes and updates. This means that all prison staff should have access to PSOs and PSIs.

■ Prison Service Instructions

Prison Service Instructions are mandatory instructions which have a definite expiry date. They are also used to introduce amendments to Prison Service Orders.

■ Prison Service Orders

Prison Service Orders are long-term mandatory instructions which are intended to last for an indefinite period.

Staff notices

These are similar to traditional posters and notices, and are used to make staff aware of up and coming events or useful information. They are usually placed on electronic notice boards which staff can access via their computers. In some cases – such as posters or printed notices – they can be placed visibly around the workplace. The noticeboards are very general and not all staff will find all the information relevant but they will act upon and read information relevant to them.

Standard operating procedures

Standard operating procedures can be stand-alone documents or supplemental information. They are a best described as guidelines to the current method of operating various procedures. The aim of standard operating procedures is to reduce variability by helping employees to make a quick decision. They often take the form of a written set of instructions detailing what the normal procedures of operating are in any given situation.

In the military it is the name given to a procedure or set of procedures which are performed when a certain situation arises. They are used where official doctrines are lacking, or it is unclear as to what to do in a specific situation.

Bulletins

Bulletins are similar to news or magazines articles, but are usually created in an electronic and digital format and can include pictures or images to make them appealing to the eye and more interesting than a standard staff notice. All the services have some form of bulletin and this can take the form of a newsletter which may be published daily, weekly or even monthly, depending on the nature of the service and the issues.

Consider this

Why is it important to have specific formats for written communications?

Assessment activity 20.1

1. Discuss with your tutor at least four different examples of formal written communication used in the public services. **P1**

2. Highlight two occasions when it may be necessary to complete a formal written communication in a uniformed public service and why this was the most appropriate method of communication. **M1**

Grading tips

P1 You need to provide evidence of research into four different forms of formal written communication used in the public services and you should be able to describe the purpose of each communication and the type of information contained in each.

M1 You need to show why it is necessary to use formal written communication on two occasions in the uniformed public services, and you must explain why the written communication was the most appropriate method of communication.

Radio is one of the most important forms of communication in the public services. It enables communication in the form of words and codes to be sent over vast distances and is not reliant on cables.

The most common type of radios used across the public services are the two-way hand held version. Simply speaking, this type of radio is made up of a transmitter and a receiver. The transmitter converts sounds into electromagnetic waves, which travel through the air. These are then picked up by a receiver and converted back into identifiable sounds.

One of the first wireless radios used by the public services was the PYE radio. This was used by the military during the Second World War. It was subsequently used by the police in 1947 in their patrol cars.

However, it should also be noted that the use of mobile phones is now on the increase. In time mobile phones will replace the more traditional radio as the main means of verbal communication in most public services.

The use of radios

The main differences between the types of radio used are:
- battery life and power supply
- number of channels
- weight and size
- frequency range.

Consider this

The choice of radio used by each public service will depend on a variety of factors. For each of the following, state the key characteristics and features that a radio should have:
- police officer
- paramedic
- soldier.

The biggest advantages of radios are their size and their usefulness for communicating quickly when outdoors. The downside is the relatively short distance that many are able to send and receive messages. Put briefly, the larger the unit, the greater the wattage, and therefore the further a message can be sent and received. An average retail radio model can usually manage one to three miles. The more sophisticated versions used by the public services operate over much greater distances.

There are many other problems associated with the use of radios, for example picking up transmission from outside individuals such as taxi firms, messages being listened to by members of the public and short battery life. The first two problems are virtually impossible to eradicate, as the airwaves are open to all. Frequency ranges are allocated by the government in line with international agreements to different groups, which means that you could pick up other people's messages whether you intend to or not.

To combat this, the public services are moving away from traditional radio frequency transmissions, and are developing and using a range of high-tech equipment and services. Some of them are described in this chapter.

Public service	Radios used for
Army	Base to unit contact Person to person contact in the field
Royal Navy	Ship to shore contact
Royal Air Force	Ground to air contact Contacting other mobile vehicles, for example refuelling tankers, ambulances, fire engines
Police	Contacting officers in vehicles, on horses or on the beat Communication between officers when pursuing suspects
Fire	Contacting officers when out with vehicles Officer to officer contact when fighting fires
Coastguards	Ship to shore contact Ship to ship contact when out searching for a lost craft/person
Ambulance	Base to ambulance personnel providing details of locations Ambulance personal to hospitals providing details of a patient's condition and estimated time to arrival at A&E
Prison service	Contacting officers on patrol in and around the prison establishment

Table 20.4 Some of the most common uses of radios in the public services

The armed forces, however, use more powerful, but more bulky versions, which cover far greater distances.

Radio communication within the Army

Within each public service, different types of radios are used. The Army uses a variety of radios which tend to be more powerful and cover a greater distance than standard radios; however they tend to be more bulky.

■ CLANSMAN

For many years the CLANSMAN was the Army's preferred communication system, having replaced the LARKSPUR system. It was used as the army's main tactical radio to help keep communication channels open between command and control and fighting units in the field.

▲ Secure tactical communication is essential in the field

■ BOWMAN

This system was first introduced in 2004 and is replacing the use of the CLANSMAN radio and some of the functions of the PTARMIGAN communication system.

The BOWMAN differs from the CLANSMAN as the system incorporates both the latest advances in digital voice communication and data communication technology.

Improvements offered by the BOWMAN radio system are:

- **Secure tactical communication:** There is no longer any need to encode and decode radio messages using a paper code
- **Enhanced situational awareness:** All BOWMAN radios have built in geographical positioning systems which will notify other radio users of their exact location which will reduce the need for open radio traffic, as troops can be located using this system
- **Reliable data network:** The system is even more secure in transferring digital communications, due to the quality of the software.

■ PTARMIGAN

PTARMIGAN remains the core equipment for the British Army Tactical Trunk Communications System. In time it will be replaced by a more advanced system called FALCON.

The system consists of a network of electronic exchanges or trunk switches connected by a satellite and multi-channel radio relay. It is a mobile battlefield system designed to create a secure communication network. It offers a range of communication formats such as voice, data, telegraph and fax. The PTARMIGAN also has a single channel radio access which allows easy access to command and control.

TYPE PRC 354 (VHF)	TYPE PRC 355 MANPACK (VHF)	TYPE HF RADIOS	TYPE High Capacity Data Radio (HCDR)	TYPE Personal Role Radio (PRR)
Description Used at section level and replaces the PRC 349 and 350.	**Description** Replaces the PRC 351 and 352. Used as the basic platoon radio and half the size and weight of a 351.	**Description** The Harris 5800 is the most common radio used. In the manpack form, the PRC 325 replaces the 320 and is smaller and lighter.	**Description** HCDR provides a high capacity data network. It complements the HF and VHF radios by providing the primary means for the transfer of large amounts of operational data between the various command and control centres.	**Description** A small transmitter-receiver that allows infantry soldiers to communicate over short distances. It works effectively through physical barriers such as brick walls. PRR are issued to every member of an eight-strong infantry section.
Frequency 30 – 88 MHz	**Frequency** 30 – 88 MHz	**Frequency** 1.6 – 30 MHz	**Frequency** Internet	**Frequency** Channels 256
Range 5km using a 2 metre whip antenna	**Range** Up to 30km	**Range** Up to 32km using a whip antenna Up to 800km using a near vertical incidence antenna. Unrestricted range using a skywave antenna	**Range:** N/A	**Range** 500 metres
Weight 1.2kg without batteries (heavier than the PRC 349)	**Weight** 3.2kg without batteries	**Weight** 4.5kg without batteries	**Weight** 11.3kg without batteries	**Weight** 1.5kg
Dimensions 94mm x 44mm x 195mm	**Dimensions** 88mm x 185mm x 234mm	**Dimensions** 267mm x 81mm x 43mm including battery box	**Dimensions** 275mm x 138mm x 381mm	**Dimensions** 380mm (longest dimension)
	Includes the Advanced Digital Radio plus (ADR+) radio waveform system			

Table 20.5 Radio systems currently in use in the Army

Radio frequency

All radio frequencies range from 3 Hz to 300 GHz

- High frequency (HF) is found between 30 Hz and 300 Hz
- Very High Frequency (VHF) is found between 300 Hz and 3 GHz
- Ultra High Frequency (UHF) is found between 3 GHz and 30 GHz

Common uses for VHF are FM radio broadcasts and TV transmission. VHF is also used by terrestrial navigation systems, marine communications and aircraft communications. UHF is also used for some TV transmissions but its most common use is for modern mobile phones.

Radio communication with the police

■ Airwave

Airwave is a digital radio communications network designed for the police, to provide a secure and flexible communications network. Airwave was introduced in 2000 and the government withdrew all of the existing VHF radio frequencies used by the emergency services in 2006.

Key features of Airwave:

- Airwave is a private mobile radio communications service
- the network is based on TETRA (Terrestrial Trunked Radio)
- the radio network operates on the 380 MHz to 400 MHz band
- it allows speech, data and image communications
- it replaced conventional analogue radios
- it ensures digital voice quality, which reduces any possible misunderstandings in messages
- it operates as a radio, mobile telephone and data terminal (for example, Automatic Vehicle and Person location)
- people can no longer listen into the police service transmissions as it is encrypted
- it operates nationally, so different constabularies can communicate easily
- it includes an emergency button on the terminal that an officer can press if he or she is in danger.

Other forms of communication

Fax machine

These are machines used to scan a paper form and transmit it as a coded digital image over the telephone system. The receiving machine then prints a copy of the original. A fax machine is made up of an image scanner, a phone, a printer and modem.

Fax machines are particularly useful in sending documents over long distances and unlike postal mail they are instantly delivered. The drawbacks can be the type of information you can send and the quality. With the emergence of e-mail they are becoming more outdated, as e-mail and a computer scanner or scanner/printer offer the same benefits without any of the drawbacks.

Object video

Object video is used to monitor and count people easily; it is useful in surveillance – particularly at large events such as football games and concerts. It can convert the video images collected easily and instantly into raw data and this can be used to detect, track and identify people who are behaving criminally or suspiciously.

Object video is essentially the intelligence software embedded and used in video tracking within CCTV systems, as a way of locating easily a moving object in real time using the camera network. It will alert the system operator automatically to help them identify any potential or current problems. Operators can use the software to fully analyse the situation as the data can be played back and contains both visual images and audio.

Lingu@net

Lingu@net is a virtual multilingual language centre. It offers on-line resources to help people learn a foreign language. Its aim is to promote a greater capability in languages across the European Union countries. It could be used amongst the public services to help police, fire or army officers to be more competent in additional languages – this will in turn help them interact with people in their wider communities. Apart from accessing the resources, people take part in e-mail exchanges, read and post weblogs and take part in live chats with other people.

Microwave

Microwave is electromagnetic radiation, with wavelengths which are longer than infrared but shorter than radio waves. Microwaves can be found between the frequencies of 300 MHz and 3 GHz and can be seen as a form of light energy.

Microwaves have several uses. Firstly, it is used within conventional microwave ovens found in most people's homes. However, it has been used in broadcasting and telecommunications systems. Before the invention of fibre optics it was used to conduct most long-distance telephone calls. Radars also use microwaves to detect the range and speed of certain objects. It is used by some mobile phone and cable TV networks.

Bluetooth

Bluetooth is a form of wireless radio technology which is a common feature found on mobile phones, PDAs (personal digital assistants) and stationary and mobile PCs such as laptops. It uses short-wave radio frequencies and allows cable-free connectivity between mobile devices by enabling connection between these electronic devices. This allows the sharing and transfer of data between devices. The main limitation of Bluetooth is that it is a very short-range communication method (around 10 metres), but the benefits are that it is essentially a cost-free way to send information and data between devices. It is also a fast method of transferring small pieces of information in comparison to transferring via the Internet.

Satellite communications

SATCOM stands for Satellite Communication. An artificial satellite is used to aid telecommunications by reflecting or relaying a radio signal from space back down to earth. It is the most powerful form of radio, which can cover far larger distances and wider areas, and can communicate words, pictures and other forms of information. This system is used to extend the range of a communication signal. There are hundreds of communications satellites in orbit providing this type of service. Satellites are also widely used for military communications between fixed stations and mobile units such as ships, aeroplanes and land vehicles in order to coordinate large-scale manoeuvres over long distances.

Video link

This allows visual and verbal communication between at least two people or two groups of people who may be great distances apart. The people involved can speak to each other in real time and hear each other's responses. This method works by using a series of cameras which are linked and allow people both to be seen and to see others. A common use of video-link technology is within courts. It can be used to hear evidence from people in custody or young people who can't attend a formal hearing in

person. This clearly has financial and security advantages. This can be used by the military and police when sharing information nationally and internationally.

Consider this

List the advantages of video links to the following services:

- court/prison service
- police
- armed forces.

Internet telephone

The advancement and growth of the Internet has meant that people no longer need to use a conventional telephone network to communicate with each other. A combination of hardware (modem, microphone and headphones) and software (an Internet provider) will enable people to use the Internet as the transmission medium for telephone calls. The benefits of this system are that it can provide free telephone calls and communication to anyone in the world who has similar Internet hardware and software. The limitations are that this system currently doesn't offer the same sound quality as a direct telephone conversation.

Morse code

Morse code could be seen as the original method of sending text messages. It involved using a series of electronic pulses, which were a mixture of short pulses (called a 'dot') and long pulses (a 'dash').

The code was devised by Samuel F. B. Morse in the 1840s to work with his invention of the telegraph and allow long-distance electromagnetic communication. Even though sending a message was slow, it was reliable and wireless, and was not affected by conditions such as noise, fading or interference. Morse code today can be transmitted in a number of others ways such as by audio tone, by a radio signal, by mechanical devices or visual signals. Morse code is very limited in its practical use today, but it is still used by military radio operators to send messages in certain circumstances.

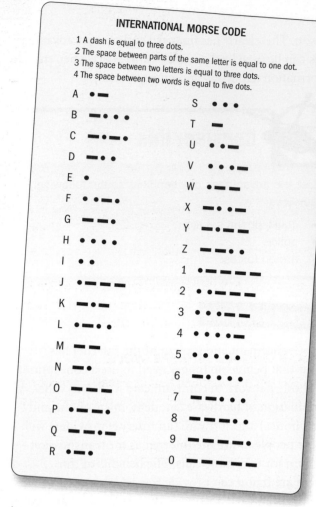

The 1922 Chart of the Morse Code Letters and Numerals

INTERNATIONAL MORSE CODE

1 A dash is equal to three dots.
2 The space between parts of the same letter is equal to one dot.
3 The space between two letters is equal to three dots.
4 The space between two words is equal to five dots.

Consider this

Can you think of a situation or situations when the military may use Morse code?

Theory into practice

Try writing out the following phrases in Morse code, using 'dit' and 'dah'. Remember to put a space between each letter, and a longer space between each word:

1. I am in location
2. Send reinforcements.

Try tapping out a word to a partner for them to translate.

Heliograph

This is a system of communication using light as a means of transmission. Using the same basic coding as Morse code, messages are sent using short and long flashes of light. This is achieved either by beams made using a special button on a torch or lamp, or by simply turning it on and off. In emergency situations, a mirror can be used to catch light from the sun and make flashes.

Theory into practice

Try passing a message over a distance of at least 200 metres using a heliograph. The message should be no more than 20 words.

Wireless networking

The term wireless networking is commonly associated with telecommunications, however it covers all types of networks that are wireless – such as computer networks.

Wireless telecommunications networks are generally operated by some type of information transmission system that uses electromagnetic radio waves to carry information along that network.

There are many different types of wireless networks; these include:

- **Wireless LAN:** Wireless Local Area Network. This uses radio waves instead of wires to transmit data back and forth in a computer network
- **Wireless MAN:** this connects several wireless LAN systems together
- **Wi-Fi:** this also involves computers; it transmits radio waves that are picked up by Wi-Fi receivers that are attached to different computers
- **Fixed Wireless Data:** this is used to connect two or more buildings together in order to share information via a network, without physically wiring the buildings together
- **Global System for Mobile Communications:** this is a common way for a mobile phone to call another phone. It involves three stages:

1. the phone connects to the base station (nearest antenna to sender)
2. the base station connects to the operation and support station
3. the operation and support station then connects to the switching station (nearest antenna to receiver), where the call is transferred to its destination.

See below for further explanation on how mobile phones work.

▲ Could electromagnetic radiation from mobile phones harm us?

Mobile phone

A mobile phone is simply a telephone that communicates by radio waves rather than along cables, and due to its size can be easily carried by a person. Currently there are over a billion handsets in circulation around the world.

A mobile phone should not be confused with a cordless telephone (which is simply a phone with a very short wireless connection to a local phone outlet). Another key feature of a mobile phone is the texting service, also known as SMS (Short Message Service), which is the means of sending a short written message from one phone to another or to an e-mail address.

■ How mobile phones work

When Person A talks into a mobile phone it converts the sound of their voice into radio waves. The radio waves

Case study: Mobile phones – is there a health risk?

A vast number of experiments have been performed to see if the electromagnetic (EM) radiation emitted by mobile phones and base stations can damage our health. While there is no compelling evidence of a risk, there are some uncertainties.

Electromagnetic radiation is certainly capable of damaging biological tissue, but precisely how depends upon its frequency. High-frequency EM radiation, such as ultraviolet, gamma or X-rays, can break chemical bonds in living tissue. Lower-frequency EM radiation is too weak to cause this kind of damage but is still capable of damaging tissue.

Microwave ovens illustrate what high-power, low-frequency EM radiation can do to raw meat, operating at up to around 900 watts and using EM waves of 2.45 GHz. GSM mobiles, on the other hand, use lower frequencies and are limited to a maximum average power output of 0.25 watts at 900 MHz and 0.125 watts at 1800 MHz. But most of the time they transmit at just one tenth of this.

The heating effect of radio frequencies is due to tissues absorbing the oscillating field of the wave. EM fields exert a force on charged ions and dipoles such as water in the tissues, producing heat from electrical resistance as they try to move or reorient themselves. Computer models have shown that radiation from a typical mobile phone can cause a maximum temperature rise of around 0.1°C in the brain.

Base stations, with antennas on masts between 10 and 30 metres high, produce more powerful beams of EM radiation. But the power of the beams falls rapidly with distance. The main beam from a base station hits the ground around 50 metres away, and at this distance the maximum power from a typical 60-watt antenna is around 100 milliwatts per square metre. The heating effect from this is about 5000 times less than that produced by a mobile phone antenna.

There are around 51,000 base stations in the UK.

Source: New Scientist, 15 February 2003

1. **According to this article, what are the uncertainties regarding the safety of mobile phones?**
2. **Conduct further research into the possible health risks from mobile phones, and create a table of the arguments for and against.**

are then transmitted through the air to the nearest base station. The base station then sends the call through the telephone network until it reaches Person B. When Person B receives the call on their mobile phone their message travels through the telephone network until it reaches the nearest base station to Person A. The base station then sends out radio waves, which are detected by Person A's mobile phone and converted back into speech.

Roaming network mobile phone

This service allows mobile phone users to extend their connectivity and service in a location that is different from where their phone is registered – for example using the phone in a different country.

Roaming means that the mobile phone automatically visits another network, allowing a person to make and receive voice calls, send and receive data, or access other services such as the Internet and e-mail whilst outside their normal geographical coverage area.

This is a very common service as all wireless network operators will offer full national coverage and will allow subscribers to use their mobile phones internationally, as network operators have made roaming agreements to enable subscribers to use another network's service.

Paging

Paging is a way of delivering a message to someone within a defined operating area. This is done through a wireless device known as a pager or beeper. It allows the sender to transmit a signal via the radio waves from a phone or other device to the receiver. This can be in the form of a simple alerting signal or in more sophisticated devices it can be either a visual text or e-mail message, or an audio message. It is a one-way communication device so messages cannot be returned through it.

Pagers were in everyday use during the 1980s and 1990s, but the growth of the mobile phone has meant they are only used within certain environments – for example, in a hospital to contact a doctor to notify them that they are wanted, or to contact retained firefighters and lifeboat crews.

Pagers use satellite networks to pass on information, so they can be more reliable than mobile phones as they are not affected by physical barriers such as buildings, and cannot be traced, unlike phones that use terrestrial based networks which may break down or have coverage problems.

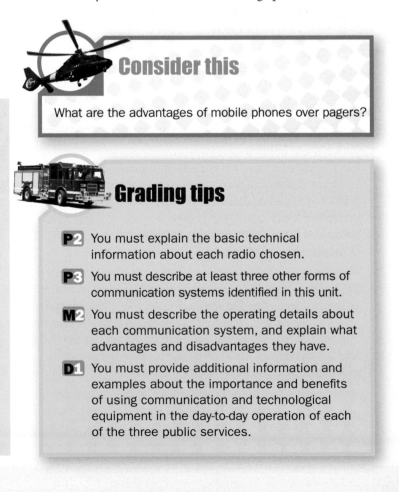

Consider this

What are the advantages of mobile phones over pagers?

Assessment activity 20.2

You have been asked by your tutor to create a visual display which describes:

1. Three different types of radio communication systems used by the various uniformed public services. **P2** Include a clear description of three other forms of communication systems used by the uniformed public services. **P3** Your display should also demonstrate that you have analysed the advantages and disadvantages of three communication systems. **M2**

2. Your tutor also feels that a supporting leaflet that analyses the importance of using communication and technological equipment in the daily operation of three uniformed public services would help other learners gain comprehensive understanding of its importance. **D1**

Grading tips

P2 You must explain the basic technical information about each radio chosen.

P3 You must describe at least three other forms of communication systems identified in this unit.

M2 You must describe the operating details about each communication system, and explain what advantages and disadvantages they have.

D1 You must provide additional information and examples about the importance and benefits of using communication and technological equipment in the day-to-day operation of each of the three public services.

Radio communication

Voice procedures and security

The purpose of voice procedures is to ensure that messages are sent and received from one person to another clearly, simply and accurately, and that the callers cannot be identified by anyone who does not have authorisation to be listening in. To ensure further security, many radio systems are encrypted to protect communications between certain groups. When, for example, the police use the Airwave system, they should ask the recipient if they are 'free to speak' before passing on the information, to ensure no unauthorised persons hear the transmission. Also, the Airwave system only allows one transmission at a time and will not allow anyone to transmit over the current one.

A range of voice procedures are covered in this section which are common to the uniformed public services.

Radio discipline

The following rules for radio discipline are common throughout the public services, only phrased differently:

1. Use correct voice procedures
2. Be alert continually for communications
3. The radio must not be switched off unless the person at base says so
4. Ensure you are using the correct frequency
5. Answer calls immediately
6. Listen before transmitting
7. Press the button before you start to speak
8. Release the button immediately you have finished.

Radio accuracy

Clear speech is necessary to ensure the accurate dissemination of information from the sender to the receiver when conducting a radio transmission.

Inaccurate transmissions can cause confusion and in certain circumstances – such as a terror attack or conflict within a war zone – could compromise the safety of the public and public services.

The following factors are important when making an accurate radio transmission:

1. **Brevity** – keep the transmission concise and avoid general chat and irrelevant information
2. **Clarity** – keep the transmission comprehensible by applying RSVP:
   - **Rhythm:** speak in a normal speech pattern
   - **Speed:** do not speak too fast
   - **Volume:** keep every word at the same volume and don't shout or speak quietly
   - **Pitch:** keep it slightly higher than usual, but not too high as this may cause alarm.

Prowords

These are common words and phrases used when transmitting messages. Prowords are easily pronounceable words or phrases. By keeping to a common protocol and a limited number of phrases it avoids confusion for the person receiving the message. For example, in the English language alone there are numerous ways of greeting someone, for example: hello, hi, hiya, good morning, good afternoon, good evening. Limiting this to 'hello' cuts out confusion and allows the person listening to the message to concentrate on the information being communicated instead of trying to fathom what is essentially unimportant. A simple 'hello' at the beginning of a message also indicates that nothing has gone before and has been missed. Using Prowords also saves time as one or two words often stand in the place of many.

■ Examples of Prowords
- **I spell** I am about to spell out a word or group of letters using the phonetic alphabet.
- **Figures** I am going to send you a number figure by figure.
- **Hello** The greeting used at the beginning of a communication.

- **This is** Used to introduce the speaker.
- **Send** Go ahead with your transmission.
- **Message** I am about to send you an important communication. You will need to write this down.
- **Over** This is the end of my transmission. A reply is required and you are free to transmit.
- **Out** This is the end of my transmission. No reply is expected.
- **Wait out** Your transmission has been received and a further transmission on the same subject will follow later.
- **Long message** Used at the beginning of a message which is longer than 20 seconds. The message is broken into 20 second chunks with a pause between each. The person receiving the message replies '**Roger so far**' after each chunk. There is also a pause of five seconds after each chunk to allow other radio users to transmit urgent messages. The phrase '**Long message**' therefore not only tells the person receiving the message to expect the information in chunks, but also advises other radio users that this frequency will be in use for some time.
- **Roger** Your message has been received satisfactorily.
- **Wrong** What has been said is incorrect, the correct version is:
- **Radio check** This phrase is used to establish whether or not all radio users can hear, it is used as a test call.
- **Say again** Please repeat your last transmission.
- **I say again** I am repeating my last transmission (used when a message is rebroadcast).

Tips for preventing confusion

1. Keep the microphone close to but not touching your mouth.
2. Avoid talking quickly.
3. Don't shout.
4. Use short easily recognisable words.
5. Keep conversations short.
6. Listen before you speak.
7. Think about what you are going to say before you start the communication.
8. Don't make unnecessary transmissions.

Consider this

Devise and pass on a simple message using a number of Prowords.

Authentication

Authentication involves the security measures used to establish the validity of a transmission or message, or as a means of verifying an individual's identity.

Authentication is used to ensure that the individual is who he or she claims to be. This is usually done within the public services by the use of call signs and code words. In non-public service transmission this may take the form of a username or password.

■ Call signs

These are used to identify individuals or groups communicating over the airwaves. They are code names aimed at making the communication more secure and ensuring that individuals are identified accurately. 'Hello, this is Paul' is likely to illicit the reply 'Paul who?' whereas 'Hello, this is Papa one zero' makes identification easier. If a number of units are taking part in one activity, a common call sign is often used but with a different number. For example, Papa One, Papa Two, Papa Three. In the army the commander is always called 'Sunray'.

■ Code words

These are used to serve two main purposes: speed of transmission and security of information. The police, fire and ambulance services often use code words or abbreviations when transmitting information. Examples of code words are 'RTI' for Road Traffic Incident, and 'DOA' for Dead On Arrival. This is usually done to speed up communication time as lives may be at risk, if not on this call out then the next. The armed forces also use such codes, often known as TLAs (Three Letter Abbreviations). For example, '2ic' is Second in command, and 'RMS' is Regimental Sergeant Major. This type of communication is used routinely in ordinary conversation as well as via the radio.

Codes which are used for security reasons are often associated with a specific operation. For example, a large-scale police operation to catch a gang of drug dealers may be given the code name 'Tiger's Eye'. This would be known only to the officers involved and would be used throughout the operation. As police radio signals could be intercepted and listened to by criminals, such code words do not allow them to identify when they are to be arrested and thus escape.

However, some organisations, such as the ambulance service, use a code name to describe a specific type of incident, for example a problem at a football match. The reasoning behind this is often to keep the information from individuals such as the press, or to avoid panic which could cause problems on the roads and prevent access to ambulances.

Phonetic alphabet

An example of an internationally recognised voice procedure/protocol is the phonetic alphabet as used by NATO. It is important that a standard coding be used so that different armed forces and countries within NATO can communicate. It is also routinely used by all British public services. When transmitting individual letters, for example a car number plate, or spelling out the name of a location, this system aims to solve the problem of mishearing such letters as m/n, b/d/p, or f/s. The quality of sound received via a radio is prone to interference. An unexpected crackle could mean the difference between an ambulance arriving at the right location in time to save a life or not. Therefore it is vital that the information is transmitted accurately.

The coding is as follows:

A	Alpha	J	Juliet	S	Sierra
B	Bravo	K	Kilo	T	Tango
C	Charlie	L	Lima	U	Uniform
D	Delta	M	Mike	V	Victor
E	Echo	N	November	W	Whiskey
F	Foxtrot	O	Oscar	X	X-ray
G	Golf	P	Papa	Y	Yankee
H	Hotel	Q	Quebec	Z	Zulu
I	India	R	Romeo		

Consider this

Work out the following words being spelt using the phonetic alphabet:

1. romeo alpha delta india oscar
2. charlie alpha mike papa
3. sierra echo romeo victor india charlie echo sierra

Work out a short message and transmit it to a partner using radios and the phonetic alphabet.

Did the message come through intact?

Net control

There are various types of net control and these include:

- **One to one** – Radios are designed to transmit one message at a time. Therefore the most common form of communication is in the form of one radio holder speaking to another. However, this feature only applies to transmitting messages. Any number of radio holders using the same frequency can listen in on a conversation.

- **Radio Net** – A group of radio holders working on the same frequency with a view of communicating with each other. One radio holder, normally at the control base, serves as the control. The other radio holders are known as substations and often have a common coding system as shown in the diagram on the next page.

Radio procedures

Look at Figure 20.1, which illustrates a radio control and four substations:

- the control has the call sign 'zero four'
- the substations use the call signs 'alpha one four', 'bravo two four', 'Charlie three four' and 'delta four four'
- the substations reply alphabetically but the control always goes first.

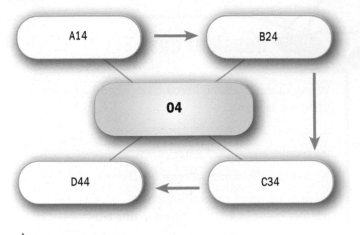

▲ Figure 20.1 Radio control and substations

Theory into practice

1. Imagine you are the radio controller for the ambulance service. Devise and transmit a radio communication using **standard voice procedures** giving the exact location and approximate casualty situation of a road traffic accident.

2. Imagine you are an army soldier who is injured and has been separated from the unit whilst on patrol behind enemy lines. Your radio's battery life is low and the reception is weak. Devise and transmit an appropriate message requesting immediate evacuation. You will need to give details of your medical condition, your location and that of the enemy as well as the risk they pose to your rescuers.

Radio procedures

When using radios, the public services follow specified procedures and protocols to ensure that the information sent over the wavelengths is both secure and accurate. In a radio net there are four main types of call:

1. Single call: from one station to another
   e.g. 'hello B24, this is A14'

2. Multiple calls: from one station to two or more stations
   e.g. 'hello 04, A14 and B24, this is C34'
   In this example 04 would respond first followed by A14 and B24 in that order.

3. All stations call: from one station to all stations
   e.g. 'hello all stations, this is D44'

4. Collective call: a call which is designed to be received by two or more preselected stations
   e.g. 'hello echo echo one, this is 04'
   The stations A14 and D44 have been given this call sign collectively.

Assessment activity 20.3

1. You have been asked by your tutor to demonstrate and send a message by radio using standard voice procedures from one uniformed public service. **P4**

 **Grading tips**

P4 To achieve P4 you must be able send a simple radio transmission by demonstrating an understanding of the radio procedures.

Transmission procedures

On any transmission network messages are usually dealt with in a routine order by being handled in sequence by the operator; however, urgent messages will take priority over routine messages. Urgent messages within the public services will generally be ones where a person needs immediate assistance.

There are many types of technological equipment and systems used by the uniformed services to aid them in their various roles. This section illustrates some of the equipment used by the police, the fire service and the Armed Forces.

Criminal justice agencies

The police, probation and prison services use a range of technological systems to help them in protecting the public and detecting crime, including the ones described below.

Electronic tagging

This is a tracking device normally attached to an offender's ankle, with a monitoring unit installed in the offender's home which is connected directly to the telephone line.

The offender is then monitored to ensure they adhere to their particular curfew order. If the tag isn't functioning within the range of the base during curfew hours, or if the base is disconnected from the phone line, then the police are automatically alerted and the offender is likely to be re-arrested. It should be noted that this is not a full location tracking system and that is why it is only used at certain times of the day (usually at night) or is connected to certain locations, for example the home. It is a realistic alternative to prison and after being piloted between 1995 and 1997 in areas such as Manchester, it was rolled out nationally in 1999. Most prisoners sentenced to at least three months but less than four years are eligible for release up to 60 days early on an electronically monitored curfew, provided that they pass a risk assessment and have a suitable address.

Closed-circuit television (CCTV)

Closed-circuit television is a common security system which involves the use of mobile controlled video cameras to monitor a specified area. The images are watched in a control room through a series of TV monitors.

▲ CCTV is used in public places like town and city centres to detect incidents and deter criminals

CCTV has commonly been used to monitor airports, banks, car parks, department stores, and restricted areas such as army bases. However, it is increasingly being used in public places. It operates 24 hours a day, every day of the year, and this has raised the 'protection versus privacy' debate to the forefront.

Public areas such as city centres and motorways are monitored by the police to help detect incidents, watch for suspicious behaviour and to help coordinate a quick and effective response by the police. The images and footage can be very useful as evidence for investigations. It is also hoped that the presence of CCTV systems will protect the public by deterring criminal activity.

CCTV systems have helped the police to increase the chance of detection of a variety of offences such as:

- shoplifting
- pickpocketing
- possession of drugs
- assault
- unauthorised taking of motor vehicles
- public order offences
- truancy
- littering.

This has led to increased arrests in these areas.

Advantages	Disadvantages
• Reduces the fear of crime • Deters crime and anti-social behaviour • Assists traffic management • Provides evidence to assist in the prosecution of offenders • Enhances community safety • Encourages greater use of the town centre, car parks, etc • Assists the emergency services • Enhances personal safety • Provides instant imaging information to the police • Improved public safety • Reduction in crime • Reduction in the fear of crime	• Increased deployment to non-priority incidents • Difficult to identify • Displacement of crime • Time-consuming nature of the work • Image quality • Authentication of CCTV images • Technical difficulties with CCTV • Disclosure of images – under the Data Protection Act, 1998 • Individual privacy

Table 20.6 Advantages and disadvantages of CCTV

Consider this

Research this question or debate it as a small group:

Are CCTV cameras a deterrent or an invasion of privacy?

Another public service that uses CCTV is the prison service, especially to monitor stairways and communal areas such as TV rooms. The footage is usually kept for 30 days and can be used as evidence in investigations of e.g. complaints against staff by prisoners, bullying and violence between prisoners.

X-ray machines

An X-ray is produced by using electromagnetic radiation to produce an image of an object. One of the key reasons for taking an X-ray is to detect something located inside an object or person.

To take an X-ray, an imaging system is needed which basically consists of a generator, an image-detection system and positioning hardware. This works by sending a controlled voltage to the generator which creates a beam of X-rays (electrons). The beam is projected on to the object or person, and some of the X-rays will pass through the object or person, whilst some are reflected back. The image-detection system and positioning hardware help to create an image based on the reaction to the beams.

One of the most common uses of X-rays on a day-to-day basis is at airports, in the fight against terrorism and drug smuggling.

At airports X-ray machines are used to screen luggage non-invasively, to examine for possible bombs, drugs or weapons. These machines use a very low dose of radiation and are not harmful to use.

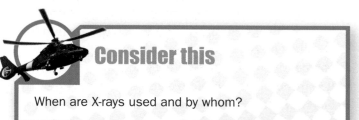

Consider this

When are X-rays used and by whom?

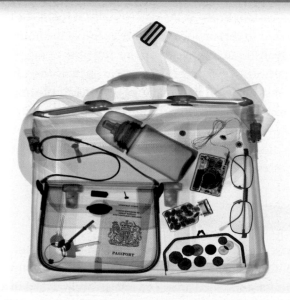

▲ X-rays are commonly used at airports to detect illegal objects

Hand-held metal detectors

These are ideal for body searches when looking for offensive weapons. They are used in a variety of environments such as nightclubs, courts and schools.

They are also used for crowd control, for checking packages and letters for metal objects, and anywhere where hidden metal needs detecting. When a metal item is detected an audio signal will sound and a red LED will be activated.

Case study: Anti-weapon initiative

The British Transport Police used hand-held metal detectors during 'Operation Shield' in February 2006. This was an initiative to help cut down on the number of knife attacks and anti-social behaviour, and it took place at a number of British railway stations. This operation involved both hand-held and walk-through metal detectors. Operation Shield resulted in over 20,000 people being scanned, with over 160 weapons being recovered and 150 arrests.

Further initiatives included the police in certain areas, such as Denbighshire, giving hand-held metal detecting devices to door staff at pubs and clubs, so that people could be searched before entering the premises, to help detect knives and guns.

Fire service

In order for the fire service to conduct its roles of tackling fires and dealing with difficult search and rescues, it uses a range of technological equipment and systems to help it.

Firelink project

Not all fire services within the country have the same radio system, which makes direct communications between them very difficult. Also, many of the radio systems are more than 20 years old.

The Firelink project intends to create a nationwide fire and rescue service radio communications system, similar to the 'Airwave' system used by the police. Firelink will create and utilise digital technology and digital networks. It is intended to help the fire and rescue service respond to all types of incidents including terrorism and natural disasters, and also to improve communication links with other emergency services. It will involve a national link between all fire and rescue service control rooms and fire vehicles. The main benefit is to be able to mobilise resources effectively and efficiently in response to a 999 call.

The Firelink project will include the installation of radio terminals, global positioning system units and mobile data terminals in all fire vehicles that are linked directly to the fire control rooms.

Firelink will offer a number of benefits over the old radio communication systems, including greater security by preventing unauthorised access, ensuring that fire vehicles and firefighters can remain in contact with the control room through mobile network roaming, create greater quality verbal communication between firefighters and the control room, creating a quick way of transferring all types of data and ensuring an automatic vehicle location system to pinpoint where appliances are at any given time. It is hoped that the Firelink system will start to be used at an operational level in 2008.

Key terms

Satellite navigation This is a navigation system which uses information transmitted via satellites to track the position of objects, vehicles or locations. It is widely available for use in vehicles using a global positioning system (GPS).

Satellite navigation systems (the general term is **Global Navigation Satellite System** – GNSS) were originally developed and designed for military use. In particular, such systems were used for a number of things such as missile tracking after launch to ensure that they hit their target precisely. This would ensure that the weapons could be used effectively, and also that the number of innocent casualties was kept to a minimum.

The fire service, along with the other uniformed services, use satellite navigation (usually abbreviated and known as 'sat nav') to ensure they can respond quickly to an emergency by choosing the best route of travel to an emergency. This form of satellite navigation involves the use of a small box in the fire engine which uses global positioning satellites (GPS) to work out the vehicle location and plan the quickest route to an intended destination. This is displayed on an electronic map, and verbal directions are also used. The system can also be used by the fire control room to identify which vehicle is nearest to the emergency.

Vehicle mounted data system

The fire service responds to thousands of incidents on a daily basis ranging from fires, road traffic collisions, rescue operations and chemical spills.

To deal with these incidents effectively it is essential that firefighters attending these calls are able to access as much information relating to the individual call-outs as possible.

In these situations it is not practicable for the firefighters to access the service's Intranet or paper documents to find out about any procedures they are unsure about in dealing with the situation.

In these cases they will have to rely on the information control room and the vehicle mounted data system to access the information and data needed whilst travelling to, or in attendance at, an incident.

The vehicle mounted data systems are touch screen computer systems installed into each of the fire engines which allow a wireless data link for firefighters to access a wealth of up-to-date and potentially lifesaving information held at headquarters. This information could include building plans, design specifications of cars, road maps and risks associated with certain chemicals. The data system includes a printer so that fire fighters can print off the information that is relevant to the situation and use it at the scene.

Firefighters' equipment

The modern firefighter's uniform consists of a light but strong helmet made of Kevlar and fibreglass with a visor to protect the eyes. The tunic and over-trousers are fire- and water-resistant, to provide protection for fire fighters against extreme temperatures. Reflective strips make the clothing more conspicuous in dark or smoky conditions. Water- and chemical-resistant boots and lined heat-resistant gloves are also part of the protective clothing worn.

When entering a burning building, firefighters will wear breathing apparatus which provides them with clean air to breathe in smoky conditions. The air tank can last up to 60 minutes and the **automatic distress signal** unit attached to the breathing apparatus will be activated if a firefighter is immobile for more than 20 seconds. This system was introduced in 1991 to help identify a firefighter who may be trapped or unconscious and in need of rescuing by their colleagues.

Thermal imaging cameras

Thermal imaging cameras are invaluable tools for firefighters, enabling them to see through the thickest smoke and darkness to provide a clear picture of the scene that is not available to the naked eye. This can save time when assessing the scene by rapidly identifying the

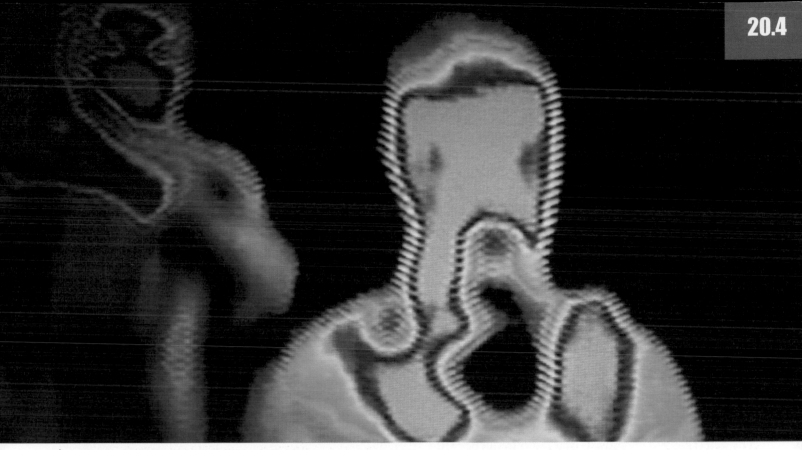

▲ Thermal imaging cameras are an invaluable resource for firefighters

source and spread of a fire, and quickly and accurately locating casualties in burning buildings.

Thermal imaging cameras work by detecting objects that are giving off heat as long wavelength infrared radiation, which thermal imaging cameras convert into a visible light picture on the camera's screen. The picture is presented in various colour combinations, enabling firefighters to see clearly the degree of heat emitted by objects around them.

Geophone

The geophone is a device used in conjunction with a seismograph which is placed on the ground to detect vibrations under the earth. It converts ground movement (displacement) into voltage which is recorded and analysed. The deviation of this measured voltage from the base line is called the seismic response. This device has many uses, but is used by the fire service to help detect and rescue people who are trapped or stuck underground.

Armed forces

Simulators

Simulators and simulations are used by all the uniformed public services as a way of putting their skills into action in a situation which is as realistic as possible. The Army, for example, has used battle simulators since 1992 to help train tens of thousands of soldiers a year in battle techniques. Training using simulators helps to prevent loss of life in real situations that soldiers face in countries such as Iraq and Afghanistan. Simulators are beneficial as many soldiers can be trained at the same time. Simulators use computer-generated imaging and digital video technology which is interactive and has dual-screen systems.

One such simulator used is the Combined Arms Tactical Trainer. This allows soldiers to practise their skills in a number of virtual vehicles along with the realities of combat against a number of enemies in a number of virtual environments from grass plains to harsh deserts. The advantage of these simulators is that they can be used as a training tool, and the battle can be played back in a lecture theatre to scrutinise and analyse the decisions made by the soldiers, and they get another chance to put new techniques into place. The key skills that can be developed include marksmanship, use of force judgement, shoot/don't shoot decision-making and small unit tactical training.

Another use of simulators within the army is to help soldiers in their ability to drive a range of heavy vehicles and to gain a driving licence if they haven't got one. This substantially reduces the cost of driving (for example, no fuel consumption), and helps soldiers to do this in a safe and flexible environment.

■ Nuclear quadrupole resonances sensors

Nuclear quadrupole resonance (NQR) is a technique used to help detect explosives. The sensors are designed to detect landmines and explosives that are concealed, for example, in the ground or in luggage.

The detection system consists of a radio frequency (RF) power source, a coil to produce the magnetic excitation field and a detector circuit which monitors for a radio frequency (between 0.5 and 6 MHz) and an NQR response coming from the explosive component of the object. From the intensity of the signal it is possible to estimate the quantity of explosive and from the radio frequency the identification and characteristics of the explosives can be revealed.

Unlike the better known technique of nuclear magnetic resonance (NMR), no static magnetic field is needed, so that portable probes can be used. Furthermore, signals are only seen in solids or solid-like materials, and because of the highly compound-specific nature of NQR frequencies, there is little, if any, interference from other nitrogen-containing materials which may be present. These advantages make it an excellent method for the detection of explosives in luggage, parcels, letters and landmines.

Man-portable surveillance and target acquisition radar (MSTAR)

This radar was developed in the 1980s and replaced the Radar GS No 14 (ZB298) during the Gulf War in 1991. It works by detecting movement – it can detect targets such as an individual person or a vehicle (including helicopters), and it has the capability to work in both day light and night time conditions, and due to its durability it can work in any weather conditions. It is operated from either a lightweight tripod or from a warrior artillery observation post vehicle, and it weighs only 30 kg. It is used mainly for reconnaissance and surveillance.

It has a detection range of up to 30 kilometres and can be used to direct artillery and mortar fire onto a specified target, and detect the fall of the shot.

The radar head is connected by cables to the radar display which is an electro-luminescent screen that can be overlaid with a 1:50,000 map grid. It also shows the areas of ground visible to the radar and those that are masked by terrain. It runs on a standard army field battery.

Intelligence, surveillance, target acquisition and reconnaissance equipment (ISTAR)

ISTAR equipment includes image-intensifying goggles, lightweight thermal imagers and laser target markers. It works through thermal imaging which turns heat into light and allows the user to see through darkness, rain or undergrowth. People are detected through their body heat which appears as bright lights, and vehicles are made visible through the heat from their engines and tyres.

These images can be used on the battlefield to determine the location, intent and combat strength of the enemy forces. The information gathered can be used by the commander to formulate a battle plan along with considering the lay of the land.

There are different types of thermal imagers used within the armed forces for example:

- **Lion** is a lightweight thermal imager used at platoon level to detect targets at medium range
- **Sophie** is a thermal imager used at company level to detect targets at long range
- **Tads** is a thermal imager which can be fitted as a sight on to the long-range L96 sniper rifle used by sniper teams
- **Spyglass** and **Otis** are larger and more powerful thermal imagers which are used by artillery observers and are normally mounted on the Warrior Observation Post Vehicle along with the MSTAR.

Importance of using different types of technological systems

There are many reasons why the uniformed public services use technological systems. These include the need for effective and quick communication between various internal teams. This in turn allows the uniformed services to respond appropriately and quickly to the communication and intelligence they receive. The ongoing advances in communication also allow the various uniformed public services to interact easily with each other, whether this is the police, fire and ambulance service working together on a major incident, or the three armed forces working together in a conflict zone.

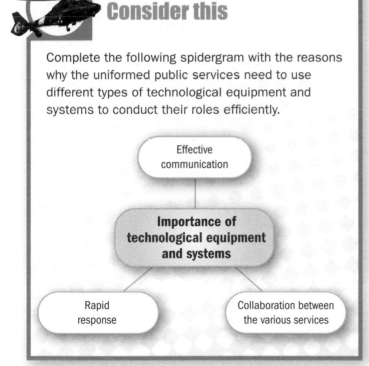

Consider this

Complete the following spidergram with the reasons why the uniformed public services need to use different types of technological equipment and systems to conduct their roles efficiently.

- Effective communication
- **Importance of technological equipment and systems**
- Rapid response
- Collaboration between the various services

There are many advantages and disadvantages in the use of technological systems within the public services. Some of the advantages are:

- **speed:** the public services can receive and act upon information quickly and effectively
- **time:** advances in technological systems and equipment often mean that collecting and transferring data and information is quicker, thus freeing up public service workers to spend more time on other elements of their role
- **reliability:** the technology used today is very trustworthy and constantly improving
- **versatility:** the range of technological systems used by the public services means that they can be resourceful in the way they deal with a given problem or situation
- **space efficiency:** a lot of the technological systems are small enough for a public service worker to carry on their person, and others are continually being modified and improved to be smaller and more efficient to use
- **ease of use:** even though technological systems are sophisticated and often complex, they are managed and modified in such a way that the basic functions of the equipment or systems can be used with little training by public service workers
- **innovation:** with technological systems and equipment being continually updated this means that the public services will show originality and modern practices when conducting their roles
- **communication:** communication networks and the way public service workers communicate internally and externally have developed substantially since 2001, for example Airwaves (used by the police), and Firelink (fire services)
- **cost-effectiveness** – advances in technological systems and equipment often have a high initial set-up cost, but often in the long run will give great saving for the public services.

Within any organisation, including the public services, there may be some disadvantages for the continuous development of technological systems and equipment, such as:

- **unemployment:** the more technologically developed an organisation becomes, the more likely it is that they need fewer employees. This may mean that the public services will cut the level of recruitment as they look to reduce staffing numbers

- **privacy:** the more open communication becomes, the more likely that privacy and data protection issues will be breached – such as e-mail hacking, intercepting calls and stealing or misplacing sensitive information
- **system failure:** no matter how advanced and reliable a system or piece of equipment is, there is still a chance that it could fail and put people in danger
- **change for change's sake:** sometimes perfectly good systems and equipment are replaced unnecessarily because of the demand for more advanced systems or equipment, so money is wasted or invested in finding unnecessary alternatives.

Assessment activity 20.4

In the form of a leaflet which includes images, you are to describe three different types of technological equipment used by one of the uniformed public services. **P5** The leaflet should also include a detailed explanation of the benefits of using technological equipment in that public service. **M3** Finally, your leaflet should analyse the importance of using communication and technological equipment in the daily operation of at least three uniformed public services. **D1**

Consider this

Can you think of any other advantages and disadvantages of the use of technological systems within the public services?

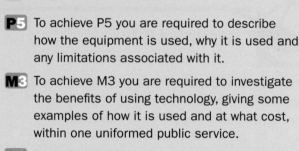

Grading tips

P5 To achieve P5 you are required to describe how the equipment is used, why it is used and any limitations associated with it.

M3 To achieve M3 you are required to investigate the benefits of using technology, giving some examples of how it is used and at what cost, within one uniformed public service.

D1 To achieve D1 you are required to provide additional information about the importance and benefits of using technological equipment in day-to-day operations of each of three uniformed public services.

Knowledge check

1. List five reasons why communication is important in the public services.

2. List the different forms of written communication that can be found within the following services:

   - armed forces
   - fire service
   - ambulance service.

3. List three circumstances when verbal communication would be more effective than written communication within a selected public service.

4. State one advantage and one disadvantage of the Internet.

5. State one advantage and one disadvantage of e-mails.

6. State one advantage and one disadvantage of an Intranet.

7. Give three examples of how radio is used within the different public services.

8. List the main radio frequencies used by the public services.

9. State one way that 'other' forms of communication are used within the identified public services (varying your answers):

   - armed forces
   - fire service
   - police service
   - ambulance service.

10. List five commonly used 'prowords' within the public services.

11. What is the phonetic alphabet for the following letters: P U B L I C?

12. Give three examples of specialist technological equipment used by the armed forces.

13. Name three examples of specialist technological equipment used by the police service.

14. Give three examples of specialist technological equipment used by the fire service.

15. List five examples of how various communication equipment has improved the public services.

Preparation for assessment

You are conducting a seminar on communication and technology in the uniformed public services for a class of new army recruits.

1. During the seminar you need to describe four different examples of formal written communication used in the police service and explain two occasions when it may be necessary to complete a formal written communication in the police service and why this was the most appropriate method of communication. **P1 M1**

2. As part of the seminar you are to conduct a radio communication demonstration. To ensure the demonstration goes well you must ensure that three different types of radio communication systems used by the armed forces are described. You also need to describe three other forms of communication systems used by the armed forces, as well as analysing the advantages and disadvantages of the three communication systems mentioned in your demonstration. **P2 P3 M2**

3. You wish to demonstrate your ability to use a radio by sending a message using standard voice procedures associated with the uniformed public services. You should analyse the importance of using communication in the daily operation of the armed forces and two other uniformed public services. **P4 D1**

4. Your presentation should describe three different types of technological equipment used by the armed forces. It should also include a detailed explanation of the benefits of using the technological equipment in the armed forces. Finally you should analyse the importance of using technological equipment in the daily operation of three other uniformed public services. **P5 M3 D1**

Grading criteria	Activity	Pg no.		
To achieve a pass grade the evidence must show that the learner is able to:			To achieve a merit grade the evidence must show that the learner is able to:	To achieve a distinction grade the evidence must show that the learner is able to:
P1 Describe four different examples of formal written communication used in the public services	20.1	160	**M1** Explain two occasions when it may be necessary to complete a formal written communication in a uniformed public service and why this was the most appropriate method of communication	
P2 Describe three different types of radio communication systems used by the uniformed public services	20.2	168	**M2** Analyse the advantages and disadvantages of three communication systems	**D1** Analyse the importance of using communication and technological equipment in the daily operation of three uniformed public services.
P3 Describe three other forms of communication systems used by the public services	20.2	168		
P4 Send a message by radio using standard voice procedures from one uniformed public service	20.3	172		
P5 Describe three different types of technological equipment used by a selected uniformed public service.	20.4	180	**M3** Explain in detail the benefits of using technological equipment in the role of one public service.	

Custodial care of individuals

Introduction

This unit is intended to give you an insight into the work undertaken by staff employed in the custodial care sector by looking at the key elements involved in care and control of individuals in custody. You will identify and investigate the many different issues, and become aware of how custodial care workers balance and maintain care and control of people in custodial care. Custodial care workers offer a legal duty of care to individuals under their control, but care cannot be at the expense of the required level of security and order in the institution.

You will gain a clear understanding of how care and control of individuals is balanced against the need for security within each establishment. You will also explore the development of individuals throughout their sentence, as well as the protocols used for the reception and discharge of both individuals and property into and out of the institution.

You will look at the need for security and the potential risks to both the individual and the institution. This will include exploring the factors that influence security, including physical and dynamic security, which includes the framework of the institution and the human approach through applying the security procedures.

You will also identify the development and resettlement of offenders and gain an understanding of offending behaviour as well as what stages an offender must go through before they are released.

After completing this unit you should be able to achieve the following outcomes:

- Understand security measures in the custodial environment
- Know how control is maintained in the custodial environment
- Understand the receiving and discharging procedures of individuals and their property
- Know how offending behaviour can be dealt with and positive relationships maintained prior to resettlement preparation of individuals in custody.

Thinking points

This unit is critical to anyone who wishes to join the prison service or work within the field of custodial care. It is also helpful to people looking at a career in the police or the criminal legal system as they will gain an insight into what happens to offenders who receive a prison sentence and the amount of aftercare needed to look after them and prepare them for integration back into society.

Anybody who works within a custodial institution needs to understand the importance for security within such an environment, whether this is physical or through following strict procedures and practices.

- Think about what security equipment and security procedures are required to maintain control and order within a prison.

This means that people looking at a career within the identified career routes need to be aware of how control is maintained within such a secure environment and how to deal with security breaches. Furthermore, you should have an understanding of key issues regarding receiving individuals into custody and discharging individuals from custody.

- Think about what needs to be done before a person can either enter or leave custody.

It is also important that all public service workers are aware of how to deal with offending behaviour both inside and outside a custodial institution, and what part uniformed services such as the police and prison service, along with non-uniformed services such as the probation and voluntary services, might play in the successful resettlement of offenders. It is important to have an understanding of how positive relationships are formed and maintained, as well as what is and is not appropriate behaviour between custodial care workers and individuals in custody.

- Think about the value and importance of building positive relationships with individuals in a custodial environment.

This chapter will primarily focus on the rules and procedures with regard to convicted adult male offenders; there are often some variations on rules and procedures for young and female offenders along with the treatment of unconvicted people within the prison environment. For example, young people in custody are managed by the Youth Justice Board, not the prison service. The levels of security and the measures in place often depend on the type of prison that an offender is sent to. In the United Kingdom there are five categories of prison and four security levels for adult male prisoners:

- **Local prisons** – these are for unconvicted and short-term prisoners. These prisons are also used for male adult offenders immediately after conviction, until their security level is decided upon
- **Dispersal prisons** – for high-security prisoners
- **Training prisons** – for long-term prisoners who do not need high levels of security
- **Category C prisons** – which are closed prisons but have less internal security
- **Open prisons** – for prisoners who are not a risk to the public or likely to escape.

The four security levels are:

- **Category A:** these are prisoners whose escape would be highly dangerous to the public or national security
- **Category B:** these are prisoners who do not need the strictest conditions of security but need to be prevented from escaping
- **Category C:** these are prisoners who cannot be trusted in 'open prison' conditions
- **Category D:** these are prisoners who can be trusted to serve their sentences in open conditions.

For women and young offenders there are only three security levels:

- **Category A**
- **Closed:** this is similar to Category C
- **Semi-open** or **open:** this is similar to Category D.

Adult male remand (unconvicted) prisoners are in most cases treated as Category B prisoners until the outcome of their trial is determined. Adult female remand prisoners will be held in Closed conditions.

Prisoners will be allocated to a prison which suits the nature of their offence, the length of the sentence imposed, meets the security level needed and suits the individual circumstances of the prisoner, for example the closest prison to their family. Most prisons will cover several different categories and security levels. For example, a prison could be both a local and a remand prison, and also a high-security prison holding Category A prisoners.

Security in a custodial environment

It is important to keep control and offer stability inside a prison to maintain safety and security. There are many security measures that are in place inside a prison to maintain security and ensure things run smoothly. Good security is more than just the physical design of the prison. It is also about the conduct and professionalism of prison staff along with having sound and workable policies and procedures to maintain cohesiveness and avoid chaos.

Security in a custodial environment can consist of a number of elements, such as:

- **Physical security:** this covers elements such as walls, bars, locks and technology such as closed-circuit television
- **Dynamic security:** this covers elements such as intelligence gathering from prisoners and staff and monitoring such things as mail and phone calls made and received by the prisoners. It also includes monitoring prisoners and accounting for their movements, as well as regular cell searches by prison officers. This approach helps to tackle drugs and violence in prisons indirectly
- **Procedural security:** this covers security procedures such as assessing prisoners to make sure that they are kept in the appropriate prison to suit their security conditions.

Physical security

Physical security covers all measures that either prevent or deter an inmate from accessing a certain area, or measures that ensure they do not escape. Physical security can be as simple as a locked gate, or as elaborate as surveillance and detection equipment.

The most obvious ways in which prisons maintain security are through the walls, bars and gates that provide a formidable physical barrier; these are often combined with surveillance and detection technology such as CCTV, spotlights and motion sensors. Therefore physical security has two key objectives:

- to create obstacles that prevent escape or restrict free movement within the custodial environment
- to notice and detect any suspicious behaviour through security measures such as alarms, cameras and patrols. This allows a quick response from prison officers when such behaviour is detected.

When designing your prison you should consider the following layers of physical security:

- **Environmental design** – consider the layout of the prison and issues such as lighting and open spaces

- **Mechanical and electronic access control** – consider including gates, fences and locks
- **Intrusion detection** – consider alarms and detection systems throughout the prison
- **Visual monitoring** – used to support intrusion detection. You need 'watching eyes', because prison officers will only offer a limited coverage of the custodial environment at any one time due to its sheer size.

Using your diagram, explain the importance of the different types of security to a colleague.

■ Cells

These are critical for the successful security of a prison as they are the accommodation for inmates within the prison, and the place where a prisoner will spend most of their time whilst in a custodial environment. They are locked and inmates will only leave the cells for work, education, rehabilitation programmes, visits or exercise and recreational time. In some cases an inmate may only leave their cell for a short period of time over a 24-hour period. The cells are often subject to daily cell checks and searches to ensure high levels of security and safety are maintained.

▲ Prisoners are likely to spend most of the day in their cells

■ Prison officers

Prison officers have a critical role in physical security as they will have the job of patrolling the prison and surrounding areas to ensure that they are secure. They will also guard critical areas such as the main entrance and cell blocks. Throughout the day and night they will conduct routine checks of all security areas – some will be frequently checked whilst others will be checked when necessary. They will also have the role of responding quickly to alarms or calls for backup from colleagues as well as questioning and reporting suspicious behaviour.

■ Search area

The search area will cover the whole prison, however some areas will be searched on a regular basis (routine) whilst other areas will be checked when security concerns or information available suggests a need for a search (non-routine). Areas used on a regular basis or accessible by prisoners will be searched frequently – especially areas where equipment is used and stored such as workshops and communal areas. The general search area of a prison will consist of all routes used by the prisoners, such as prison blocks and corridors, and these will be patrolled.

■ Search equipment

There is a range of specialist equipment that can be used by prison officers and staff, especially when searching for the concealment of drugs and weapons in search areas such as prison buildings and individual cells. The need for sophisticated equipment is necessary, as prisoners are finding more ways of smuggling and concealing items. This type of equipment can be used to carry out quick searches, and cause minimum disruption to prisoners and staff alike.

One of the most common types of search equipment is portable visual inspection equipment, which is designed to enable visual searches of difficult areas and locations such as toilets, waste pipes, ceilings and even inside cell walls and doors.

The intensity of search and the equipment needed will of course vary according to the intelligence available.

Specialist visual equipment such as videoscopes, fibrescopes, infrared telescopes and CCTV are commonly used in prisons.

- A fibrescope will be used for access into small areas such as drains. It is a flexible fibre optic cable with an eyepiece at one end and a lens at the other, and images are provided directly to the eye or on a separate monitor display
- Infrared telescopes are used to produce images inside a darkened room, such as in prison roofs. The receiver will see these images on a monitor screen and the image will appear as a black and white image produced by the infrared illumination.

Consider this

More basic search equipment can include mirror kits and rods, torches and guard dogs.

In what situations would these be used and when?

Can you think of any other forms of search equipment?

Dynamic security

Dynamic security is often referred to as the human dimension of prison security and includes all the 'social' measures used to ensure security. Prison officers are essential to this type of security being successful.

The key features of dynamic security measures are:

- diverting prisoners' energy into constructive work and meaningful activities
- creating decent regimes which give prisoners a degree of freedom, and programme opportunities either based on education and training or treatment
- developing positive relationships with prisoners by treating them with respect
- creating a framework of incentives for good behaviour and sanctions for bad behaviour.

All these features help to create a more constructive regime within the prison.

■ Good relationships between prison staff and prisoners

Dynamic security is created in prisons by building a rapport and relationship with the prisoners in order to build a more secure prison environment. This gives prisoners a stake in prison life, so reducing their grounds for resisting and threatening security.

This approach aims to help individuals develop and reform so that on release they can follow the social rules of the community. In dynamic security, the prison considers the wider concept of security, by both protecting the public, and by creating an environment based on humanity and rehabilitation. This will encourage prisoners to look to changing their ways and not try to escape.

■ Role of the personal officer

One of the most common ways of building up a rapport and relationship with prisoners on a daily basis is

Case study: A prisoner's story

Frank has undergone an offender assessment (OASys) before starting a 9-month prison sentence for GBH. Two months into his sentence Frank has started to suffer from a loss of appetite and seems depressed. Eric, a prison officer, has noticed that Frank looks sad and allocates him a listener – a specially trained fellow prisoner – who establishes that Frank may need to do something constructive to help him adjust. Frank has a good educational background so Eric recommends him for work, and within one week Frank is working in the prison stores and has started to integrate well with other prisoners and even to enjoy his time in custody. During his time in prison Frank didn't get into any trouble, and was released early owing to his excellent behaviour.

1. What are the long-term benefits of this approach?

2. Why could this approach to maintaining security be criticised by members of the public?

through the allocation of personal officers. These officers will have responsibility over a particular number or particular group of prisoners, such as young offenders. A prisoner will normally be allocated a personal officer on their first day at prison.

Key aspects of their role are:
- to give advice and guidance to prisoners on a daily basis
- to identify prisoners in need, such as those who may be depressed and suicidal
- to monitor a prisoner's progress both formally, by writing regular reports, and informally through observations
- to help deal with any complaints a prisoner may have
- to help them arrange and attend visits
- to help the prisoner liaise with probation staff in order to help deal with any resettlement issues whilst in prison.

Any prisoner who does not have a personal officer should be able to get the support mentioned above from the officer in charge of their wing. In addition prisoners can talk to a prison listener (trained by the Samaritans), chaplain or directly to the Samaritans.

■ Intelligence systems

Another aspect of dynamic security is looking for and monitoring intelligence, including collecting any relevant intelligence such as patterns of unusual behaviour, and ensuring that this information is shared with all relevant parties. This also includes building up and maintaining good working relationships with external agencies such as the police and the courts by sharing intelligence of criminal behaviour and activities.

■ Importance of a secure environment

All these elements of dynamic security combined create a range of 'situational' security measures and make it harder for individuals to pose a potential security threat. Dynamic security also involves the management of the entry and exit of people from outside the prison, and procedures such as identifying the people entering and exiting a prison. Other security measures which form part of dynamic security include limiting access to the prison, bag searches and the wearing of visitor badges. All these measures can help to ensure a secure prison environment.

In creating a safe environment, physical security and dynamic security need to be backed up with and complemented by procedural security. Procedural security is often seen as the final part of a successful security system, and it is the methodology behind which the security is managed. This includes, for example, operational procedures for the screening and searching of staff and visitors to the prison. It also covers policies such as minimum staffing levels and how to move prisoners safely about the prison.

■ Importance of security procedures

Procedural security within a prison covers a range of policies and practices in relation to security and includes aspects such as information management (for example, data protection and using secure ICT systems which are protected by passwords and firewalls). It also covers a range of legal obligations which must be carried out by the prisons and their staff, such as ensuring prisoners' human rights are not infringed. This aspect of security management is fundamentally based on ensuring that staff are aware of their duties and responsibilities and how to deal with the various situations that may arise.

Consider this

Within the prison itself, there are controls and security procedures on what property and materials prisoners may have access to, whether it be within the prison, or the property that can be brought in for them. This is done in order to restrict the use of items that may be used to present a risk to prison security and personal safety.

In small groups – give five examples of property and materials that prisoners may have restricted access to, and explain why this is. Consider a range of reasons when feeding back your answers.

■ Security risks

Procedural security includes a range of protocols, such as how violent incidents are managed, and prison officers in this case will have had the necessary training to deal with aggressive and threatening behaviour. They will use and follow procedures such as:

- the use of verbal de-escalation techniques – acting in a manner that may help defuse the situation
- self-defence and breakaway techniques, including control and restraint to ensure that they only use reasonable force which is appropriate to the situation
- the application of seclusion techniques, such as isolating the movement of individual prisoners or locking down an entire wing or the whole prison.

■ Documentation and record keeping

Overall procedural security will look to ensure that security risks such as physical risks to prisoners or prison staff are unlikely, through a well-managed risk containment system. This will include risk assessments which have identified the risks and harm levels of various activities. Procedural security uses a robust documentation system followed by all staff. Necessary documents are completed when an incident occurs, to ensure that there is a written record of any incident that occurs – this is a legal requirement. This in turn will be used to assess whether the prison needs to re-address its standard working policies and procedures on security, and may lead to further development in its security techniques and additional training for staff.

So far we have identified three different forms of security and a well-managed and secure prison will be one that doesn't rely on one single form of security alone but combines all three.

Assessment activity 21.1

After negative media coverage on the poor security within your local prison, you have been asked by your local MP to create a presentation that can be used in several local community forums to increase confidence in the amount and level of security in place in UK prisons.

To do this you have been asked to:

1. Outline the main security considerations in a custodial environment. **P1**

2. Explain clearly how combining security elements can improve the overall security of an establishment, using appropriate examples. **M1**

3. Analyse the main security measures, showing why it is important that no one measure is allowed to dominate within a custodial environment. **D1**

Grading tips

To achieve **P1** you must be able to outline the security considerations in a custodial environment. You must be able to state the different elements that contribute to physical, procedural and dynamic security. You should be able to describe examples of physical elements such as walls, cells, fences, gates etc. This must also contain a short description of each as well as any limitations. Dynamic security should include the role of the personal officer as well as showing examples of how a constructive regime, intelligence, staff vigilance and a secure environment are essential for prison security. Procedural security should include a list of security procedures which the prison service has in place to detect or prevent breaches to security.

To achieve **M1** you need to explain how security elements are combined to be effective and why this is done.

To achieve **D1** you need to analyse why it is important to ensure that no one measure is allowed to dominate.

Searches

A key method of control within a prison is the conducting of a search. Any prisoner or member of staff entering a prison may be searched. Visitors, including children and babies, may also be searched if consent is given. For example, visitors who are visiting friends and family as part of an official prison visit are only allowed to bring the following items into the prison and their visit will be limited to the visiting areas of the prison only:

- personal clothing (not hats or sunglasses)
- loose change for the purchasing of refreshments (not notes or large amounts)
- babies' dummies, feeding bottles, baby food, change of nappy.

All other items must be stored in lockers before entering the prison.

Search procedures

To ensure that all types of visitors to the prison, including prison officers, don't bring in any unauthorised items, they will be subjected to a rub-down search and all bags and overcoats will be passed through a metal detector. All other types of property and items brought into the establishment will be searched and all visitors are subjected to routine passive screening by drug detection dogs and camera surveillance whilst within the prison grounds.

Consider this

What are the potential dangers from visitors who are not searched thoroughly on arrival?

■ Respecting individuals

It is important that these searches are conducted correctly and only in authorised situations, as unauthorised or improper searches of a prisoner may amount to misconduct and lead to disciplinary action against the prison officer on the grounds of common assault (including sexual assault).

It is therefore important that any person searched is treated courteously and considerately, and only a person of the same sex as the person being searched can carry out a rub-down and strip search.

Consider this

There are a range of rules regarding the conducting of searches on prisoners. Here is an extract from the Prison Rules relating to searches:

PRISON RULES 1999 section 41 (1) – (3) state regarding searches that:

1. Every prisoner shall be searched when taken into custody by an officer, on his reception into a prison and subsequently as the governor thinks necessary or as the Secretary of State may direct.
2. A prisoner shall be searched in as seemly a manner as is consistent with discovering anything concealed.
3. No prisoner shall be stripped and searched in the sight of another prisoner, or in the sight of a person of the opposite sex.

Give examples of when a prisoner may be searched other than when they first enter the prison.

■ Prisoners' property

All incoming property brought in by the prisoner will be searched and recorded. The prisoner will sign a receipt agreeing on the inventory of items collected and stored. Also any unauthorised items found on the prisoner or concealed or deposited anywhere within a prison may be confiscated.

■ Rub-down search

A rub-down search is a basic personal search and is less intrusive than other forms of personal searches, such as a strip search or an intimate body search.

During this search the person being rubbed down remains clothed. The prisoner officer conducting the search will follow this procedure in conducting the search.

Firstly, using an open hand with the fingers spread out comfortably, they will check the front of the prisoner's body from neck to waist, then the sides of the body from under the armpits to the waist and then the front of the prisoner's waistband. They will then check the prisoner's back from collar to waist, then the rear of the waistband and the seat of the trousers. They will then check the front of the abdomen and the front and sides of each leg. Finally the searcher touches the seat of the trousers outside the clothing and runs their hands down the inside of each leg starting at the crotch.

This form of search is the most frequently used and anyone who enters the prison, whether it is a prisoner, staff or a visitor, will be subjected to such a search.

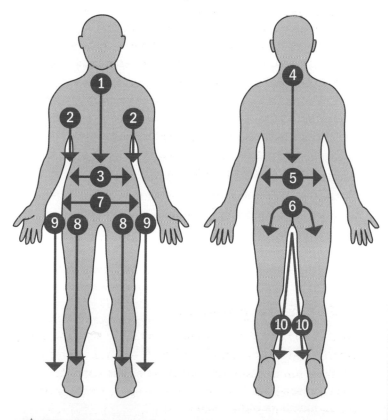

▲ Procedure for a rub-down search

A prison officer can also conduct a personal search if they have reasonable grounds to suspect that a prisoner may possess something that could jeopardise the security of the prison or the safety of persons in the prison.

However, this personal search is limited to outer clothing and sometimes a more intrusive type of search will be conducted – these include a strip search and an intimate body search.

Case study: Female prison officer wins payout over 'rub-down searches'

Daily Mail, 31 August 2006

Carol Saunders, 42, a female prison officer, won a landmark sexual discrimination case and was awarded £145,000 in an out-of-court settlement after being made to carry out intimate 'rub-down' searches of male inmates.

She had claimed it was 'degrading, distasteful and dehumanising' that she had been made to perform physical searches on male prisoners.

She said they subjected her to taunts such as 'higher, miss, higher' during leg searches and 'take as long as you like', leaving her angry and embarrassed.

Prison officers were not permitted to perform the intimate 'rub-down' searches – involving touching the crotch and buttocks – on inmates of the opposite sex when Mrs Saunders joined the service in 1987.

But five years later, after pressure from women warders who said their career prospects were being hampered, the rules were changed so female officers could search inmates of either sex.

A Prison Office spokeswoman said the rules on rub-down searches had now been changed.

'Since the tribunal judgement, female prison officers are no longer compelled to carry out rub-down searches on male prisoners if they do not wish to', she said.

Male prison officers have never been permitted to search female inmates in this way.

Strip search

This search involves the removal of clothing in a private room and involves only half of the body being naked at a time. The person being searched must be given the reasons for such a search and give consent, and no part of the body can be directly touched except for the hair, ears and mouth.

The search is conducted by the person to be searched holding their arms in the air, or standing with their legs apart, to enable a visual examination to be made by the prison officers. The prison officers should be of the same gender and there should be at least two of them. Reasonable care should be taken to protect the person's dignity and the search should be carried out as quickly as reasonably practicable, and the person should be allowed to dress as soon as the search is finished.

Intimate body search

This type of search involves an examination of an orifice or cavity of the prisoner's body other than the mouth. This type of search can only be performed by a doctor. The doctor can ask another person, such as a prison officer, to assist in conducting the search, if reasonably required. The people conducting the search should be the same gender as the prisoner unless it is an emergency.

If the doctor finds something in the course of the search that corresponds with the nature of the search they may seize the item and give it to a prison officer as soon as practicable.

When conducting any of the mentioned searches a prison officer is allowed to use reasonable force to compel a prisoner to submit to a search. Also, if a prisoner refuses to be searched this will lead to a charge of disobeying a lawful order. Visitors and staff who refuse a search will not be able to gain entrance to the prison.

Case study: Wainwright v United Kingdom 12350/04 26 September 2006

In this case the argument was that a strip search conducted by prison officers violated both Article 8 of the European Convention on Human Rights – the right to respect for private and family life, home and correspondence, and Article 3 – the right that no one shall be subjected to torture or inhuman or degrading treatment or punishment.

The facts of the case were that Mrs Wainwright and her mentally and physically impaired son were strip searched during a visit to Mrs Wainwright's other son in prison. A number of prison rules were breached during the search. Mrs Wainwright was searched in front of a window overlooking the street; both applicants were required effectively to strip naked; neither party was shown a consent form before the search began; and the officers put their fingers in the son's armpits, handled his penis and pulled back his foreskin (in spite of the rule that only a person's hair, mouth and ears should be touched).

The ECHR upheld the Wainwrights' claim that the strip searches breached Article 8 of the Convention. They stated that even though they were 'conducted in accordance with the law' and pursued the 'legitimate aim' of fighting drugs in the prison, the ECHR held that prison authorities must comply strictly with procedures set down for searching visitors to a prison, and must 'by rigorous precautions' protect the dignity of those being searched from being assailed any further than is necessary.

The officers' failure to do so amounted to a breach of Article 8 for which each applicant was awarded 3,000 Euros in compensation.

However, the ECHR held that the treatment did not reach the level of severity required to breach Article 3. In order to violate that article, the search must have 'debasing elements which significantly aggravate the inherent humiliation of the procedure' or have 'no established connection with the preservation of prison security and prevention of crime and disorder'.

1. What was the outcome of the case?

2. What are the future implications of this case for
   a) prison staff
   b) members of the public?

■ Scanning search

This is another form of search commonly used within a prison, and consists of the use of electronic devices such as a hand-held scanner or arch style metal detector. These devices can be used as a quick way of searching prisoners, staff and visitors when entering the prison, and such a search can be done without a person removing their general clothes (except perhaps a coat or shoes), and without them being touched by another person.

The nature and security levels of the prison will determine the type of scanning devices used. For example, a body orifice security scanner (BOSS III) has been trialled in HMP Woodhill which is a Category A prison. BOSS III takes the form of a chair which detects small metal objects hidden inside and on the body, such as mobile phones and weapons. It is primarily used when new prisoners enter the reception area before entering the prison, to ensure items that can be used to assist in escapes, drug deals and serious assaults on prisoners and staff don't enter the prison. It is currently being used in all high-security prisons within the UK.

Control measures

Prisoners have certain basic rights, which survive despite imprisonment. These include rights of access to the courts and of respect for one's bodily integrity. Prisoners do lose a range of civil rights, such as the right to vote.

The prison authorities are governed themselves by a range of legislation which include the Prison Act 1952 and the Prison Rules 1999, which ensure that they treat and respect prisoners' rights.

However prisoners themselves do need to follow the rules set down by a prison, and breach of the rules such as by fighting or stealing will be dealt with by the prison. In some cases breaches of prison rules can see extra days added to a sentence.

Prison discipline procedure

All institutions, including prisons, require a means of enforcing their rules and procedures and ensuring that prisoners receive effective sanction for breaches.

Most of the misconduct that takes place in prisons can be dealt with informally through good management and relations. However, certain types of misconduct require formal discipline and this is essential to the maintenance of good order and discipline in a prison.

Offences that infringe Prison Rule 51 – which is any offence that goes against good order and discipline – will lead to formal disciplinary procedures against a prisoner.

There are 25 categories of offences that go against prison discipline, which a prisoner can be found guilty of under Prison Rule 51. Do you think that the following activities are covered by Rule 51?

- Drug possession
- Racially threatening and aggravated behaviour
- Physical assaults on another
- Attempting to escape
- Intoxication
- Destroying or damaging prison property

Through appropriate research, give five other examples of activities that go against good order and discipline and in turn breach Rule 51.

Why do offences like these need to be dealt with formally?

The procedures for prison discipline are set out in the Prison Discipline Manual (PSO 2000, Adjudications Manual 2006). This manual gives power of investigation for all charges to independent adjudicators, governors and controllers of private prisons and sets out all disciplinary offences and punishments. It should be made available to all prisoners and its key aim is to provide fair and just treatment for prisoners within the prison discipline system, by ensuring that all adjudications are conducted in accordance with the law and without discrimination.

The member of staff against whom the alleged offence was committed or who witnessed the particular incident will lay a charge by completing a form F1127A (Notice of Report) which is handed to the accused. A charge must be laid and within 48 hours of the discovery of the offence.

F1127A - NOTICE OF REPORT
COPY FOR PRISONER

Charge number ☐

First name(s) .... Surname ....

Number ....

You have been placed on report by ....

for an alleged offence which was committed at.................. hours on.............................(date)

at .... (place)

The offence with which you are charged is that you:

Contrary to Rule .... Paragraph...................... Prison/YOI Rules
(Delete as appropriate)

The report of the alleged offence is as follows:

Signature of reporting Officer ....

Your case will be heard at .... hours on............................(date)

You will have every opportunity to make your defence. If you wish to write out what you want to say you may ask for writing paper. You or the adjudicator may read it out at the hearing.

You may also say whether you wish to call any witnesses.

This form was issued to you at.. hours on............................(date)

by..(name of issuing officer - block capitals)

..................................☐

OR016 Printed by HMP Albany

▲ Prisoner report form

Key features of the prison discipline procedure

- the charge must be in sufficient detail and the prisoner should have the opportunity to hear what is alleged against them and to present their case
- in cases where the charge is not serious, it will be dealt with by a prison governor
- pending the enquiry by the governor, a prisoner who is to be charged may be segregated
- the prisoner should be given the opportunity to seek legal representation or assistance, including a 'McKenzie friend' (a lay adviser/assistant)
- if legal representation is refused, the prisoner may still request an adjournment in order to get legal advice from a solicitor
- prisoners are entitled to copies of statements or other written material that is to be used in evidence against them
- if an award of additional days is given, the case will be referred to an independent adjudicator. In such cases, the independent adjudicator must conduct a first hearing within 28 days of the referral
- independent adjudicators are district judges (magistrates) who sit in the prison to hear such charges
- where cases are referred to an independent adjudicator, there is a right to be legally represented at the hearing
- at the hearing the prisoner will be allowed to put questions to witnesses who gave evidence against them and to call witnesses relevant to their defence
- the case must be proved by the prosecution to the criminal standard of 'beyond a reasonable doubt'
- the maximum number of additional days that an independent adjudicator may order to be served as punishment for an offence is 42. If a prisoner is found guilty of more than one offence arising from the same incident, the punishments may be ordered to run consecutively
- following an **adjudication** before an independent adjudicator, an application can be made to the Chief Magistrate at Bow Street to review the punishment awarded. However there is no right of appeal regarding the guilty verdict itself, except through judicial review

- where alleged indiscipline amounts to a serious criminal offence the police may be asked to investigate and a prosecution may result.

Adjudication

Key terms

Adjudication The judicial process by which an arbiter or judge reviews evidence and makes a judgement or decree to determine the level of guilt, and if guilt is established a suitable punishment will be imposed.

If the charge against a prisoner is deemed to be serious then the prison governor may choose to adjourn the adjudication for referral to an independent adjudicator who will be better equipped to deal with the incident. Independent adjudicators, who hear the case and charges laid, are approved by the Lord Chancellor in the same way that judges are selected for normal criminal cases.

The adjudication process has two purposes within a prison:

- to help maintain order, control, discipline and a safe environment by investigating offences and punishing those responsible
- to ensure that the use of authority in the establishment is lawful, reasonable and fair.

Punishments

If a guilty finding is reached through the above process, then a range of punishments can be imposed. The punishments available where a minor report charge is proved are described below.

A verbal caution

A caution is available for any case where a warning seems sufficient to recognise the offence and to discourage its repetition. A caution cannot be combined with any other punishment resulting from the same charge, nor can it be combined with the activation of a suspended punishment.

Forfeiture of specified privileges

A prisoner may have their privileges withdrawn for a maximum period of 42 days for adult prisoners and 21 days for young offenders. The privileges to be forfeited must be specified at the hearing and only the privileges that fall within Prison Rules may be withdrawn as a punishment and these are often the privileges that are stated in the prison's Incentives and Earned Privileges Scheme (IEPS).

The following items are not normally covered by IEPS:

- attendance at educational classes and educational materials such as books
- radios and newspapers
- the purchase of postage stamps
- phone credits and the use of the telephone, unless the circumstances of the offence are directly related to their abuse
- the gym
- religious activities, such as attendance at worship or visiting a chaplain.

Extra work

This is available only to young offenders. The extra work given will be outside normal working hours and for a maximum period of 21 days from the date punishment is imposed, and not for more than two hours on any given day. The work to be carried out is done under normal circumstances and at the normal pace.

Other punishments

Other more serious punishments are available to both independent adjudicators and prison governors:

- additional days added to sentence
- stoppage of earnings
- cellular confinement
- exclusion from work
- removal from wing or living unit
- suspended punishments
- referral to police

Additional days added to sentence

These may only be imposed by an independent adjudicator. Where an adjudicator, such as a prison governor, considers that a charge warrants a punishment of additional days, the charge will be referred to an independent adjudicator.

Stoppage of earnings

These may be imposed by any adjudicator and they may stop all or part of a prisoner's daily pay earned while in prison, excluding sums paid into a private bank account to which the prison does not have access. The maximum amount is 84 days' full pay for adult offenders and 42 days' full pay for young offenders.

Cellular confinement

This may be imposed by any adjudicator with the maximum period of cellular confinement being 21 days for adult prisoners and 10 days for young offenders. The punishment can only be imposed when a medical practitioner or registered nurse has completed a Segregation Safety Algorithm or Assessment. They are also required to visit the prisoner on a daily basis.

Exclusion from work

This may be imposed by any adjudicator with the maximum exclusion period being both 21 days for adult and young offenders. For adult prisoners the punishment must not in itself involve forfeiture of any other privileges except those that are incompatible with exclusion from associated work. For young offenders the punishment differs as it covers removal from particular activities other than training courses, work and education.

Removal from wing or living unit

This may be imposed by any adjudicator with a maximum period for removal from wing or living unit of 28 days for adults and 21 days for young offenders. They will be held in a cell or room away from the wing or living unit for the set time, but the prisoner must be allowed to take part in normal compulsory regime activities, including work, education, physical activity and training with other prisoners and none of their basic privileges are lost.

Suspended punishments

This may be imposed by an independent adjudicator, who may order any punishment other than a verbal caution to be suspended for up to six months so that it will not take effect unless the prisoner commits another disciplinary offence during the suspension period.

■ Referrals to the police

Any serious criminal offence must be reported immediately to the adjudicator for a decision about whether the police should be informed. Where the police are asked to investigate, a disciplinary charge must nevertheless be laid within 48 hours of discovery of the alleged offence. In such cases the adjudicator must open the adjudication and adjourn the hearing pending the outcome of the police investigation. The independent adjudicator is not involved at this stage.

If no prosecution results from the referral, or if the Crown Prosecution Service decides that a prosecution cannot continue, the adjudicator must consider whether to proceed with the disciplinary charge. If they do proceed they will follow the same standard disciplinary procedure and use the range of punishments mentioned.

Incentives to behave

All prisons will have incentives as a way of encouraging prisoners to earn things such as extra time out of the cell, the right to attend certain classes, to spend more of their own money in the prison canteen, to have extra visits or to have a cell of their own.

■ The Incentives and Earned Privileges Scheme

Prison Rule 8 requires every prison to provide a system of privileges which can be granted to prisoners in addition to the minimum entitlements. The prison service introduced an Incentives and Earned Privileges Scheme (IEPS) in July 1995, and prisoners have the opportunity to earn additional privileges through good and responsible behaviour, participation in hard work and other constructive activities. In turn they can lose these privileges if they misbehave or fail to participate in prison life.

The aim of the scheme is to:
- provide privileges that can be earned by prisoners through good behaviour and performance, and can be removed if prisoners fail to maintain acceptable standards

- encourage responsible behaviour by prisoners
- encourage hard work and other constructive activity by prisoners
- encourage sentenced prisoners to make progress within the prison system
- create a more disciplined, better controlled and safer environment for prisoners and staff.

The scheme ensures that privileges above the minimum are earned by prisoners through good behaviour and performance. Privileges earned can substantially affect a prisoner's daily life in prison and include:
- extra and improved visits
- eligibility to earn higher rates of pay
- access to in-cell television
- opportunity to wear own clothes
- access to private cash on top of their prison wages
- time out of cell for association.

Take it further

Why might the following non-material incentives be beneficial for prisoners and the prison environment?

1. Positions and jobs of trust.

2. Community work outside the prison.

3. Opportunity to prepare own meals.

4. Opportunity to build relationships and mix with other prisoners and staff.

5. Movement to a less secure unit or prison.

6. Additional responsibility and choice regarding prison life such as time and frequency out of cell.

■ The three-tier system

This is a scheme of graded privileges and standards within a prison, which operates on three tiers or levels, namely basic, standard and enhanced. All prisoners entering the prison system will start off on the standard privilege level and this will be reviewed within their first month.

Basic

The basic level is a minimum standard of facilities to which someone is entitled to regardless of their behaviour and performance, such as entitlement to visits, letters, telephone calls, provision of food and clothing and any other minimum facilities provided by the prison to all prisoners such as the prison shop, exercise and association. Prisoners will be allowed and expected to participate in normal prison activities such as work, education, treatment programmes and religious services.

Standard

The standard level provides prisoners with a greater volume of the allowances, privileges and facilities than those on basic privileges. This is likely to include more frequent visits, more time for association and the provision of in-cell television. Standard-level prisoners are also eligible for higher rates of pay for work and a higher allowance of private cash.

Enhanced

Prisoners on enhanced level will receive the same privileges as those on a standard level but in greater volume. This is likely to include additional visits in better surroundings with more flexibility over actual visiting times, additional time for association, more private cash, and priority consideration for certain prison jobs and higher rates of pay.

Take it further

You are a prison governor and have been asked to create a guidance leaflet on what constitutes good behaviour and good performance within your prison. You have sought government guidance and they have given you a list of possible criteria. You have decided to illustrate the use of these criteria by adding a range of examples under each heading for prison staff to use. The headings are:

- Effort and achievement in work and activities
- Non-violent behaviour
- Non-discriminatory behaviour
- Civility
- Mutual respect
- Fairness
- Supporting others
- Respecting prison rules and routines
- Health and safety.

■ Loss of privileges

Prisoners may lose an earned privilege or move to a lower privilege level if they demonstrate a pattern of declining behaviour or performance. Normally a single incident of misbehaviour or short-term failure of performance should not automatically result in a change of status, but may be taken into account when reviewing the prisoner's general suitability to be granted or retain privileges.

Other control measures

There are many other ways of keeping control in a prison other than the formal disciplinary system or the incentives scheme. Other control methods include confiscating property of prisoners, changing their work or education, keeping certain prisoners away from other prisoners, restraining prisoners and even placing prisoners in a special cell. The prison staff cannot use these methods as formal punishments but can use them to control or prevent trouble within the prison.

■ Segregation

Prisoners can also be segregated, but only on the grounds of maintenance of good order and discipline, or for the prisoner's own protection, for a maximum of three days. As with the cellular confinement, a medical officer will need to assess the prisoner before the segregation can take place. Longer periods of segregation need to be authorised by the Secretary of State for Justice and they will require written reasons for the segregation. They have the power to segregate for up to a month, then the case will be reviewed on a monthly basis. In extreme cases a disciplinary transfer may take place; for example when a prisoner is considered to be too disruptive or subversive. Transfer to another prison may be temporary, for a period of up to one month for a cooling-off period. It will then be up to the governor at the alternative prison to consider if it is necessary for the prisoner to be segregated further.

■ Restraints

Prison officers are instructed not to use force unless absolutely necessary and when necessary to use no more force than is absolutely necessary to bring the situation under control.

To help deal with violent or unmanageable prisoners, prison officers on the authority of the prison governor may place them temporarily in a special cell – these cells are either ones stripped of all furniture except for a mattress or have cardboard furniture that cannot cause injury to the prisoner or others. Prisoners should only be held in these special cells whilst they are a threat to others and usually this is less than 24 hours.

The prison governor may also order prisoners to be put in physical restraints if they feel it is necessary to prevent injury to the prisoner or others, to help prevent damage to prison property or to help deal with a prison disturbance. This usually takes the form of body belts, which are leather belts placed around the waist with handcuffs attached, which are used in the normal fashion to help restrain movement. This procedure is rare and only used in extreme cases and anyone placed in such a restraint needs approval of the prison medical officer and should not be restrained for a period greater than 24 hours.

It should be noted that should a prisoner be held, either unnecessarily or for too long, in a body belt or other restraint, this can constitute assault and give the prisoner legal grounds for a prosecution.

■ Restraint techniques

Restraint techniques are used only as a last resort in order to bring a violent or uncooperative prisoner under control when all other methods such as persuasion and negotiation have been exhausted. These techniques should only be applied for the shortest period of time possible and should only be used with a team of at least three officers with a fourth deployed to control the legs.

The level of force used in bringing the situation under control should be reasonable, proportionate, and no more than is necessary in the circumstances. The restraint team should aim towards releasing and relaxing the holds and locks imposed on the prisoner if the prisoner is compliant as this reduces the risk of injury to the team and the prisoner.

When staff arrive at an incident, such as a fight between two prisoners, they should not put themselves in danger but wait until they have enough staff to attempt to deal with the situation – in this case at least six officers (three for each prisoner). Before the arrival of sufficient staff the officers should use reasonable force to protect themselves and others and after a restraint takes place the prisoner should seek medical attention as soon as possible. Finally a record of all restraints should be kept and prisoners should be aware of the avenues of complaint open to them.

Consider this

How would you deal with the following situation?

You are on a night shift and the fire alarm is sounded at 2am on your wing. You are the first to arrive and find that the cell is on fire with one prisoner on the ground, who appears to be unconscious whilst another is at the cell door with an object in their hand and they are threatening to cut you up if you enter. You can see another officer approaching but due to staffing levels you are unsure about how long it will be until further assistance arrives.

What do you do in this situation and what force may be reasonable to deal with the incident?

Gareth Myatt, from Stoke-on-Trent, choked to death in April 2004, three days into a six-month sentence, after staff used a technique known as a 'seated double embrace' to restrain him when he refused to clean a sandwich toaster. The 15-year-old complained of being unable to breathe, but was ignored. An inquest reached a verdict of accidental death.

Consider this

Use the Internet to research the Gareth Myatt case further. Following this case should there be a ban on restraint techniques within prisons? List and consider the pros and cons before making a final decision.

Assessment activity 21.3

You have been asked by your tutor to create a professional leaflet that describes the control measures in place in a custodial environment **P3** and explains the purpose of incentives schemes in relation to addressing offending behaviour and the maintenance of control **M2**.

Grading tips

To achieve **P3** you need to describe a number of different methods available to ensure that control of the individual is maintained while in custody.

To achieve **M2** you need to investigate and explain how incentive schemes assist in addressing offending behaviour and help to control individuals.

Receiving individuals into custody

The first place the prisoner will come to on arriving at prison is the reception. The prison term for booking in new prisoners is called 'processing' and prisons can vary in their reception procedures, but all prisons will conduct the following as a bare minimum when receiving a prisoner into custody:

1. The prisoner's property will be searched and listed by the reception officer and some items will be put into safe-keeping by being placed in a sealed bag for storage and returned to them when they leave prison. Other items will be kept by the prisoner. For example, a prisoner will not be able to bring in food or their own toiletries and will instead be supplied with basic essentials such as soap and toothpaste as part of a reception pack. All the prisoner's cash will be paid into an account which is controlled by the prison, and the prisoner will not automatically have access to the money. The amount they can actually spend weekly varies according to whether they are convicted or unconvicted, and whether they are on a basic, standard or enhanced regime.

2. The prisoner will provide and confirm personal details and be given a prison number. This will remain with them throughout their sentence, even if they are transferred to a different prison. This number is issued to help keep track of their property, personal details and other relevant files.

3. The prisoner will undergo a strip search and should be offered the chance to have a bath or shower. They will also have a medical examination in order to assess their health on entering the prison, so that they can be given proper care whilst they are in prison. For example, the medical examination will aim to identify prisoners who have drug problems or suffer from HIV, so that any medication that they need can be provided.

4. Convicted prisoners may have their own clothes exchanged for the appropriate prison dress, and will have their photo and fingerprints taken. They may be asked to provide a urine sample for a drugs test.

The prisoner should also, as soon as feasibly possible, have a reception interview with an allocated personal officer (a prison officer) or prison probation officer, who is there to help the prisoner if they don't understand something regarding the booking-in process, if they have any questions or if they need any additional advice or support.

If the prisoner has not been able to talk to their solicitor before leaving court, then the reception officer will help in contacting the solicitor to arrange a visit.

The prisoner will be inducted into the prison to help them settle into prison life; this involves a seminar which explains how the prison works and what each prisoner's responsibilities are. They will be given a copy of the Prisoners' Information Handbook and made aware of where they can locate a copy of the Prison Rules. They will then be taken to the wing and allocated a cell.

Property procedures

Prisoners may retain a reasonable amount of their personal property with them while in custody, but some limitations and restrictions are necessary to maintain good order and discipline, and security. The rules vary from prison to prison on what property prisoners may possess and this is influenced by the status, size and security level of the prison.

When a prisoner enters a prison, their property – if not on their person – will be checked against the Prisoner Escort Record. If on their person it will be searched and recorded at reception and all unauthorised items will be stored away or disposed of in accordance with the prison's rules.

7. an electric shaver
8. batteries for personal possessions
9. toiletries for personal use
10. one wedding ring or other plain ring
11. one medallion or locket
12. photographs and pictures
13. unpadded greetings cards, postage stamps and envelopes
14. a calendar, address book, diary and personal organiser
15. medication and disability aids.

▲ Prisoners may be allowed to have pictures, reading matter and a sound system in their cells

Items retained by prisoners

Prisoners must be allowed to have in their possession any items related to religion, such as religious books or artefacts. Unconvicted prisoners may retain books, newspapers, writing materials and other means of occupation unless it is misused for a purpose that threatens good order, discipline or security. The possession of any other item is at the discretion of the prison, according to the rules of that prison, and dependent upon the prisoner's privilege level. Since the introduction of the Incentives and Earned Privileges Scheme, many prisons have limited the range of items that can be retained by the prisoner, or even disallowed any items being retained at all, as prisoners must buy all items through the scheme. However, the following items are usually allowed to be retained and owned by prisoners in their cells although this list is not exhaustive:

1. newspapers, magazines and books
2. a sound system including records, cassettes, CDs and earphones
3. cigarettes, tobacco and cigars
4. board games and electronic games including consoles
5. writing and drawing materials
6. a standard wristwatch

Consider this

Should prisoners be allowed any luxuries whilst in prison? What are the pros and cons for arguing that luxuries should be allowed?

Receiving, storing and releasing property

The amount of property that prisoners may retain in their possession is limited by the policy on 'volumetric control'. This aims to ensure that cells and prisons don't become cluttered, so that search procedures are not unnecessarily hampered, and that the quantity of property which accompanies prisoners is manageable. As a standard rule, prisoners are allowed to keep about six cubic feet of property (two large boxes) plus one oversize item, such as a sound system. However the prison can authorise on request a greater volume to be held. Some items, such as religious items, legal papers and one set of personal clothes and bedding, are exempt from the rule. The items that are controlled include education materials, food, consumables, utensils and equipment associated with hobbies. Prisoners who exceed the volume controls are encouraged to hand or send the excess items out to friends or relatives.

■ Storing property

Property can be stored within the prison or by the prisoner in their cell and this will cover property such as personal clothing, personal disposable items and prison issue items; however, items that are not likely to be needed or are unauthorised within the prisons will be stored at the Branston National Distribution Centre (NDC).

Once the items are stored at the NDC the prisoners will not be allowed to gain access to them unless there is an exceptional circumstance or until they are released. For those due to be released, the date on which the property is required must be specified by the prison, and 10 working days' notice is normally needed. Property belonging to a discharged prisoner will only be sent to the prison for collection, and not to any private address.

■ Receiving property

In some prisons prisoners can receive property such as items of personal clothing. This may be done by family or friends handing items in to the prison property desk, or in some cases items may be sent by post. It is then checked and either returned to the sender or given to the prisoner, depending on its suitability – for example, its value, whether it is an authorised item, or its size. Money handed in by family or friends is held by the prison in a personal account for the prisoner and money sent by post is often requested in the form of a postal order. It is often possible for prisoners to buy things from approved mail order companies if these items are not available through the prison shop and carry no security implications or risk. Prisoners are generally not allowed to transfer ownership of their property to other prisoners, unless the prison is satisfied that such transfers are voluntary and for acceptable reasons (for example, not the result of bullying or taxing, or in exchange for illicit items). Generally, prisoners are not allowed to send money out of the prison unless it is checked (for example, the money is not being sent to suspected criminals or drug dealers) and approved by the prison beforehand.

Finally, if a prisoner is transferred to another prison, their property is stored for them by the prison, and their private cash account will be transferred to the new prison. Any articles belonging to a prisoner which remain unclaimed for a period of more than three years after they leave prison will be sold or disposed of.

We need to remember that the prison at all times retains the right to confiscate any item within a prison, no matter what it is, if it threatens the security and safety of the prison.

Discharging individuals from the custodial environment

Before the date of the prisoner's release, a member of the prison probation staff will put the prisoner in contact with probation staff in their local area who will supervise the prisoner's licence.

They will also help the prisoner contact support agencies, who can help with accommodation, training, education or employment after release, and specialists who can help prisoners deal with particular issues such as alcohol or drug abuse, gambling addictions and behavioural problems such as anger management.

These issues are also covered when prisoners attend a pre-release course run by the prison resettlement team, which will address general issues that they will have to deal with on release such as housing, work, benefits, health, addictions and families.

Before a prisoner is discharged they will go through a parole board meeting, where probation staff will demonstrate that the prisoner will cooperate with any conditions set in a parole licence, that they will meet regularly with probation staff during their licence period, and that they have accommodation arranged which can either be their own home, a family or friend's home, or a registered hostel.

Shortly before they are discharged the prisoner will have a discharge interview to confirm where they will live, and to establish if they have or need additional support, for example a community care grant if the prisoner is short of items such as clothing and household items.

The prisoner will also be examined by the medical officer shortly before they are discharged. If they are not well or fit to leave prison they will stay in prison until they are ready for release or in some cases a family member, prison officer or friend will be requested to travel with them on their release.

When a prisoner is released from custody, they will have their private property returned and also their private cash, including any additional prison earnings that are outstanding. They are likely to receive a travel warrant to help them get home by public transport, and a discharge grant which is roughly equivalent to one week's benefit to support them until they get their first benefit payment or first wage.

Prisoners will in most cases be released before 8.45am but will have breakfast first and if the release date falls at the weekend or on a bank holiday they will be released on the last working day which is usually a Friday. However if a prisoner is being released on parole, normally the release date will be the first working day after the parole release date.

Early release from prison on licence

Prisoners serving a sentence of more than 12 months in prison may be released early on licence. Being released on licence means that they are still serving a prison sentence but they can live in the community instead of being in prison. Whilst they are on licence, there are a number of conditions they must follow and the period of time these conditions are in place depends mainly on the length of the original sentence.

Common licence conditions include:
- not to commit any further criminal offences
- to have a good standard of behaviour
- to keep in touch with a designated probation officer and follow the rehabilitation plan
- to live at an address that has been approved by the probation officer
- to take part in approved voluntary work schemes or paid work
- not to travel outside the UK
- to adhere to the home detention curfew agreement
- not to associate or make contact with certain people
- not to live in or enter certain locations or areas.

If any of these conditions are not adhered to then the prisoner is likely to go back to prison, or receive a warning from their probation officer. If they have committed another criminal offence whilst out on licence, they will also go to court for that offence and if found guilty, the new sentence will be added on to the original sentence.

Home detention curfew (tagging)

Any prisoner who receives a sentence of less than four years could be released on a home detention curfew before the end of their sentence. This curfew involves a small electronic tag attached to the prisoner's ankle, which will monitor their location. The condition of the curfew means that at certain times of the day or evening the prisoner has to stay inside at an agreed address. Usually the curfew runs from 7pm to 7am the next morning but can be adapted to suit job and training arrangements. As with any licence, if the prisoner breaks the conditions set they are likely to be recalled to prison.

Temporary licence

In certain circumstances a prisoner will be allowed to leave prison on a temporary licence before the end of their sentence. Being released on a temporary licence is given to prisoners when a service or activity cannot be provided by the prison itself. For example, it may be granted to prisoners to help them attend certain training courses that are not provided inside the prison, to do community work or to help them adjust back into the community.

There are a number of different types of temporary licences and these include:
- **Special Purpose licences:** given to prisoners in exceptional personal circumstances such as to visit dying relatives, attend a funeral, to get married, to receive special medical treatment or for religious reasons
- **Resettlement Day Release licences:** given to prisoners to allow them to participate in reparative and community service work or employment and work skills training/education
- **Resettlement Overnight Release licences:** given to prisoners to help maintain family ties and to make arrangements for accommodation, work or training on release
- **Childcare Resettlement licence:** given to prisoners in open or semi-open conditions or in a mother and baby unit when they have sole caring responsibility for a child under 16 years of age.

To ensure the security of the community the following groups will be ineligible for any type of temporary licence:

- Category A prisoners (those who are an escape risk)
- prisoners subject to extradition orders
- prisoners who are remanded on further charges which are waiting further convictions.

Additionally, Category B prisoners are not eligible for the two resettlement release licences. The prison governor can refuse release of any prisoner, if their release is likely to undermine public confidence in the administration of justice. Governors also have the power to recall a prisoner to prison at any time, whether the conditions of their release have been broken or not.

Sex offender register

If a prisoner who has been convicted of certain sex offences is released early they will be placed on the register for a predetermined amount of time and they are required to follow the conditions of the licence. They will also have to give the police their details including their current address and keep them informed if they move.

Pre-release conditions

All prisoners will undergo a risk assessment prior to early release on licence. The list of factors given below is not exhaustive, and there may be other issues that lead to the creation of pre-release conditions.

Here are some of the considerations:

- Is the prisoner a significant risk to the public? If so, the application should be refused.
- Where will the prisoner live, and is this a suitable environment?
- Would any victims be protected and safe?
- Would there be family support?
- Has the prisoner addressed any drug or alcohol problems?
- Has the prisoner fully complied with the conditions set for previous periods of release?
- Has the prisoner been well-behaved in prison?
- Is the prisoner debt free or with no outstanding fines to the court?

If any of the answers to these questions is 'no', then early release should be reviewed and initially refused.

Consider this

Using the guidance from Prison Rule 9 on temporary release, imagine you are a prison governor, and decide whether or not you would allow temporary release for the following prisoners:

1. Prisoner A is a Category A prisoner. He has heard that his father is critically ill after having a heart attack, and is not expected to recover or regain consciousness.
2. Prisoner B is required to meet police officers at the scene of a murder that he has alleged to have witnessed.
3. Prisoner C has been offered the opportunity of employment as an electrician on his release, but needs to do a specialist course to allow him to take up this position.
4. Prisoner D is worried about his divorce settlement, and would like to visit his solicitor to discuss it further. He is only 4 weeks into a 3-year sentence.

Assessment activity 21.4

You have been asked by your tutor to visually demonstrate, through a videoed role-play, the process of receiving and discharging individuals and their property into and from the custodial environment. You should make sure that the role-play includes sufficient verbal commentary which clearly describes the processes involved in receiving and discharging individuals and their property into and from the custodial environment. **P5**

Grading tips

To achieve **P5** you must clearly describe the entire process of receiving and discharging an individual and their property into and from the custodial environment.

Internal relationships

As prisoners and prison staff spend a great deal of time together, good relationships between both parties are important, but need to be appropriate, and not overly friendly. All prison staff need to be supportive and encourage prisoners to engage in positive behaviour that will help them to rehabilitate. This can be achieved if all prison staff liaise closely with each other, especially those working within different teams in a prison, such as those concerned with education, health and rehabilitation.

Consider this

List five reasons why it is important for prisoners and staff to build good relations within a custodial environment. Discuss these reasons with a colleague.

Role of prison officer

It is important that all prison officers build a positive and professional relationship with prisoners. This is so that tasks and duties such as supervising prisoners, maintaining order, carrying out security checks and searching procedures can be done in a safe and amicable atmosphere. This also means there is less requirement to employ physical control and restraint over prisoners as well as creating a culture which takes account of everyone's rights and dignity. This in turn will help create an environment free of bullying by both staff and prisoners and also leads to a more supportive setting for prisoners.

Provision of support for prisoners whilst in custody

Within prisons there are different courses to support individuals during their sentences in order for them

▲ Prison officers can create a positive environment through professional and supportive relationships with prisoners

to integrate back into society; these include a number of courses which help them develop their interaction, communication and relationship skills. Some of these are described below.

■ Healthy Relationships Programme (HRP)

This programme is primarily for male offenders who have either been convicted of or admit to abusive and violent behaviour towards their spouse or partner. The programme is designed to reduce the risk of further violence in their future intimate relationships.

■ Choices, Actions, Relationships and Emotions (CARE)

This programme is primarily for female offenders whose offending is related to difficulties with emotion regulation. The programme is designed to help offenders identify and label emotions and develop skills for managing emotion.

A range of more general offending behaviour programmes are addressed later within the chapter.

External relationships

When prisoners leave the custodial environment they may need support and guidance from a variety of different sources.

Consider this

Research these agencies and list the kinds of support they could offer.

Research and list three other agencies that offer either emotional or relationship support.

Consider this

List the support prisoners may need from the following groups:

- family and friends
- employers
- police
- probation officer
- local council
- social services.

Support organisations

Another source of external support to prisoners may be provided by a variety of charitable and statutory support groups. These can offer prisoners a range of support from basic financial help and advice, to help in dealing with relationship and emotional issues.

These agencies can offer support to prisoners with both emotional and relationship issues:

Counselling and therapy

Another way prisoners can gain support for helping to build better relationships is through counselling and therapy.

Counselling is all about trained counsellors listening and helping people discuss their emotional issues such as relationship problems, mental health issues and suicidal tendencies. The role of a counsellor is not to tell a person what to do but to help them identify the issues behind their problems to allow them to deal with them, and in some cases act as a mediator.

Prisoners may also receive therapy. The two most common are behavioural and cognitive therapy:

- **Behavioural therapy** helps prisoners identify any unusual thoughts or feelings they may have, and helps them to address these. This is done through a series of rewards given when they confront the issues and factors that influence these thoughts.

- **Cognitive therapy** helps prisoners to recognise unusual thoughts or events that could potentially result in unwanted feelings and negative behaviour. This is done by helping prisoners to amend their initial thoughts and replace them with a different perspective.

These two approaches are often combined and prisoners will take part in both types of therapy to help them address and change their perceptions, feelings and thought processes in order to change their behaviour and aid emotional development.

▲ Figure 21.1 Agencies and support groups available to prisoners

The following techniques are examples of topics covered during these types of therapies:

- Challenging certain thoughts and perceptions
- Communication and body language strategies
- Coping strategies
- Thought stopping and control
- Relaxation and meditation

Dealing with offending behaviour

Assessment of individual behaviour

Every prisoner entering prison will be assessed; this will include a psychological assessment and part of this assessment will identify any behavioural characteristics or personal circumstances that may lead them back into crime upon release.

These assessments primarily focus on issues such as:

- alcohol and drugs problems, as these are often linked to crime
- social factors that can increase the likelihood of re-offending
- personal factors that can increase the risk of re-offending.
- intervention strategies, in order to reduce prisoners' levels of risk and increase their quality of prison life.

Consider this

Here is a list of common risk factors which are associated with offending and re-offending behaviour. A combination of these factors will further increase the likelihood of re-offending on release:

- lack of qualifications
- unemployment
- no accommodation
- substance addictions
- mental health issues
- social and behavioural problems.

How could these be addressed? Suggest at least one strategy for each, and state whether it could be tackled within a prison or outside after release.

Behavioural factors

Prisoners' behavioural issues that lead to re-offending can stem from a number of physical, social, psychological and emotional factors. Here are a few examples:

- **personality** – some people tend to be more aggressive and impulsive than others and this can often be linked to offending behaviour
- **medical conditions** – Attention Deficit Hyperactivity Disorder (ADHD) and autism can lead to misunderstanding and a belief that these people behave in an anti-social manner
- **family issues** – lack of parental involvement or lack of parental supervision can lead people to offend as they have no role models or safeguards on what is and is not acceptable behaviour
- **education** – people with poor levels of attainment, high levels of truancy or little commitment to obtaining qualifications will often demonstrate negative behaviour, as they become frustrated with the limited opportunities they have during or after their time in education
- **society** – people living in disadvantaged or neglected neighbourhoods will witness and often replicate criminal activities, and an increased availability of substances such as drugs and under-age drinking will also increase the possibility of offending behaviour
- **peer groups** – associating with certain people can lead to offending behaviour.

■ Why do people continue to re-offend?

There are many common triggers that can lead people to re-offend; these include poor thinking and problem-solving skills such as decision-making, little self-control and poor social skills.

People who re-offend tend to not identify or foresee potential problems, and lack the ability to recognise the full range of possibilities when they are dealing with a problem. They tend not to be able to disassociate from offending peers. Such people have a propensity to be more impulsive, and are more prone to aggressive and hostile behaviour which will lead them to getting into trouble with the police and courts.

▲ Crime is often linked to peer pressure and under-age drinking

Dealing with and changing offending behaviour

To help prisoners deal with their offending behaviour they will have to address a number of issues. One way that this can be done is by allowing prisoners to talk about how they think and feel about their crimes. Prisoners will reflect on and try to understand the harm and anguish they cause to other people through their behaviour. This includes both the victims of their crime and their own family and friends. Both these can be addressed through taking part in role-play and practical exercises.

Finally, a great deal of time and resources are spent on prisoners learning new techniques to help them develop in areas such as coping mechanisms, problem-solving strategies and decision-making skills. The most common way of addressing offending behaviour is through a range of offending behaviour programmes.

Offender Behaviour Programmes

All prisons will offer a range of specialist programmes designed to help prisoners to change their behaviour so that they are less likely to re-offend after release from prison.

The prison service, through the Offending Behaviour Programmes Unit, currently provides 13 different Offending Behaviour Programmes (excluding Drug Treatment Programmes). Some of the programmes offered are described below.

■ Enhanced Thinking Skills (ETS)

This is one of the most popular programmes offered within prisons. It helps offenders to develop thinking skills, so that they can deal with behaviour associated with offending. It covers issues such as impulse control, logical reasoning, morality, social values and inter-personal problem solving.

■ Controlling Anger and Learning to Manage It (CALM)

This programme is for offenders whose offending is associated with poor emotional control. It aims to enable offenders to reduce the intensity, occurrence and duration of negative emotions which are associated with their offending. These emotions include anger, anxiety and jealousy.

■ Cognitive Self Change Programme (CSCP)

This programme is for offenders who are high-risk violent offenders. It helps them to develop skills to help control their violence, and includes both group and individual sessions.

■ Sex Offender Treatment Programmes (SOTP)

There are a range of programmes available for sexual offenders, and the nature and appropriateness of the programme will be measured according to the level of risk and the needs of the offender.

■ One-to-One Programme

This programme involves the use of psychological and social methods on an individual basis to help change the thoughts, attitudes and values that contribute to offending behaviour.

■ Think First Programme

This is a group work programme which helps offenders to confront, challenge and change their thoughts, attitudes and values that can cause offending behaviour.

■ Drug Treatment Programmes

There are a range of programmes which encourage prisoners to address their substance use. These include:

- the Voluntary Drug Testing scheme
- the Peer Support scheme
- Prison-Addressing Substance Related Offending (P-ASRO) programme
- Counselling, Assessment, Referral, Advice and Throughcare (CARAT) team.

It should be clear that most help available to prisoners is in the form of intervention programmes/treatments provided by both the prison psychology department and OASys teams. Only in exceptional cases will external counsellors be used.

You have been asked by the prison service to create a written booklet which includes appropriate illustrations. This will be given to trainee staff to help them.

The booklet needs to cover the following topics:

a) outline the importance of positive relationships for individuals in custody both internally and externally **P4**

b) identify how offending behaviour is addressed in custody, including a description of the aims of at least one accredited offending behaviour programme **P6**

c) explain how developing positive relationships and addressing offending behaviour benefits the individual and society **M3**

d) Analyse the ways offending behaviour is addressed and the need for individuals to address their offending behaviour while in custody and before being released from custody. **D2**

Grading tips

P4 To achieve this, you will need to outline the importance of the development and maintenance of positive relationships, both internally and externally, of individuals inside the custodial environment.

P6 To achieve this, you should identify the ways that offending behaviour is addressed in custody. You must also be able to describe the aims of a specific accredited offending behaviour programme – including its purpose, duration and expected outcome.

M3 To achieve this, you need to explain how developing positive relationships and addressing behaviour benefits the individual and society.

D2 To achieve this, you need to analyse the ways offending behaviour is addressed, and the need for individuals to address offending behaviour while they are in custody and before being released from custody. You should provide examples to explain the main triggers that are connected to an individual committing a crime, and identify the most appropriate programme for their chosen offending behaviour.

Preparation for resettlement

Inside and outside the custodial environment

Resettlement is the period when offenders and their families receive support from the prison, the Probation Service, and a range of voluntary and statutory agencies, so that a prisoner can prepare for life after prison. Resettlement work begins within the custodial environment and continues after release back into the community. The ultimate aim is to help offenders return to a normal life and integrate back into society, by ensuring they have employment and training (including education), suitable accommodation, and are able to cope with life without re-offending.

Resettlement work within prison includes anything that helps them to become independent and law-abiding citizens, such as:

- offering education, training and employment opportunities whilst in prison
- preserving family ties, through allowing frequent visits
- addressing any addiction problems
- tackling their offending behaviour and improving their life skills
- job clubs, which give advice and assistance on jobs, including how to prepare a CV and interview techniques.

The role of the probation officer

Probation officers play a significant role in the resettlement of offenders both within and outside the custodial environment. Their aim is to reduce the likelihood of further offending, to ensure the proper punishment of offenders, to rehabilitate the offender back into the community and reduce crime.

Their key roles include:

- the preparation of written reports for the courts, including pre-sentence reports which advise courts about the security risk posed by individual offenders, and how that risk should be contained
- managing and enforcing Community Orders made by the courts, including probation orders

- assisting in sentence management during their custodial sentence, including arrangements for eventual release
- arranging support and monitoring progression and rehabilitation
- interacting with offenders, their families and their victims
- managing and supporting offenders released early on licence
- comprehensive management of documentation and personal records of offenders.

Outside the custodial environment there are a range of agencies that support offenders – these are often arranged by the probation officer who will monitor and manage their rehabilitation. Some of these agencies are described below.

The National Association for the Care and Resettlement of Offenders (NACRO)

This agency is primarily a crime reduction organisation, with the aim of making society safer by finding practical solutions to reducing crime. A large part of this role is to work with ex-offenders by providing offenders with up-to-date information on housing, employment, training, education, benefits, debt advice and counselling services. It also runs a helpline to ensure that ex-offenders, their families and friends can easily access this information.

UNLOCK – The National Association of Reformed Offenders

This agency advises and assists serving and former prisoners who want to lead a crime-free lifestyle. It gives them a voice by campaigning to create better facilities for prisoners after release, so that ex-offenders can leave crime behind and rebuild their lives. A key aim of UNLOCK is to overcome the social exclusion of ex-offenders, thus helping them to break the cycle of re-offending and so benefit society as a whole.

Bridging the Gap

This agency aims to reduce re-offending by helping released prisoners settle back into the community. This support includes help with claiming benefits, pursuing accommodation, training opportunities, and links with employers who are willing to recruit ex-offenders.

Knowledge check

1. What are the three main types of security and how do they differ?

2. What are the key duties of a personal officer?

3. List the other three public service agencies apart from the prison service that will use visual search equipment such as infrared telescopes.

4. What are the different types of searches that can be conducted on prisoners?

5. In what ways is minor misconduct dealt with in the prison environment?

6. What does the term adjudication mean?

7. State three common punishments given to prisoners who break the rules.

8. What is the main purpose of the Incentives and Earned Privileges Scheme (IEPS)?

9. What other methods of control do prison officers have over prisoners?

10. What are the key elements of receiving a prisoner into custody?

11. What internal support mechanisms are available to prisoners?

12. What external support mechanisms are available to prisoners?

13. Why is it important to address offending behaviour?

14. What are the key roles of a probation officer?

15. What is the main role of NACRO?

Preparation for assessment

The Home Secretary has chosen to visit your prison in response to a series of national negative media stories on poor security and control measures within prisons, the conducting of inappropriate searches, over-generous incentive schemes for prisoners, inhuman treatment of prisoners by staff during all aspects of the prison system, and insufficient work on addressing offending behaviour.

During the visit, which is also open to important dignitaries and the media, you have been asked to do the following:

1. Conduct a formal verbal presentation that clearly outlines the main security considerations within a prison. **P1** Explain how combining security elements can improve the overall security of a custodial establishment. **M1**

The presentation should conclude with an open group forum which allows the dignitaries to ask questions and allows you to analyse the main security measures, showing why it is important that no single measure is allowed to dominate within a custodial environment. **D1**

2. Conduct a series of demonstrations which correctly shows the different types and methods of searches undertaken by staff in a custodial environment. Include a verbal commentary on each one. **P2**

3. Prepare a visual presentation, including images which describe the control measures in place in a custodial environment. **P3** Explain the purpose of incentive schemes in relation to addressing offending behaviour and the maintenance of control. **M2**

4. Create a short written report which will be given to the dignitaries on arrival, which clearly outlines the importance of positive relationships for individuals in custody both internally and externally to the custodial environment. **P4** Include a detailed explanation of how developing positive relationships and addressing offending behaviour benefits the individual and society. **M3**

5. Create a script which will be used by a local drama group on the day of the visit, which clearly describes the process to receive and discharge individuals and their property, into and out of the custodial environment. **P5**

6. Create a leaflet which will be given to dignitaries which identifies how offending behaviour is addressed in custody, and describe the aims of one accredited offending behaviour programme. **P6** Analyse the ways offending behaviour is addressed and the need for individuals to address their offending behaviour while in custody and before being released from custody. **D2**

Grading criteria	Activity	Pg no.		
To achieve a pass grade the evidence must show that the learner is able to:			To achieve a merit grade the evidence must show that the learner is able to:	To achieve a distinction grade the evidence must show that the learner is able to:
P1 Outline the main security considerations in a custodial environment	21.1	191	**M1** Explain how combining security elements can improve the overall security of an establishment, using appropriate examples	**D1** Analyse the main security measures, showing why it is important that no one measure is allowed to dominate within a custodial environment
P2 Describe the different types and methods of searches conducted by staff in a custodial environment	21.2	195		
P3 Describe the control measures in place in a custodial environment	21.3	202	**M2** Explain the purpose of incentives schemes in relation to addressing offending behaviour and the maintenance of control	**D2** Analyse the ways offending behaviour is addressed and the need for individuals to address their offending behaviour while in custody and before being released from custody.
P4 Outline the importance of positive relationships for individuals in custody both internally and externally to the custodial environment	21.5	212	**M3** Explain how developing positive relationships and addressing offending behaviour benefits the individual and society.	
P5 Describe the process to receive and discharge individuals and their property, into and from the custodial environment	21.4	207		
P6 Identify how offending behaviour is addressed in custody and describe the aims of one accredited offending behaviour programme.	21.5	212		

Understanding aspects of the legal system and law making process

Introduction

The English legal system can appear very complex and daunting at times, with its long history, traditions, and use of Latin and legal language. However, it is the fundamental basis for any study of law that you may go on to use in later life in higher education, a legal career or in a uniformed public service.

The first part of this unit explores the structure and framework of the courts, the personnel involved in the administration of the law and the types of cases heard in the various courts. Since attendance in court can be a commonplace occurrence for many individuals who have a career in the uniformed services, it is really important that you are familiar with the courts and the people you are likely to encounter there.

We will then look at how law is made by the courts and by Parliament. This includes the sources of law and the development of the common law through precedents. This will show you that the law changes over time to reflect what is considered to be right or appropriate at a given point in history. You will look at the role of Europe in the creation of legal rules, although this is covered in more detail in *Unit 8: International perspectives for the uniformed public services*.

After completing this unit you should be able to achieve the following outcomes:

- Understand the hierarchy of the court system
- Know the role undertaken by the personnel of the courts
- Understand how legal rules are created by precedent
- Understand how statutory rules are made and interpreted.

Thinking points

One of the most important things you will learn from this unit is that the law is not static – it does not stay the same forever. The law is very dynamic and changes in response to the needs of the public and government of the time. This is crucial for the development of a modern and energetic society in which morals and ideas about how we should live our lives change constantly.

In the past it was illegal to have an abortion, to commit homosexual acts and to commit suicide. All those laws have changed to reflect the needs of society.

- What laws would you change if you could?

- Recently the age at which you can buy cigarettes has risen to 18; what is your view on this? What are the reasons the law was changed and are they valid?

Considering that in a few short years' time, some of you may end up enforcing civilian or military law in the police service or royal military police, or be a prison or probation officer dealing with the after-effects of how the legal system deals with people, understanding these issues is essential.

This section is concerned with examining the structure and function of the civil and criminal court structures of England and Wales. The structure in Scotland is different from that outlined here. Although the courts are notionally divided between the criminal and civil, in actual fact there are many links and crossovers between them. You will see below, when we look at the civil and criminal sections in more detail, that each has its own court structure. However, when they are placed together the entire structure looks like this.

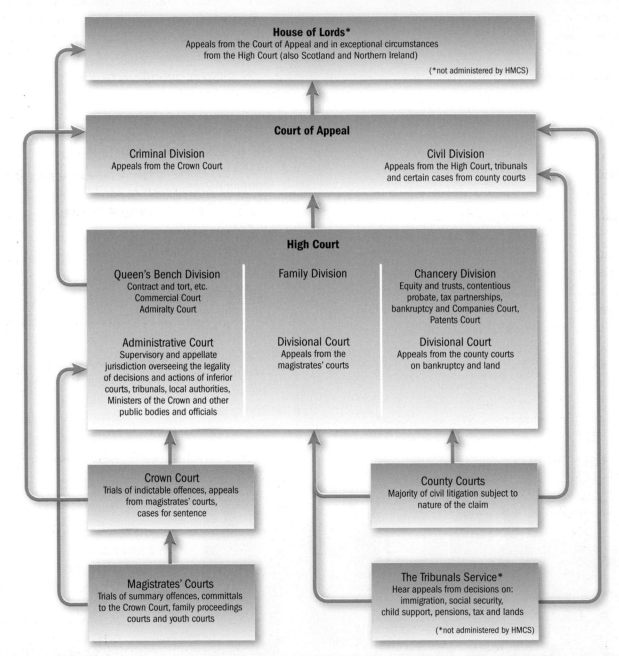

Source: Her Majesty's Court Service. Crown Copyright material reproduced by permission of the Controller of Her Majesty's Stationery Office and the Queen's Printer for Scotland.

▲ Figure 22.1 Civil and criminal court structure

We will now look at the civil and criminal structure in more detail.

Civil court structure

The civil court structure is complicated and depending on the nature of the case the following courts may be involved:

- magistrates' court
- Crown court
- county court
- High Court
- Court of Appeal
- House of Lords
- European Court of Justice.

The traditional structure of the civil courts is shown in Figure 22.2.

Civil procedure is designed to be used when one person or organisation decides that they have been wronged at the hands of another person or organisation. It does not deal with criminal matters, which are about the state being wronged by an organisation or individual.

Civil claims are usually about getting financial compensation for a wrong that has been committed. The **plaintiff** (the person or organisation claiming to be a victim) sues the **defendant** (the person or organisation they are accusing) for an amount of money to correct the breach of civil law that they claim has been committed against them.

Claims usually start in the court in which they are likely to be tried and this depends on two issues:

- the size and nature of the claim
- the complexity of the legal issues.

As a general distinction smaller cases would be heard in the county court and larger ones in the High Court. For instance, claims under £5000 are dealt with by the small claims track, which resides within the county court. In addition claims under £25,000 would normally begin in a county court and claims over £50,000 in a High Court. For claims between £25,000 and £50,000 the complexity of the case would have to be examined in order to determine which court would be most suitable.

£5000 or less	Small claims court
£5000–£25,000	Usually county court
£25,000–£50,000	High Court or county court, depending on complexity
£50,000 and above	Usually High Court

Key terms

Plaintiff The person or organisation claiming to be a victim

Defendant The person or organisation that is accused or sued

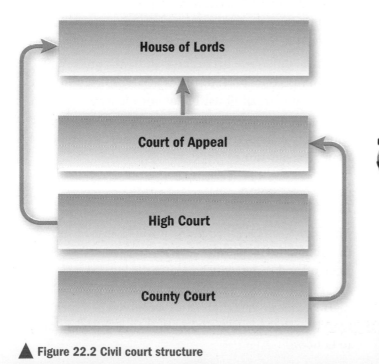

Figure 22.2 Civil court structure

(Diagram showing, from bottom to top: County Court → High Court → Court of Appeal → House of Lords)

Remember!

- Civil law exists to resolve disputes between companies or individuals.
- Civil law has its own civil courts.
- Civil law has many divisions, each dealing with a specialised branch of the law.
- The main purpose of civil law is financial redress (compensation).
- The parties involved are called plaintiff and defendant.

Small claims track

Firstly remember that the small claims track is actually part of the county court, not a separate court in itself. It is designed to deal with claims worth less than £5000, but it can be a greater sum if all parties agree to have the small claims track hear their case and the case does not require a great deal of legal preparation.

The first step in the procedure is to take out a summons and pay a small fee based on the amount being claimed. The summons must contain written details of the claim. It does not need to be in great detail but it must be clear to the defendant and the court why the claim is being made and how much it is for. Once the summons is 'served', i.e. the defendant has received it, they then have 14 days in which to send back a defence. At this point the defendant has several options:

- They may choose to pay the claim.
- They may make an admission and agree arrangements to pay at a later date.
- They may make a defence to the claim.
- They may choose to do nothing.

If no response is received the court may choose to rule in favour of the plaintiff automatically. If the defendant does defend themselves, an informal trial follows. This trial or 'arbitration' is held in private and each party will have a fair and equal opportunity to state their side of the dispute to the presiding judge, who is likely to be a district or deputy district judge.

This procedure can be quite quick and straightforward. Elliot and Quinn (1998) note that 60 per cent of cases take less than 30 minutes. The judge will then make a decision as to whether or not to award compensation. It is unusual for a solicitor to present a small claims case. The procedure is designed to be accessible by the general public, who would deal with the presentation of their own case after having an initial meeting with a solicitor to decide if their case has merit.

It is difficult to appeal against small claims judgements unless there has been a significant irregularity affecting the proceedings, or the judge is incorrect on a matter of law.

There are advantages and disadvantages to the small claims procedure, as shown below.

Advantages	Disadvantages
<ul><li>Quick, simple and cheap.</li><li>Increases public confidence by seeing justice done.</li><li>It is fully accessible to all members of the public.</li></ul>	<ul><li>It may involve complex cases.</li><li>The paperwork could be simplified.</li><li>There are problems enforcing successful claims.</li><li>The financial limit needs regular updating to keep in line with inflation.</li></ul>

Table 22.1 Advantages and disadvantages of the small claims procedure

County courts

County courts deal with low-level civil law matters. They were created by the County Courts Act 1846 and a large number of civil claims are heard in these courts every year. There are around 250 county courts in England and Wales, which are presided over by a circuit judge who sits alone to make judgements. It has jurisdiction over matters such as contract, tort, recovery of land, partnerships, trusts and inheritance and of course the small claims track, which was discussed above.

The county court has a fast-track procedure that can be used to reduce the waiting time in county court. This is mainly used for cases between £5000 and £15,000.

The main difference between small claims procedure and county court procedure lies in the arbitration stage. Small claims are dealt with in an informal manner by a judge who undertakes the role of arbiter whereas county court proceedings are heard in open court in a much more formal manner.

The High Court

The High Court is based at the Royal Courts of Justice in London, but it also sits at 'district registries' across England and Wales, which are usually located inside existing Crown or county court buildings. These district registries mean that High Court cases can be heard anywhere in the country without the necessity of going to London.

The court is split into three divisions:

- Queen's Bench
- Chancery
- Family.

■ Procedure

The procedure in the High Court is much more formal than the small claims track or county court. The first stage in this procedure is to issue a **writ**, which is drafted by a barrister or solicitor and is then served on the defendant. A writ is a document very like a county court summons and it is the most common form of starting an action in the High Court. The writ tells the defendant who the plaintiff is and why they are making a claim. If the defendant does not respond within 14 days the judge may make a decision by default on behalf of the plaintiff. If the defendant intends to defend themselves against the claim they must complete and return an 'acknowledgement of service' form, which states their intention to defend. The defendant must then submit a document called a 'defence'. This document answers the claims made by the plaintiff and sets out any new facts which the plaintiff did not know or did not disclose. The plaintiff can then deny the defendant's 'facts' or reply to them in a document called a 'reply'. This procedure will continue until both parties have exchanged every point they think is relevant. At this point the pleadings are closed and the judge can see clearly the matter that he or she must decide on. Following this a trial is conducted, with each side having its own witnesses. The judge then makes an appropriate decision regarding the case. The cost of a High Court trial can be very expensive and this can stop people making a claim.

▲ The High Court is at the Royal Courts of Justice in London

High Court procedure – example

There was a contract between Tom Groves and Cohen's Bakeries which specified that Tom would deliver 8 tonnes of minced beef at £5000 per tonne. Tom delivered the beef but Cohen's have not paid him.

- Tom issues a writ for £40,000 against Cohen's Bakeries.
- Cohen's Bakeries send back their 'Acknowledgement of Service' form.
- Cohen's Bakeries submit their defence, which states that the beef was not the quality that was promised by Tom.
- Tom submits his reply and says that the beef was of the quality he promised.
- Pleadings are closed.
- Trial.
- Judgement.
- Costs.

Key terms

Writ A document starting an action in the High Court. It tells the defendant who the plaintiff is and why they are making a claim.

The Court of Appeal

Like the High Court, the Court of Appeal also sits within the Royal Courts of Justice in London. It has two divisions, criminal and civil, which hear appeals from the lower courts in each structure. The appeals system has two main functions:

- to put right any incorrect or unjust decisions made in the courts below them
- to help promote consistent development of the law.

The criminal division is presided over by the Lord Chancellor and hears appeals from the Crown court. The civil division is presided over by the Master of the Rolls and hears appeals mainly from the High and county courts.

The civil division hears appeals from:

- the High Court
- the county courts
- certain tribunals such as employment and immigration.

The Court of Appeal hears cases where the plaintiff or defendant are not happy with the original results of the case in the lower courts. Not just any case can go to appeal; there must be a sound reason why the plaintiff or defendant needs to appeal, such as the first trial was not conducted correctly or brand new facts have come to light. There are approximately 40 judges who sit in the appeal courts. These judges often sit in both the civil and criminal appeal courts.

House of Lords

This is the highest court of appeal in the UK. It hears civil and criminal appeals from England and Wales and may also hear certain cases from Scotland and Northern Ireland. The judgements of the House of Lords bind all courts below it. It hears about 70 cases a year and it operates on a majority judgement. The judges in the House of Lords are commonly called Law Lords, but their correct name is the Lords of Appeal in Ordinary, and there are currently 12 of them. They are equivalent to supreme judges in other countries and when the new UK Supreme Court is expected to be operational (in 2008) they will become the first Justices of the Supreme Court.

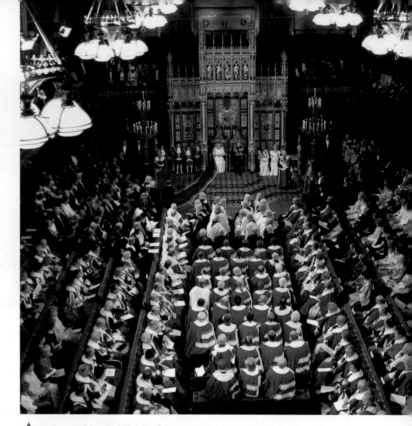

▲ The House of Lords is the highest court of appeal

 **Case study:** **The case of Diane Pretty**

The case of 43-year-old Diane Pretty was heard by the House of Lords in November 2001. Mrs Pretty had been paralysed by motor neurone disease that left her unable to end her suffering by committing suicide. She went to the courts in order to receive assurances that her husband would not be punished if he helped her to end her own life – a process called 'assisted suicide'. The piece of law she used to support her case was the Human Rights Act 1998. The five Law Lords who heard the case refused to give such an assurance on the grounds that the Human Rights Act 1998 was designed to protect lives, not end them.

1. **What crime would Diane's husband have been guilty of if he'd helped her die?**
2. **Why couldn't Diane simply end her own life?**
3. **Do you agree with the decision of the Law Lords?**
4. **What are the implications of the judicial system approving assisted suicide?**
5. **Do you think that assisted suicide ought to be legal in this country? Explain your reasons.**

European Court of Justice

The European Court of Justice has 27 judges and 8 advocate generals who are appointed by the collective governments of the European Union for a term of 6 years. They are chosen from the best judges each nation has and they must be completely independent and very skilled at their role.

The European Court of Justice has very clear jurisdiction on what it can and cannot do. Table 22.2 shows these roles.

Jurisdiction	Explanation
References for preliminary rulings	This is when the member states of the EU ask the court to clarify the meaning of a piece of European law so that it can be correctly interpreted and applied in all of the member states. The clarification given by the court is binding on all EU member states.
Actions for failure to fulfil obligations	This type of action allows the court to establish that a country has not fulfilled its obligations under European Union law.
Actions for annulment	This is when the court hears a case that asks for a directive, rule or decision made by the EU to be annulled (got rid of).
Actions for failure to act	This when the court hears cases where there has been a failure to act from a European Union institution.
Appeals	Appeals on points of law only can be brought before the Court of Justice against judgements and orders of the Court of First Instance.
Reviews	Decisions of the Court of First Instance on appeals against decisions of the European Union Civil Service Tribunal may, in exceptional circumstances, be reviewed by the Court of Justice.

Table 22.2 Jurisdiction of the European Court of Justice

Criticism of civil procedure

Criticism	Detail
Expense	The costs of the case can amount to more than the original claim was worth. This means people or companies can end up losing money in civil proceedings even if they win. The Woolf report found that this happened in 40% of cases where the original claim was worth £12,500 or less.
Delays	The civil justice procedure deals with a tremendous volume of cases and it is over-stretched. According to the Woolf report the current average waiting time in the county court is 79 weeks.
Injustice	If people cannot afford a lengthy trial they may have to accept an out-of-court settlement from the other party for a lower sum. This can create a sense of injustice.
Too complex	The procedure can be difficult to track and follow.
Enforcement	It can be difficult to enforce judgements and make sure that people who are successful in the civil courts can actually get their money from the other party.

Table 22.3 Criticisms of civil procedure

Case study: Civil law

Susan has had a disastrous haircut in a town centre salon. She complained at the time but the salon refused to put the problem right. Susan was left £90 out of pocket for the haircut and had to pay a further £100 to another salon to have her hair put right. She wants to sue the original hairdresser, but doesn't know how to go about it.

1. **Which court would Susan use to sue her hairdresser?**
2. **Describe the steps she would have to go through to conduct a claim.**
3. **What amount should Susan claim in compensation?**

Criminal court structure

The criminal court structure contains some of the same institutions we examined in the civil court system. Figure 22.3 shows the main courts in the criminal court system.

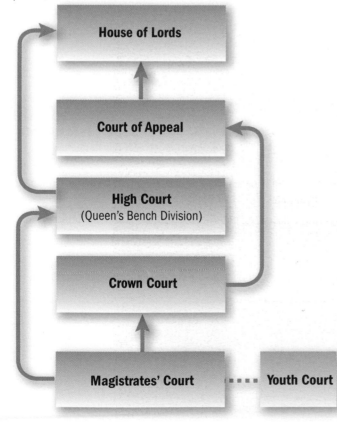

▲ Figure 22.3 The main courts in the criminal court system

House of Lords

Court of Appeal

High Court
(Queen's Bench Division)

Crown Court

Magistrates' Court ····· Youth Court

Youth court

Magistrates' courts may deal with cases that involve people under 18 but only if they are tried with an adult. Young people also appear in the Crown court if they are being jointly tried with an adult whose case needs to be heard in that court. Homicide and rape cases will always be heard in the Crown court. The youth court may also send a young person to the Crown court if the offence is very serious and the sentencing powers of the youth court are thought to be insufficient to punish the young offender properly.

However, unless the case is one of those mentioned above, 10- to 17-year-olds will have their case dealt with in the youth court. This is a specialised form of magistrates' court. As in the magistrates' court, the case will be heard by magistrates sitting in a panel of three (usually one of them will be female in the youth court) or by a district judge (magistrates' courts).

The youth court is not open to the general public in order to protect the young people involved, and only those directly involved in the case will normally be in court. A hearing in the youth court is similar to one in the magistrates' court though the procedure is adapted to take account of the age of the defendant. The magistrates and district judges who sit in the youth court will receive specialist training on dealing with young people.

The magistrates' court

The magistrates' court is the most junior of all the courts in the English legal system. The country is divided up into 'commissions' that are then further divided up into petty sessional areas, or benches. Each bench has its own courthouse and clerk. Although this is the most junior court it is a vital part of the legal system due to its caseload. There are over 400 magistrates' courts in England and Wales and each deals with business happening in the local area.

Magistrates' courts deal with:

- 97 per cent of all criminal cases
- civil family matters such as adoption, custody and maintenance
- granting of warrants and summonses and bail applications
- granting of licences, e.g. for the sale of alcohol
- juvenile jurisdiction (offenders aged 10–17)
- summary jurisdiction
- jurisdiction over some triable either-way offences
- committal for trial for indictable offences.

The courts are staffed by magistrates whose job it is to decide guilt or innocence and to provide appropriate punishments to those defendants they convict. The maximum sentence that magistrates can give for an offence is 6 months' imprisonment and/or up to £5000 fine. If they feel an offence needs a stronger punishment than they are able to give they may send the case to Crown court, which has the power to deliver harsher sentences. Around 90 per cent of people appearing before a magistrates' court plead guilty, which simplifies and speeds up matters considerably.

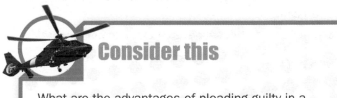

Consider this

What are the advantages of pleading guilty in a magistrates' court?

Magistrates have a long history in the English legal system. They date back to the Justices of the Peace Act 1361, which gave certain judicial powers to lay people.

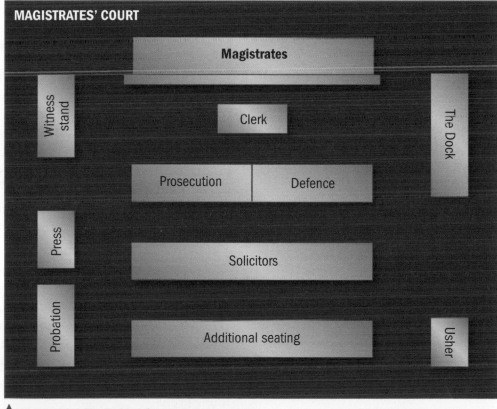

MAGISTRATES' COURT

- Magistrates
- Witness stand
- Clerk
- The Dock
- Prosecution
- Defence
- Press
- Solicitors
- Probation
- Additional seating
- Usher

▲ **Figure 22.4 The inside of a magistrates' court**

This meant that they had the ability to deal with criminal matters and some civil issues, but unlike magistrates today they were also entrusted with the running of local government. The magistrates and judges found in this court will be discussed later in this chapter.

Key terms

Lay people People who work in a profession but who are not professionally qualified.

Progress of a magistrates' court trial

1. The magistrates hear a summary of the facts.
2. The defendant enters a plea of guilty or not guilty.
3. The prosecution puts forward their case.
4. The defence puts forward their case.
5. The magistrates give a verdict.
6. If the defendant is found not guilty they may leave the court.
7. If the defendant is found to be guilty the magistrates confer and seek guidance from the clerk on a suitable sentence.
8. The magistrates deliver a suitable sentence.

Advantages	Disadvantages
• Lay magistrates are a very cost-effective and efficient way of administering justice. • Involvement of ordinary people makes the justice system appear fairer. • Groups of three are likely to give more balanced decisions. • They have local knowledge and understanding.	• Inconsistent decision making between benches. • Magistrates tend to have a bias towards the police and are more likely to believe their evidence than the evidence of the defendant. • Magistrates tend to be white, middle class and middle aged. • Cases are not heard in much detail.

Table 22.4 Advantages and disadvantages of the magistracy

Case study: Magistrates' court

Jack is a 37-year-old alcoholic. He has a long history of violent alcohol-related disorder. He was picked up in his local town centre under the influence of alcohol, behaving in a threatening manner to passers-by. He was kept in police custody overnight to sober up and then taken to magistrates' court in the morning.

1. **What powers do the magistrates have to sentence Jack?**
2. **What offence is he likely to be charged with?**
3. **What sentence do you think would be appropriate for Jack's behaviour?**
4. **What are the chances that Jack would plead guilty?**

Remember!

- There are over 400 magistrates' courts in England and Wales.
- They deal with less serious criminal offences and some civil matters.
- They deal with juveniles aged 10–17.
- There are two types of magistrate: lay justice and district judge.
- Magistrates have maximum sentencing powers of 6 months' imprisonment and a £5000 fine per offence.

Crown court

The Crown court was established by the Courts Act 1971. It was created to replace the system of Assizes and Quarter Sessions, which were outdated and unable to cope effectively with increasing numbers of criminal cases. There is only one Crown court. This is called the Central Criminal Court or sometimes the 'Old Bailey'.

▲ The Old Bailey or Central Criminal Court deals with serious criminal offences. On its roof stands a statue of Justice personified.

This one Crown court has over 90 centres from which it operates throughout cities in England and Wales. The Crown court deals with four main areas of work:

- criminal trials of indictable and some triable-either-way offences
- appeals against the decisions of magistrates
- sentencing from magistrates' court
- some High Court civil matters.

Offences dealt with in Crown court also fall into four categories, as shown in Table 22.5.

The Crown court also operates a tier system for its external centres that dictates the kind of work they are allowed to do. There are three tiers of the Crown court. The first tier deals with High Court civil matters, any kind of triable-either-way or indictable criminal offence and hears appeals from magistrates' court. The second tier deals with triable-either-way offences and indictable offences and hears appeals from the magistrates' court. The third tier deals only with class four offences and appeals. These terms are explained in more detail in *Unit 17: Understanding the criminal justice system and police powers.*

Category	Offences
Class 1	Murder, treason, offences under the Official Secrets Act. Usually tried by a High Court judge or circuit judge.
Class 2	Manslaughter, rape etc. Again, may be tried by a High Court judge or a circuit judge.
Class 3	A wide variety of indictable and triable-either-way offences. May be tried by a High Court, circuit or recorder judge.
Class 4	Robbery, assault, grievous bodily harm etc. Usually tried by a circuit judge or a recorder.

Table 22.5 Offences dealt with in Crown court

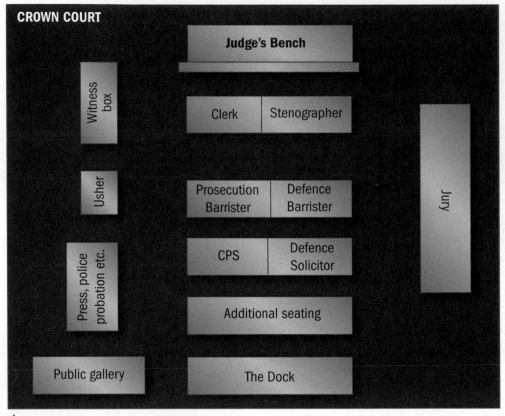

CROWN COURT

		Judge's Bench		
Witness box		Clerk	Stenographer	
Usher		Prosecution Barrister	Defence Barrister	Jury
Press, police probation etc.		CPS	Defence Solicitor	
		Additional seating		
Public gallery		The Dock		

▲ Figure 22.5 Crown court floor plan

The progress of a Crown court trial

1. Defendant pleads not guilty.
2. Jury is sworn in.
3. Opening speeches outlining the case for the prosecution and defence.
4. Prosecution witnesses are called to give evidence and are cross-examined by the defence.
5. Prosecution case closes.
6. Defence witnesses are called to give evidence and are cross-examined by the prosecution.
7. Defence case closes.
8. Closing speeches, which are summaries from the prosecution and the defence.
9. Judge sums up.
10. Jury retires to consider verdict.
11. Jury returns and a verdict is given.
12. If the defendant is found not guilty they are free to leave the court.
13. If the defendant is found to be guilty the defence will argue for a lenient sentence by providing the court with mitigating circumstances.
14. The judge gives a suitable sentence.

A jury is only used where a defendant pleads not guilty. Juries are found in only about 1 per cent of all criminal cases.

Remember!

1. There is only one Crown court, but it has around 90 centres.
2. They are usually found in large towns and cities.
3. They deal with more serious criminal offences and some High Court civil matters.
4. There are three tiers of Crown court.
5. A jury is used to decide guilt or innocence, but is only used in about 1 per cent of criminal cases.

Take it further

Describe in detail the role and procedure in a Crown court.

Criminal division of the Court of Appeal

As was already discussed in the civil court structure, the Court of Appeal consists of two divisions, criminal and civil, which are at the Royal Courts of Justice in London. The appeals system has two main functions. The Criminal Division is presided over by the Lord Chief Justice and hears appeals from the Crown court, on a variety of matters, such as:

- appeals against conviction
- appeals against sentence
- unduly lenient sentences
- points of law.

The court may allow an appeal to go ahead if they think that a conviction may be unsafe – if the judge in the case interpreted the law incorrectly or there was some sort of irregularity in the course of the trial. The court can recall all the witnesses and evidence that were used at the original trial and even new evidence can be submitted. Many countries have an automatic right to appeal built into their criminal justice system. This is not the case in England and Wales, where permission to appeal must be given by the courts.

Consider this

Should criminal convictions have an automatic right of appeal? What are the advantages and disadvantages of this?

Assessment activity 22.1

Understanding the differences between the criminal and civil courts and their hierarchies is very important. For this assessment activity you will research the following content:

- civil courts' structure – role, function and jurisdiction of small claims court, county court, High Court, civil division of the Court of Appeal, House of Lords, European Court of Justice; difference between first instance and appeal courts
- criminal courts' structure – role, function and jurisdiction of the youth court, magistrates' courts, Crown court, criminal division of the Court of Appeal, House of Lords; first instance and appeal courts.

1. Using the research you have gathered, produce an A1 poster that highlights the hierarchies and differences between the civil and criminal courts. **P1**

Grading tips

P1 This task only asks for an outline, so you can use diagrams and charts as well as text to provide your answer. Your poster needs to clearly show the hierarchies of the courts. This could be done as a labelled diagram. You should also show the differences between the civil and criminal court. You could do this using a comparison table or chart.

This section examines the role, work and training of a variety of personnel involved in the legal system.

The legal profession

Solicitor

Solicitors may work alone or in a partnership with other solicitors. They deal directly with the public and offer a wide variety of legal services, such as all pre-trial work, accident claims, conveyancing, contracts, wills, representation in court and divorce and family matters. There are around 80,000 solicitors in England and Wales. They are controlled by the Law Society, which has the power to discipline or strike off a solicitor for professional misconduct.

The training of a solicitor usually starts with a law degree followed by a legal practice course that lasts one year and a training contract that lasts two years. There are other methods of becoming a solicitor if you have a non-law degree or indeed if you have no degree at all. Solicitors are able to act as advocates in the Crown court if they have an additional qualification called an advocacy certificate.

Barrister

Barristers are considered to be self-employed individuals and are not allowed to form partnerships with other barristers. However, in practice they usually share a set of offices, called 'chambers', with other barristers in order to share costs and gain professional support and advice. They are generally associated with advocacy work, which involves representing people in court, but they may also deal with matters such as drafting documents and offering expert advice on legal issues. Barristers are not allowed to deal directly with the public. They must instead take their instructions from a solicitor.

As with solicitors the training of barristers normally starts with a law degree. They must then join one of the four inns listed below and complete their Bar Vocational Course (BVC), which can take up to two years. They must also complete 12 qualifying sessions with their inn. After this they must complete a pupillage, which is an additional year's training.

There are over 9500 barristers in England and Wales and they are governed by the General Council of the Bar, which acts in much the same way as other professional bodies such as the Law Society or the General Medical Council. Barristers must be members of one of the four Inns of Court listed below which are based in London:

- Middle Temple
- Gray's Inn
- Inner Temple
- Lincoln's Inn

There are two ranks of barrister:

- **Queen's Counsel (QC)** – These are more senior and experienced barristers who take on more complicated cases. A barrister must have at least 10 years' experience before becoming a QC. The majority of the judiciary are promoted from within the ranks of the Queen's Counsel. Since very few QCs are women or from ethnic minority backgrounds this has significant implications for the composition of the judiciary. Becoming a QC is called 'Taking Silk'.
- **Juniors** – These are less experienced barristers who deal with less complicated cases. Juniors also help QC's deal with cases in court.

Legal executive

Legal executives are similar to solicitors but they complete an ILEX qualification in law, which allows them to specialise in a particular area of law rather than dealing with the law generally. They usually have five years of experience of working under the supervision of a solicitor in a private legal firm or in the legal department of a business or local council. The type of work they do depends upon the area of law they have specialised in, which could be anything from property to contract to family law.

Paralegal

Paralegals are not qualified solicitors or barristers, but they still carry out a wide range of legal duties such as:

- legal research
- interviewing witnesses
- attending court
- clerical tasks
- providing legal information
- drafting legal documents.

Paralegals work in a variety of different environments such as law firms, advice agencies, courts, businesses. In order to be a paralegal you need a good standard of education and a good understanding of the legal system. This means you would usually have a law degree or a paralegal qualification from a recognised accrediting body.

Legal services ombudsman

The current ombudsman is Zahida Manzoor CBE. The role of the ombudsman is to ensure that complaints raised by the general public are dealt with in a fair and impartial manner. The ombudsman does not investigate the complaint themselves. They and their team just make sure that the professional bodies responsible for dealing with the complaint do a fair and impartial job. If the ombudsman decided that the complaint was not correctly handled they may implement one of the following decisions:

- recommend the complaint (or part of it) is reinvestigated
- make a formal criticism of the professional body concerned
- award compensation.

The ombudsman has the power to reinvestigate a complaint themselves, but in practice will rarely do so.

Remember!

- Solicitors have direct contact with clients.
- Solicitors deal with a wide range of legal matters including crime, family and civil issues.
- The general public cannot contract a barrister on their own. A solicitor must do it for them.
- There are two kinds of barrister, QCs and Juniors.
- Barristers deal with the majority of advocacy work in the Crown court.

Take it further

- Once you have finished your National Diploma what steps would you have to take if you ultimately wanted to be a barrister?
- List the top six skills you think are important for a barrister.

The judiciary

You will find a variety of different judges in the court system. The table below highlights the types of judges, how they are referred to and their seniority in the system.

Judge	Referred to as:	Seniority
Lord Chief Justice	Lord/Lady	Senior
Master of the Rolls	Lord/Lady	Senior
Presidents of the High Court Divisions	Lord/Lady	Senior
Lords of Appeal in Ordinary	Lord/Lady	Superior
Lord Justice of Appeal	Lord/Lady	Superior
Puisne Judges	Lord/Lady	Superior
Circuit Judges	Your Honour	Inferior
Recorders	Your Honour	Inferior
District Judges	Sir/Madam	Inferior

Table 22.6 Types of judges

▲ The ceremonial robes of judges are intended to lend impartial authority to their public appearances

Judges have a very important role in the court system. They are legal experts on points of law if the prosecution and defence are in dispute. They manage and oversee the conduct of trials and sum up to the jury in criminal cases. They also pronounce sentence if a defendant is found guilty.

Hight Court or Puisne judges

There are 106 High Court judges currently appointed in England and Wales. They are also called Puisne (pronounced 'puny') judges. They deal with the more complex and difficult cases. Although usually based in London, they travel to the major court centres in the rest of the country to try serious criminal cases and important civil cases. They also assist the Lord Justices to hear criminal appeals.

High Court judges sit in one of the three divisions of the High Court:

- Queen's Bench
- Chancery
- Family.

They are appointed by the Queen, who takes recommendations from the Lord Chancellor. Potential High Court judges have to have had the right of audience (this is the legal right to act as a lawyer or advocate in the High Court) for at least ten years and they must have been a circuit judge for two years before they can be considered for the job.

Circuit judges

Circuit judges are appointed to one of six geographical circuits in England and Wales and they hear cases in the Crown and county courts of that area. There are over 600 circuit judges in the country and they deal with a wide range of legal matters including civil, criminal and family matters.

In order to be appointed as a circuit judge a legal professional must have held the right of audience for at least ten years and they must also have served as a part-time recorder on criminal matters or as a full-time district judge. Like High Court judges they are appointed by the Queen on the basis of a recommendation from the Lord Chancellor.

District judges

District judges are full-time judges who do a wide variety of civil work such as family matters, property matters and bankruptcy. They deal with the vast majority of civil cases heard in county court and there are currently 434 district judges in post, including 18 who sit in the family division of the High Court in London. Like circuit judges they sit on one of the six geographical circuits.

In order to be appointed they must have had the right of audience for seven years. It is also usual for a district judge to have been a deputy district judge for two years.

District judges (magistrates' court)

This type of district judge used to be called a stipendiary magistrate, and they are still known as justices of the peace. They are judges who deal with longer and more complex cases that appear in the magistrates' court. This type of judge has a very wide jurisdiction in magistrates' court, including criminal cases, youth court and family matters. They also sit as prison adjudicators. Unlike lay magistrates, district judges (magistrates' court) sit alone to hear a case. There are just over 300 full- and part-time district judges who are entitled to sit in magistrates' court.

As with all other judges they are appointed by the Queen on the recommendation of the Lord Chancellor. They must have had the right of audience for at least seven years and will usually have sat as a deputy judge for at least two years before becoming full time.

Recorders and assistant recorders

These are part-time judges who often still work as barristers and solicitors. They deal with some of the least serious Crown court cases.

Remember!

- High Court judges are also called Puisne (pronounced 'puny') judges. They are the ones who hear the most serious cases in a Crown court.
- Circuit judges travel around an area of the country called a circuit. There are six circuits in the country. They deal with a wide range of legal matters including civil, criminal and family matters.
- District judges and deputy district judges hear civil cases in the county court. Usually this means dealing with small claims.
- Some district judges work in magistrates' court. They were previously called stipendiary magistrates.
- Recorders and assistant recorders are part-time judges who deal with some of the least serious Crown court cases.

Judicial independence and immunity

In order for the public to have faith and trust in the justice system it is important that judges are seen as being completely independent when they are making their decisions. This means that they cannot allow themselves to be influenced (or perceived by others to be influenced) by a variety of factors such as:

- the state
- the media
- other judges
- religion
- politics
- money.

Judges are also traditionally immune from legal actions arising from their judicial role. This is called 'judicial immunity' and it means that they cannot be sued or prosecuted for a decision they made in the course of their duties, even if new evidence comes to light in later years that the decision they made at the time was incorrect.

Removal from office

It is actually very difficult to remove a judge from office and how a judge may be removed differs between superior judges and inferior ones. Superior court judges can only be removed if both Houses of Parliament pass a resolution requiring them to go. This is an extremely rare occurrence and last happened in 1830. They can be removed if they experience a significant illness or disability that affects their ability to be a judge, but again this is not used often. Judges would far prefer to resign than be dismissed. Resignation and retirement at age 70 are therefore the main ways judges leave office. Inferior judges can be disciplined and removed from office by the Lord Chief Justice. They can also have the type and jurisdiction of cases they may oversee restricted.

Assessment activity 22.2

This activity requires you to examine the role of judges and lawyers in the legal system. In order to do this you should research the following content:

- legal profession – work, training and regulation of barristers, solicitors, legal executives, paralegals; Legal Services Ombudsman and complaints
- judiciary – organisation, selection and appointment of judges; roles in civil and criminal cases; judicial independence and immunity; removal from office.

1. Using the above research, produce a leaflet that outlines the role of judges and lawyers in civil and criminal cases. **P3**

Grading tips

P3 This task only requires an outline from you, so you don't necessarily have to provide in-depth information. Your leaflet should cover the roles and responsibilities of judges and lawyers in both civil and criminal cases.

Lay people

Magistrates

Magistrates are sometimes referred to as lay magistrates and, like district judges (magistrates' court), they are also known as justices of the peace. Magistrates are unpaid volunteers who are trained to serve as representatives of their local community. They sit in panels of three and have a trained legal advisor on hand at all times when in court (this is the clerk of the court). There are approximately 30,000 magistrates in England and Wales and they are based in around 300 courts. Even though they are volunteers they must commit to a minimum number of days in order to be able to fulfil their role. Currently this is a minimum of 26 half days. As they are not legally trained they do not deal with complex or difficult cases; instead they try low-level criminal offences in the magistrates' court and the youth court. They also have a role in referring more serious cases to the Crown court, which has the power to deal with them. Magistrates are often referred to as the backbone of the criminal justice system as they deal with around 97 per cent of all criminal cases. Magistrates also have some civil jurisdiction in family matters and financial affairs such as non-payment of council tax. Magistrates apply for the role from the local community and normally undergo a series of interviews to establish their suitability. They can be of either gender or any ethnic background but must be aged 18 or over. It is important to remember that magistrates are unpaid volunteers – they serve the community and the criminal justice system for reasons other than money.

Consider this

The backbone of the justice system is dependent on volunteers.

- What is your view on the use of volunteers in such an important service?
- Why is there a need for district judges (magistrates' court) when lay magistrates do the job for free?

Take it further

List and describe five personal characteristics that you think would be useful if you were aiming to become a lay magistrate. How do these characteristics compare with the characteristics needed in other public service roles?

The jury

The use of a jury has a long and distinguished history, but it has seen a decline in both civil and criminal cases over recent years. A jury is made up of 12 people in a criminal case and 8 in a civil case. In a criminal case they appear in Crown court when a defendant pleads not guilty. Juries are a fundamental principle of the system because the exercise of justice is by the people not the state. The guilt or innocence of a person is not decided by a judge who is in the employ of the state but by ordinary people in the community at large. Juries are not required to justify their verdict and there have been cases where juries have acquitted defendants, despite strong evidence of guilt, to show their disapproval of the law.

To qualify for jury duty you must be:

- aged between 18 and 70
- registered on the electoral roll
- have lived in the UK for at least five years since the age of 13.

Even if you fulfil these qualification criteria you may still not be allowed to serve on a jury. Alternatively, your personal circumstances might mean you can be excused from jury duty.

You are ineligible for jury duty if you:

- have a mental disorder
- are a member of the clergy
- are a judge, or otherwise connected with the criminal justice system.

You will be automatically disqualified for jury duty if you:

- have certain criminal convictions
- are currently on bail in a criminal case.

You can choose to be excused if you:

- are aged 65–70 years old
- have already done jury service in the last two years
- are an MP
- work in the medical profession
- are in the armed forces.

You can also be excused if you provide the judge with a good reason as to why you cannot serve, or you have a lack of capacity to understand the case (for example you don't understand English, or you are hearing impaired).

The jury system has some advantages and disadvantages, as shown in Table 22.7.

Advantages	Disadvantages
• Ordinary people are represented in the justice system. • Group decisions give fairer results. • Public representation makes the system more open to scrutiny.	• Juries are untrained. • Complex cases may be difficult to understand, particularly in civil cases. • It is a compulsory system.

Table 22.7 Advantages and disadvantages of the jury system

Consider this

Should jury service remain compulsory? What are the advantages and disadvantages of a compulsory system?

Assessment activity 22.3

This activity requires you to examine the role of lay people in the legal system. In order to do this you should research the following content:

- magistrates – selection and appointment, training, role and powers, jurisdiction in civil and criminal cases, removal, advantages and disadvantages
- juries – qualifications and disqualification, selection and role, summoning, vetting and challenging, advantages and disadvantages.

1. Research, prepare and present a 15-minute PowerPoint presentation, with supporting notes, which addresses the following questions:

- Describe the role of lay people in criminal court cases. **P2**
- Compare and contrast the role and function of judges, lawyers and lay people within the English courts. **M1**
- Evaluate the effectiveness of lay personnel in the English courts. **D1**

Grading tips

P2 This is very straightforward. Simply describe the role of magistrates and juries as part of your presentation.

M1 This part of the presentation requires you to compare and contrast legal personnel. This means look at the similarities and differences between judges, lawyers and lay people such as juries and magistrates.

D1 This criterion requires you to evaluate the role of lay people. This means examining the advantages and disadvantages of magistrates and juries and forming sensible and well thought-out conclusions about their effectiveness.

This section covers how the law is made by the courts.

The creation of legal rules

Much of English law is unwritten. It has developed over the centuries by the decisions judges have made in important cases. The legal system that we know now began its development during the Norman conquest of 1066, but it really began to become an organised system during the reign of Henry II (1154–1189). When Henry came to the throne justice was usually dealt with in local courts:

- **Feudal courts** – local lords dealing with issues arising from the peasantry or tenants on their land.
- **Courts of the shires and hundreds** – county sheriffs often sitting with a bishop or earl to hear more serious cases.

According to most sources of information these early courts operated on local customs and, as you would expect, these customs often differed from county to county. There was a lack of consistency in the law of the time, which meant that courts in different areas might settle the same dispute in entirely different ways.

Case study: Local customs

The rule of primogeniture (the right of the eldest son to inherit his father's land) was almost universally applied across England. However, if you lived in Nottingham or Bristol, the youngest son inherited the land. If you lived in Kent, all of a landowner's sons inherited the land in equal shares.

1. **Why were customs of inheritance different across the land?**
2. **Why would a standardised system of law be better than a fragmented system?**
3. **Why did sons inherit but not daughters?**

Henry II wanted a more standardised system of law in England and so he introduced the 'General Eyre' which literally means 'a journey'. This General Eyre created a system whereby representatives of the king went out to the counties of England to check on the legal administration that was in effect there. They would sit in local courts and listen in to how the legal problems of the time were dealt with. Over time these representatives of the king came to be seen as judges themselves and were called 'Justices in Eyre'.

Common law

The General Eyre disappeared around 200 years later and was replaced with a system of circuit judges from which our current High Court developed. By selecting the best local laws from all over the country the judges gradually changed differing local laws into a system of law which was 'common' to the entire kingdom – this is how **common law** originated. So in summary, common law is a judge-made system of law, originating in ancient customs that were brought together and extended by judges operating over many centuries.

Common law was the sole source of law in England from the time of the Norman conquest until the 15th century. From the 15th century until the end of the 19th century, common law shared power with a new body of laws called **equity.** Equity is a group of laws that developed alongside common law as a result of dissatisfied common law plaintiffs being unhappy with the way the law treated them. It developed because common law had many defects, particularly that the system was very rigid and sometimes not at all fair.

Key terms

Common law A system of law made up of judges' rulings over many centuries.

Equity A set of legal principles based on fairness rather than the rigid application of common law.

Equity and common law initially operated in conflict with one another and it wasn't until 1615 that this was resolved and a firm decision was taken by James I that when common law and equity were in conflict, equity should prevail.

Table 22.8 shows how law has changed over time.

Prior to 1066	Local customs of the time. These varied from place to place.
1066 – 15th century	Common law developed from the General Eyre and became 'common' across the country.
15th century – end of 19th century	Common law and equity. Initially in conflict, these two bodies of law became mutually tolerant.
20th century – 1973	Primary source of law is statute law, also called legislation, or Acts of Parliament.
1973 – current	UK has statute law and sometimes law from the European Union. This change came about because the UK joined the European Economic Community in 1973.

Table 22.8 Law over time

Judicial precedent

The decisions made by judges create new law for future judges to follow – they are 'binding' on the decisions of future judges when the facts are the same. This procedure is known as judicial precedent. Judicial precedent is an important part of common law. It is based on the Latin saying '*Stare decisis et non quieta movere*', which means 'stand by what has been decided and do not change the established'.

The English legal system follows the rules of judicial precedent quite rigidly when compared with other countries. This means that courts in England and Wales must follow decisions already made in a higher or superior court and appeal courts are bound by their own past decisions. In order to understand judicial precedent you must be aware of the hierarchy of the courts – that is, which courts are binding on the decisions of other courts.

Remember!

- Common law began its development during the reign of Henry II.
- It established a unified system of law that was common to the whole country.
- Common law is based on judges' decisions in important cases that are then used by other judges as a standard to follow in future cases.
- Common law began to share power with equity in the 15th century.
- From the 19th century, common law began to be replaced by statute law.

■ Persuasive and binding authorities

- **Persuasive** – This is a matter of precedent that is not legally binding, which means that although a court is likely to take the information into account when making a judgement on a case it is not necessarily bound to follow it. This might mean that the precedent came from a court in another country, such as an EU member, or a military court, and although the other court's decision is not binding on our courts it might be used as guidance by our judges.
- **Binding** – This is a matter of precedent, whereby all lower courts in the hierarchy must abide by it.

■ Ratio decidendi

'*Ratio decidendi*' is a Latin phrase that means 'the reason for the decision'. When it is used by the legal profession it refers to the legal, moral and social principles a court used to make a rationale for a particular decision in a court case. Usually the ratio decidendi is binding on the lower courts. This is because under the principle of judicial precedent, lower courts must abide by the decisions of the higher ones.

■ Obiter statements

An *obiter dictum* is a Latin phrase used in the legal profession to mean comments made by a judge about a case that do not form part of the rationale for a decision and are said 'by the way'. These comments are not legally binding on the courts below, but could be seen as a 'persuasive authority' in helping lower courts to make a decision.

How judicial precedent works and avoiding it if required

Judicial precedent creates law that all the courts below are bound by. Figure 22.6 shows the hierarchy of the courts and explains which courts would be bound by which decisions.

When a judge encounters a case where there may be a relevant previous decision made by either the court they are currently in or another one in the hierarchy they have four possible courses of action:

- **Follow** – If the facts are very similar to the previous case then the judge will choose to follow the precedent that has already been set.
- **Distinguish** – If the facts are quite different from the previous case then the judge can distinguish between the two cases and doesn't need to follow the original precedent.

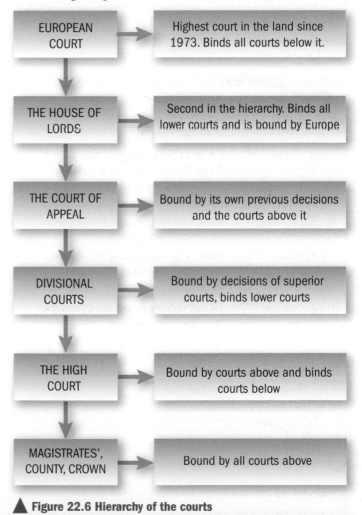

EUROPEAN COURT	Highest court in the land since 1973. Binds all courts below it.
THE HOUSE OF LORDS	Second in the hierarchy. Binds all lower courts and is bound by Europe
THE COURT OF APPEAL	Bound by its own previous decisions and the courts above it
DIVISIONAL COURTS	Bound by decisions of superior courts, binds lower courts
THE HIGH COURT	Bound by courts above and binds courts below
MAGISTRATES', COUNTY, CROWN	Bound by all courts above

▲ **Figure 22.6 Hierarchy of the courts**

- **Overrule** – If the original precedent was set in a lower court the judge may overrule it if they disagree with it. This means that although the original case still stands the judge does not have to follow its precedent.
- **Reverse** – If the decision made by a lower court is appealed to a higher one the higher court may reverse the decision if they think the lower court has misinterpreted the law. They will then substitute their own decision for the previous one.

The last two courses of action can be problematic because if higher courts overrule or reverse the decisions of lower ones they can weaken the power of the lower courts. Judges think extremely carefully in these circumstances and it is relatively rare that these options are taken. Although most law these days is created through Acts of Parliament the law may still be made and refined through judicial decisions. Indeed, interpreting the Acts of Parliament themselves often calls for judges to give clarity to the law by interpreting complex legislation.

■ Practice statements

Practice statements simply put are a way of allowing the House of Lords to move away from the practice of following the rules of precedent if they think it necessary. It does not change the rules of precedent in the lower courts. Before practice statements were allowed, the only way for the House to depart from previous decisions was by an Act of Parliament.

'Their Lordships nevertheless recognise that too rigid adherence to precedent may lead to injustice in a particular case and also unduly restrict the proper development of the law. They propose, therefore, to modify their present practice and, while treating formal decisions of this house as normally binding, to depart from a previous decision when it appears to be right to do so.'

(Lord Gardiner's statement in the House of Lords, 26 July 1966)

Case study: Interpreting legislation

The Dangerous Dogs Act 1991 created all sorts of problems that courts had to resolve. For instance the Act specifically referred to 'dogs', which left the courts having to interpret the legislation regarding bitches. In addition the law made reference to the control and destruction of various breeds of dog, but failed to give guidance on mixed-breed dogs. This left the courts in a very difficult position. In order to interpret the law judges used one of several rules such as the 'literal rule' and the 'golden rule' (see page 247).

1. **What were the difficulties in implementing this Act?**
2. **Do you think the Act was designed to control bitches as well as dogs?**
3. **Do you think dog owners were right to challenge the government on the grounds that this Act was flawed?**

Advantages	Disadvantages
• **Consistency** – Consistency in the law helps to provide a sense of equality and justice. • **Certainty** – Because of the high number of recorded cases that have gone before, lawyers are able to advise their clients with confidence. • **Flexibility** – The options available to judges ensure that the law can develop and be applied fairly.	• **Rigidity** – Judicial discretion can be limited. • **Bulk** – The sheer volume of prior cases can make understanding the law very time consuming. • **Illogical distinctions** – Judges may look for justifications not to follow a precedent and create illogical distinctions to support them. • **Accident of litigation** – The court relies upon a suitable case appearing if it wishes to alter the law.

Table 22.9 Advantages and disadvantages of judicial precedent

Consider this

Based on the advantages and disadvantages shown in Table 22.9 do you think the use of judicial precedent is a positive or negative feature of our legal system?

Grading tips

P4 Remember that precedent is about previous decisions made by the court. Describe how a court might use a precedent and why it is important to do so. Use examples to illustrate your report.

Assessment activity 22.4

Judicial precedent is a very important way that law is made and reinforced. This activity gives you the opportunity to show that you understand the system of precedent in English courts. You will need to research the following content:

• judicial precedent – development of the judicial precedent system; law reporting; binding authorities; persuasive authorities; *ratio decidendi*; obiter statements.

1. Produce a 300-word report that describes how precedents are applied in court. **P4**

This section considers how law is made by Parliament, rather than the courts.

Statute law

Put simply, statute law is law that has been formally written down and recorded in an Act of Parliament. Statute law has become increasingly important over the last 150 years or so. Statute law is made by Parliament and Parliament has three parts, each if which has a role to play in making the law.

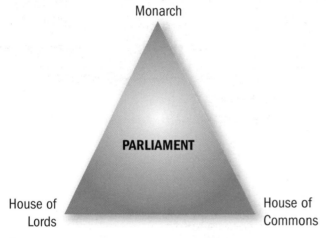

▲ Figure 22.7 Statute law has a tripartite structure

This tripartite (three-way) system was commented on as far back as 1713:

'...*every law being made in the first instance formally drawn up in writing, and made as it were a tripartite indenture, between, the lords and the commons and the monarch; for without the concurrent consent of all those three parts of the legislature no such law is, or can be made*"

(Matthew Hale, *The History of the Common Law of England*, 1713, page 1)

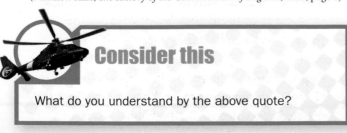

Consider this

What do you understand by the above quote?

Statute law differs from common law in the following ways:

- It was created by Parliament, not by judges.
- It is not bound by judicial precedent.
- It can abolish and replace common law.
- It is formally recorded in an Act of law.

Bills

All potential statutes begin life as 'bills'. A bill is a proposal for a piece of legislation. There are three kinds of bills:

- public bill
- private bill
- private member's bill.

A public bill is usually a proposal for a large piece of legislation that will affect the whole country. Public bills are created by the government currently in power and sometimes they are preceded by a 'green paper', which allows interested parties to consult and comment upon the ideas put forward. Examples of public bills are the Crime and Disorder Act 1998, Police and Criminal Evidence Act 1984 and the Theft Act 1968.

A private bill is usually proposed by a local authority or large corporation and will usually only affect the group of people who propose it in the first place, for instance if the building of a new motorway requires a local authority to purchase land. An example of a private bill is the Henry Johnson, Sons and Co Limited Act 1996, which was an Act that allowed the company of Henry Johnson, Sons and Co to transfer to the republic of France.

A private member's bill is usually prepared by ordinary members of Parliament who have to enter a ballot in order to be guaranteed the time in Parliament that it takes to introduce a bill. This allocated time is very important because the reason private members' bills often fail is that they do not have enough time to be debated. Sometimes private members' bills are introduced as a way of drawing attention to a particular public concern, for instance the Wild Mammals

(Hunting with Dogs) Bill drew massive public attention even though it did not succeed in becoming law in that parliamentary session. Examples of private members' bills are the Abortion Act 1967 and the Activity Centres (Young Persons' Safety) Act 1995.

Stages in making an Act of Parliament

So what procedure do these bills go through in order to become statutes or Acts of Parliament? There are seven stages that a bill must proceed through before it can become law:

1. First Reading
2. Second Reading
3. Committee Stage
4. Report Stage
5. Third Reading
6. House of Lords
7. Royal Assent.

Let's examine each stage in turn:

- **First Reading** – This is the notification to the House that a proposal is made. The title of the bill is read out and copies of it are made available. There is little or no debate at this stage.

- **Second Reading** – This is a crucial stage for the bill, as it is the main debate on the proposals contained within it. The House must then decide whether to send it forward for the next stage. In practice a government with a clear majority will almost always get its bill through this stage.

- **Committee Stage** – As you can see in Figure 22.8 this can be a complex part of the procedure. In short this is where the bill is examined in detail and the committee considers the changes it would recommend to the House. Most bills are dealt with in standing committees of about 20 MPs. However, if a bill is introduced late in the parliamentary session it may be sent to a select committee, which can hear evidence from outside individuals or agencies. The members of the committees are chosen for their qualifications and personal or professional interests. If a bill is controversial or very important, the bill is examined by a committee of the whole House instead. For private bills only, the committee stage

Figure 22.8
Stages in making an Act of Parliament

might be judicial. This means that anyone whose business or property may be affected can lodge a petition to amend a bill in order to protect their interests.

- **Report Stage** – The committee reports back to the House with suggested amendments, which are then debated and voted on by the House at large.

- **Third Reading** – The bill is represented to the House of Commons and a final vote is taken on whether to accept the proposed legislation; if the bill is accepted it is said to have 'passed the House' and is then sent on to the next stage.
- **House of Lords** – The bill then goes through a similar procedure in the House of Lords, and it must pass all of these stages in one session of Parliament. The House of Lords cannot reject most legislation passed from the House of Commons although it does retain some powers such as the ability to reject a bill that attempts to extend the duration of a government for longer than five years. The House of Lords has less power than the Commons because its members are not elected by the public.
- **Royal Assent** – When a bill has successfully passed through both Houses it must go to the monarch for approval and consent. It will then become law on a specified date. It is not usual for the monarch to give consent in person. It is normally done by a committee of three peers including the Lord Chancellor. This stage is a formality these days. The last time a monarch refused a bill was Queen Anne in 1707, when she declined to give consent to a Scottish Militia Bill.

▲ The monarch must give Royal Assent

Remember!

- Statute law is made by Parliament.
- It can abolish and replace common law.
- It is created via three kinds of bills: public, private and private member's bills.
- It is approved in a seven-stage procedure, concluding with Royal Assent.
- The monarch has not refused to sign a statute law since 1707.

As you can see, statutes can be very complicated and detailed, and this can cause tremendous problems when they are applied in courts of law. Bennion (1990) identifies several problems that can arise in statute law:

- A word is left out.
- A broad term is used.
- An ambiguous word is used.
- The events in a case were not foreseen when the statute was written.
- There are printing errors.

It is up to the courts to settle disputes as to the meanings of words or clauses in a statute. They do this by using some generally recognised rules that the judge may choose to apply. These are discussed later in this unit.

Doctrine of parliamentary sovereignty

'Parliamentary sovereignty' is a complicated phrase for what is actually a very simple concept. It simply means that Parliament is independent and is not subject to outside influences such as the church, the courts or the monarchy. Parliamentary sovereignty is associated with the 16th century, when the rule of law was asserted to be of greater importance than the rule of the church, and with the 17th and 18th centuries, when the powers of the monarch were gradually eroded and transferred to Parliament. In essence Parliament can make laws on anything it likes and does not have to be accountable to other institutions.

Delegated legislation

Parliament may create the legal framework of an Act but leave it to others such as ministers and government departments to fill in the details. This is called delegated or subordinate legislation, but it is not inferior to ordinary statutes. There are three main reasons why delegated legislation is needed:

- There isn't time in Parliament to debate all the small details of bills.
- Parliament may not be in session.
- Parliament may not have the technical knowledge or expertise to deal with the details.

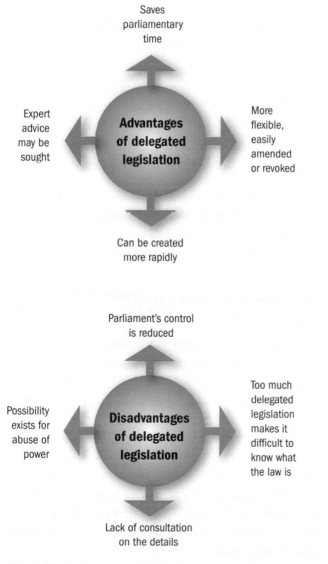

▲ **Figure 22.9 Advantages and disadvantages of delegated legislation**

Principles of statutory interpretation

There are several different ways a judge can interpret the law if what Parliament has written isn't clear:

- **The literal rule** – According to this rule the workings of the Act must be interpreted according to its literal and grammatical meaning. An example of the literal rule is the case of *Whitely v Chappell* (1868). The statute in this case was designed to prevent malpractice in elections and made it an offence to impersonate anybody entitled to vote at an election. The defendant was acquitted because he was impersonating a dead person and a dead person was not entitled to vote.

- **The golden rule** – This is an extension of the literal rule, which states that judges should interpret the law literally unless to do so would lead to an absurd or ridiculous result. For instance, in the case of Sigsworth (1935) the court decided that a man who had murdered his mother was not entitled to inherit her estate even though the Administration of Estates Act 1925 said that where a will had not been made the person's estate should go to the next of kin. In this case the next of kin was the person's murderer and this would have been a ridiculous result.

- **The mischief rule** – This was established by the case of Heydon (1584). In this rule the courts try to discover what mischief the Act of Parliament was trying to remedy and then interpret the words accordingly. An example of this is *Smith v Hughes* (1960). A prostitute claimed that she was not soliciting for business even though she was attracting the attention of male passers-by, tapping on the window of a house. The Street Offences Act (1959) made it a criminal offence to solicit for business in a public place or a street. The prostitute argued that since she was not in a public place she was not guilty of an offence. The court found that the mischief that Act had been created to remedy was to try to stop people being solicited in the street and since she was attracting the attention of people in the street she was guilty of an offence.

As with common law there are advantages and disadvantages to law made by statute, some of which are outlined briefly in Table 22.10.

Advantages	Disadvantages
• Created by an elected body that represents the people. • Law can be made on any subject at any time. Parliament does not have to wait for a suitable case to arrive in front of it. • Created by a formal procedure that includes checks and balances to ensure the law is appropriate.	• Can be difficult to interpret. • Process can be time consuming and private members' bills often fail. • The political party in power can control the legislative process.

Table 22.10 Advantages and disadvantages to law made by statute

Approaches to statutory interpretation

There are two approaches to statutory interpretation you must examine as part of your course:

- **Purposive** – This approach to understanding legislation aims to consider the general underlying purposes for its creation in the first place. The law is examined in detail and the reason the law was created. Its 'purpose' will overarch its literal meaning.

- **Integrated** – This was developed by Sir Rupert Cross in 1995. It is based on the literal rule (see above), but allows judges to interpret the meaning of the law differently if the result of the literal rule is absurd or unworkable.

European Union legal rules

The EU has a complicated system for making legislation that is outlined in the first section of *Unit 8: International perspectives for the uniformed public services* in Book 1. The role of the European Court of Justice and EU regulation, directives and decisions are also covered in that section. It is important to note that EU laws become part of UK law by virtue of the European Communities Act 1972. EU law also takes precedence over existing UK law, which must be amended if it is found to conflict with EU law.

Assessment activity 22.5

This activity requires you to consider how laws are made by Parliament and how they are interpreted by judges. You should research and include the following content:

- statutory legal rules – stages in making an Act of Parliament; public and private members' bills; doctrine of parliamentary sovereignty; primary and delegated legislation
- principles of statutory interpretation – literal rule; mischief rule; golden rule; integrated and purposive approaches to statutory interpretation.

Produce a written report that answers the following questions:

1. Describe the process when making an Act of Parliament. **P5**

2. Compare and contrast the methods of law making. **M2**

3. Outline or explain the rules of statutory interpretation. **M3**

4. Evaluate the role of the judiciary in the formulation and interpretation of legal rules. **D2**

Grading tips

P5 There are two parts to P5. First, you have to describe how Parliament makes laws. This is the procedure that moves all the way from committees, green and white papers all the way to Royal Assent. (For more information on this subject, see *Unit 1*, Book 1, page 26.) The second part of P5 requires you to outline the rules of statutory interpretation such as the literal rule and the mischief rule. 'Outline' means just a brief overview.

M2 This criterion asks you to examine the ways in which laws are made, such as judicial precedent, Acts of Parliament and EU laws, and to discuss the differences and similarities in the way they are made.

M3 M3 is a straightforward extension of the second part of P5. Here you are required to explain in more detail the rules of interpretation.

D2 This criterion asks you to examine the role of judges in creating and interpreting legal rules. Look at the advantages and disadvantages of how judges use rules to interpret the law and come up with some conclusions as to how effective they are.

Knowledge check

1. Where would you find the small claims track?
2. What cases are tried in county court?
3. What is the highest civil and criminal court in England and Wales?
4. What does 'taking silk' mean?
5. What can disqualify you from jury service?
6. Where would you find a Puisne judge?
7. What is judicial precedent?
8. What is parliamentary sovereignty?
9. What does *ratio decidendi* mean?
10. Explain the literal rule.

Preparation for assessment

You are working part time as a police special constable. Your sergeant knows that you are studying law as part of your public services course and has asked you to produce an easy-to-read guide to the legal system that can be given to civilian support workers so that they can understand the system better. Your guide should answer the following questions:

1. Outline the hierarchies of and differences between the civil and criminal courts. **P1**

2. Compare and contrast the role and function of judges, lawyers and lay people within the English courts. **M1**

3. Evaluate the effectiveness of lay personnel in the English courts. **D1**

4. Describe the role of lay people in criminal cases. **P2**

5. Compare and contrast the methods of law making. **M2**

6. Evaluate the role of the judiciary in the formulation and interpretation of legal rules. **D2**

7. Outline the role of judges and lawyers in civil and criminal cases. **P3**

8. Explain the rules of statutory interpretation. **M3**

9. Describe how precedents are applied in court. **P4**

10. Describe the process when making an Act of Parliament and outline the rules for statutory interpretation. **P5**

Grading criteria	Activity	Pg no.		
To achieve a pass grade the evidence must show that the learner is able to:			To achieve a merit grade the evidence must show that the learner is able to:	To achieve a distinction grade the evidence must show that the learner is able to:
P1 Outline the hierarchies of and differences between the civil and criminal courts	22.1	231	**M1** Compare and contrast the role and function of judges, lawyers and lay people within the English courts	**D1** Evaluate the effectiveness of lay personnel in the English courts
P2 Describe the role of lay people in criminal cases	22.3	238	**M2** Compare and contrast the methods of law making	**D2** Evaluate the role of the judiciary in the formulation and interpretation of legal rules
P3 Outline the role of judges and lawyers in civil and criminal cases	22.2	236	**M3** Explain the rules of statutory interpretation	
P4 Describe how precedents are applied in court	22.4	243		
P5 Describe the process when making an Act of Parliament and outline the rules for statutory interpretation	22.5	248		

Index

Note: Page numbers in **bold** indicate where key terms are defined.